**Verlag der Buchhandlung
Walther und Franz König
A+ Architecture in Belgium
Bozar, Centre for Fine Arts**

2006–2022

AGWA

I0811723

PREFACE
Hülya Ertas

AgwA, the name of the office led by Benoît Burquel, Harold Fallon and Benoît Vandenbulcke, is not explicitly defined by the partners. From multiple possible abbreviations the letters may form, to the obvious etymological connection to the Spanish word for water, the name suggests an intentional signification but leaves the final decision to the imagination.

Founded in Brussels in 2003, AgwA has been working on projects of various scales and programmes, each time recreating the architectural language specific to the projects, like water taking the shape of the container, while simultaneously challenging the shape and context of the design brief. Whether a school kitchen, transformation project, campus or house, AgwA starts the design process by questioning the question. This moment of reflection makes it possible to reread and sometimes redefine the programme, size and scope of the commission, leaving almost no rock unturned, taking nothing for granted. The architectural language specific to the project derives from this initial process. Thanks to this way of working, transformation projects in particular gain new importance. Dealing with the existing situation in terms of both urban context and physical attributes of the building involves many layers of complexity, such as construction history and collective memory. In many of their transformation projects, we see how the questioning of the question leads to new perspectives in deciding what to demolish and what to keep.

Developing an architectural language specific to projects does not mean that the practice does not have a designated route. Like water following a course defined by the rules of physics, AgwA projects follow some principles, such as a prudent audacity, an experimental approach to construction and structure, frugality, and criticality. In many cases, in collaborations with other architectural offices, these principles remain explicit, proof of their engagement in the design process.

The opportunity to build also means the opportunity to carry out research, during the design phase but also in reflections during and after the realization of the project. The office's engagement with the *In Practice* book series, initiated in the context of their academic activities, generates this feedback loop where AgwA's attitude of sharing knowledge and their interest in learning from others create a richness in bridging the dichotomies of theory and practice.

AgwA's work is distinguishable in its attempt not to be distinguishable as a genius effort but to achieve a clearly identifiable presence, not always humble yet never arrogant.

PRACTICE OF ARCHITECTURE

01

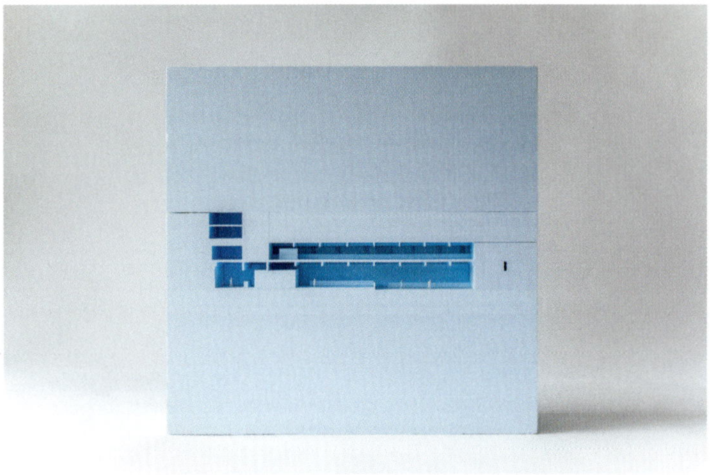

section

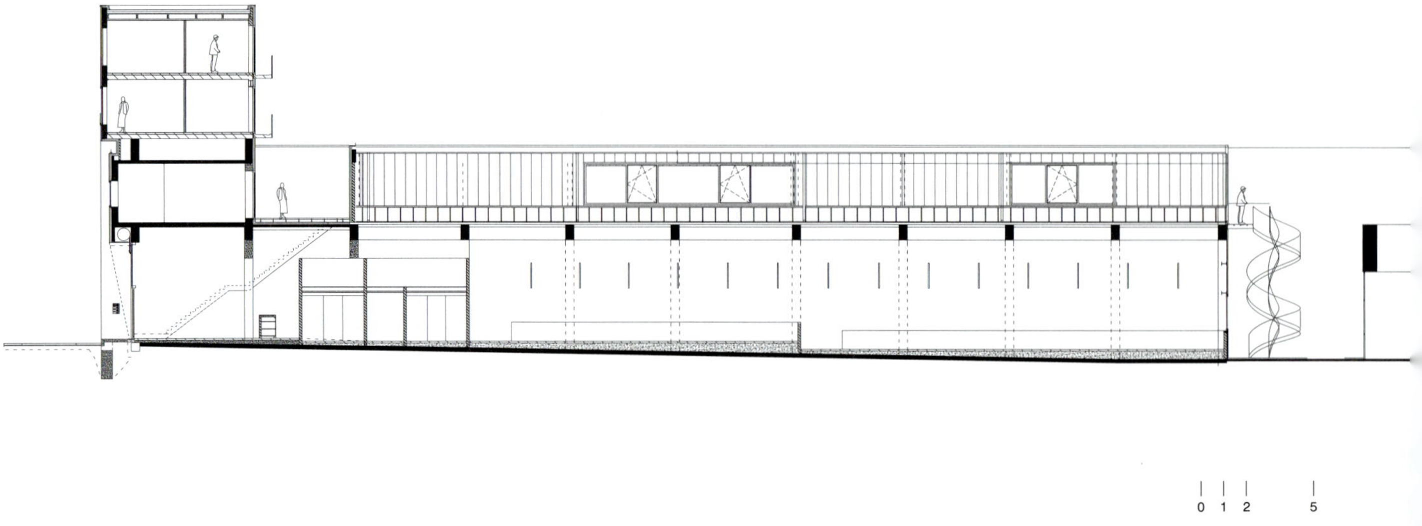

A former tyre shop was converted into a sports hall, an after-school programme and three apartments. The modernist structure was preserved, offering deep open spaces for sporting and pedagogic activities. Two apartments were added on the roof as an independent Vierendeel bridge structure clad in translucent polycarbonate. The horizontal layering of the façade contrasts with the surrounding houses. The lateral façades of the first floor are recessed and clad with polycarbonate, ensuring natural light on both levels and organizing views towards the dense interior of the city block.

see p. 244 – 253

02

03

1
cale model realized for the *NICHE*
xhibition at Bozar, Brussels (2009),
© Delphine Mathy

02
photograph of the original project
by K. Grochowski and P. Tapproge,
source unknown (c. 1970)

03
Rue du Métal / Metaalstraat (2009),
© Marie-Françoise Plissart

level +3

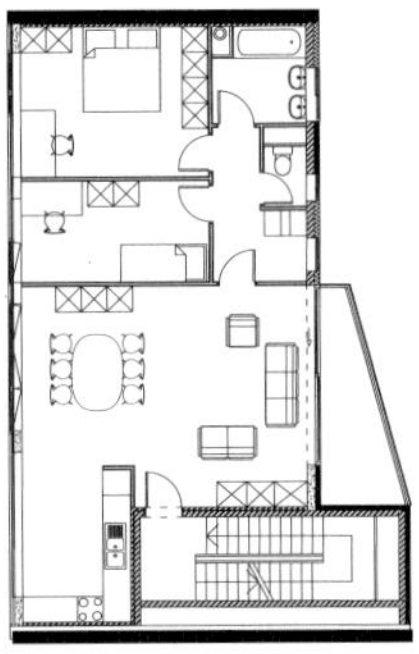

level +2

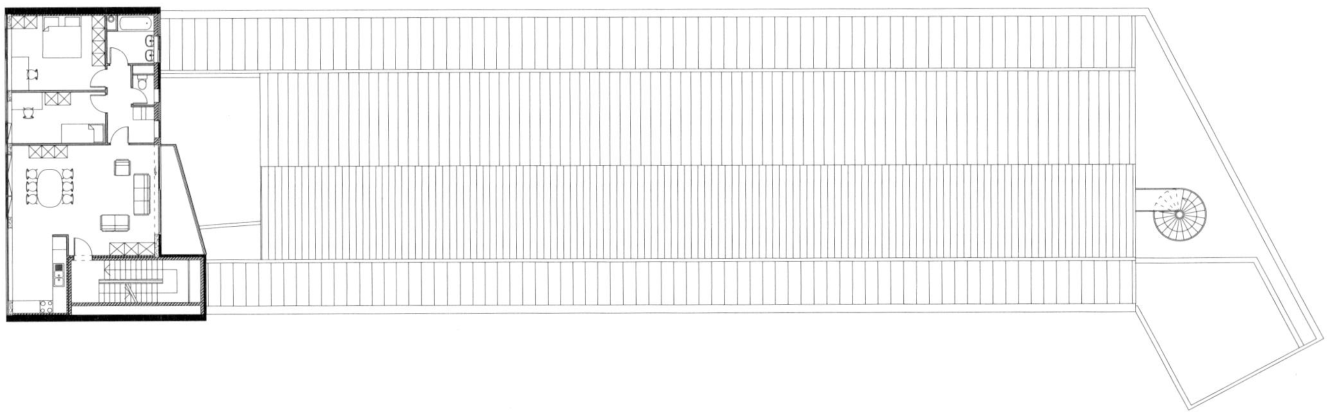

level +1

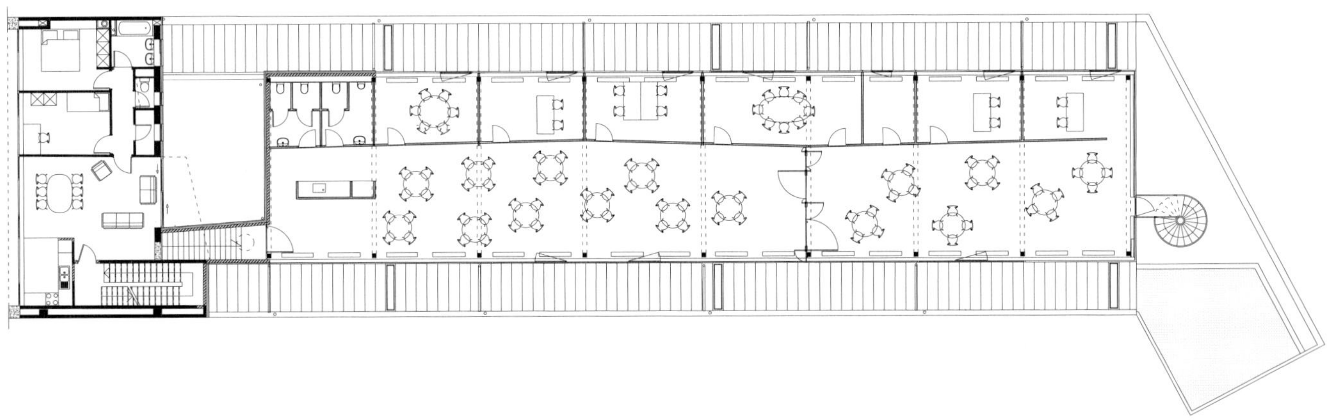

ground floor

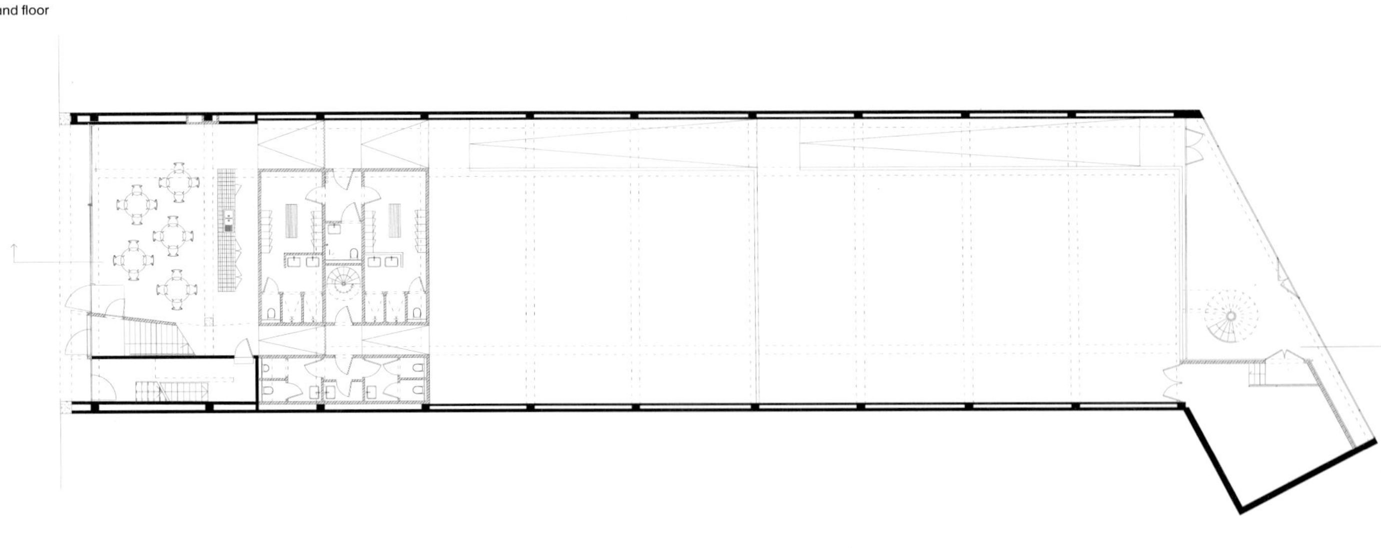

04

05

06

07

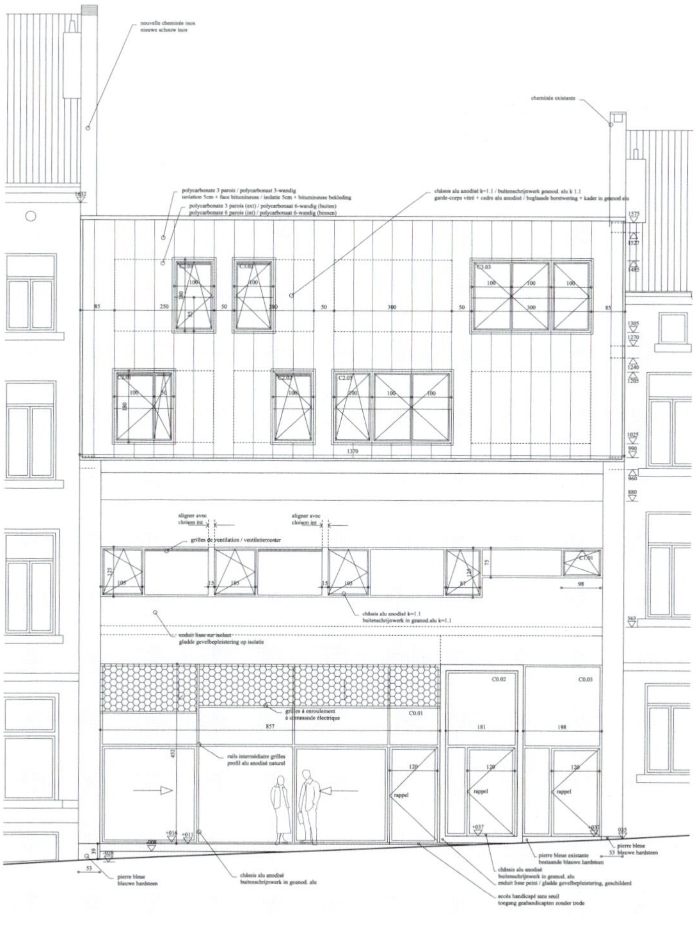

04–05
construction site (2009, 2006)

06
construction site (2008),
© Marie-Françoise Plissart

07
street elevation, building permit
(2007)

VERTIGO **theming of a rollercoaster** **2006–07** **Wavre**

01

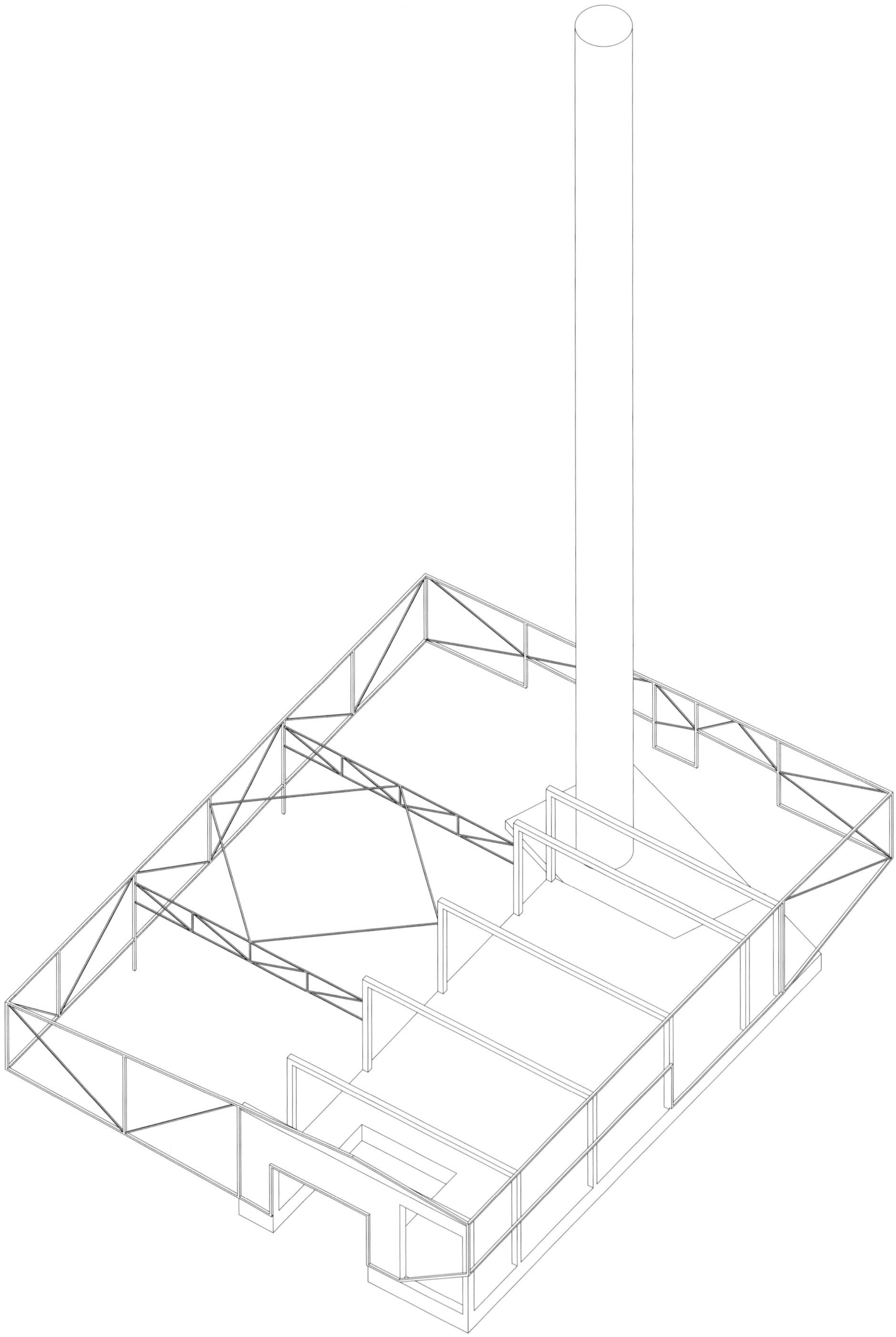

A square steel structure clad with polycarbonate in shades of blue is all that decorates the station of the Vertigo prototype ride at the Walibi Belgium theme park. Two containers make for a small shop linked to the ride. For administrative reasons, the station had to be elevated three metres above ground. A grass hill was proposed to bridge the gap. At its top, the floating blue screen both conceals and reveals the ride's machinery, in contrast with the usual *horror vacui* found in theme parks.

see p. 240 – 243

02

03

04

05

06

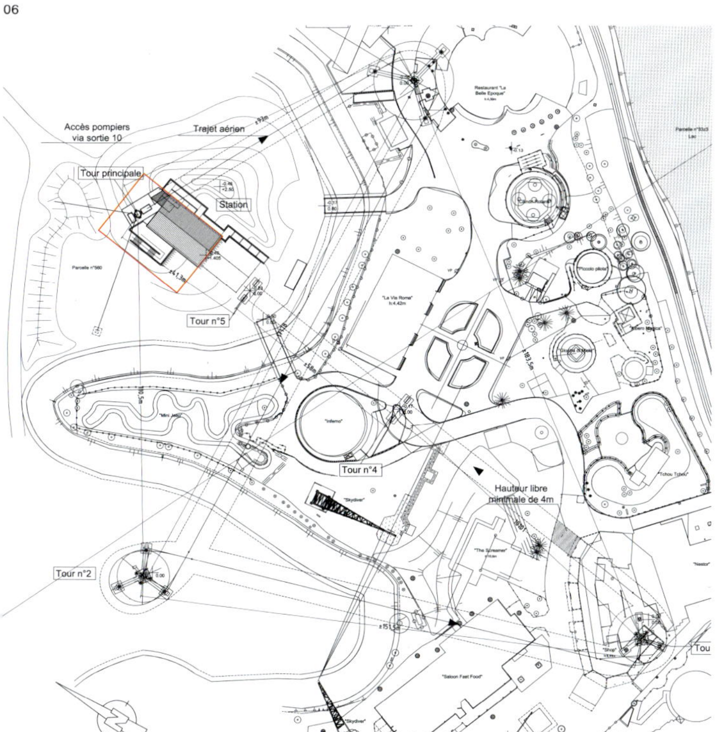

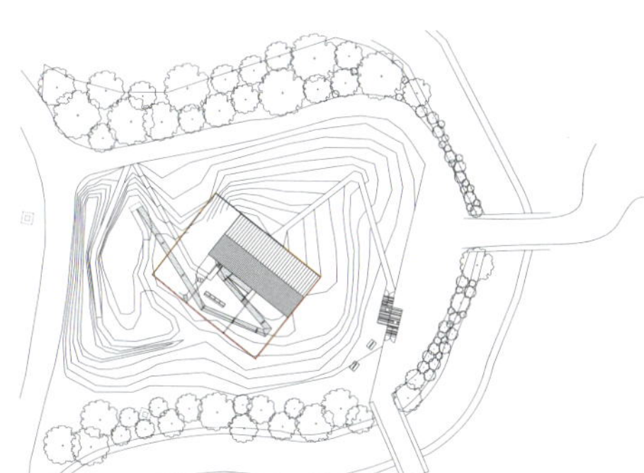

0 10 20 50

01
axonometric view of
the primary structure

02
scale model made for the AgwA:
An Architecture of Practice exhibition
at CIVA, Brussels (2013)

03 – 05
construction site

06
technical plan of the theme park
with indication of the project

07

08

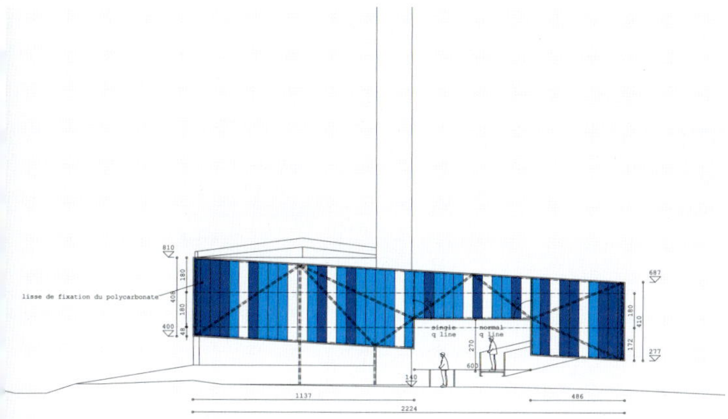

09

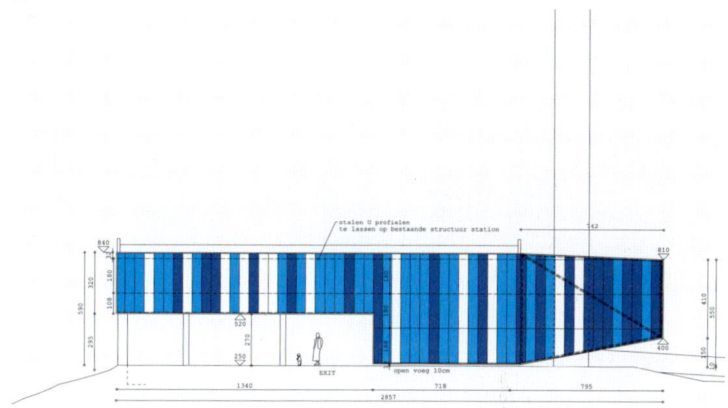

0

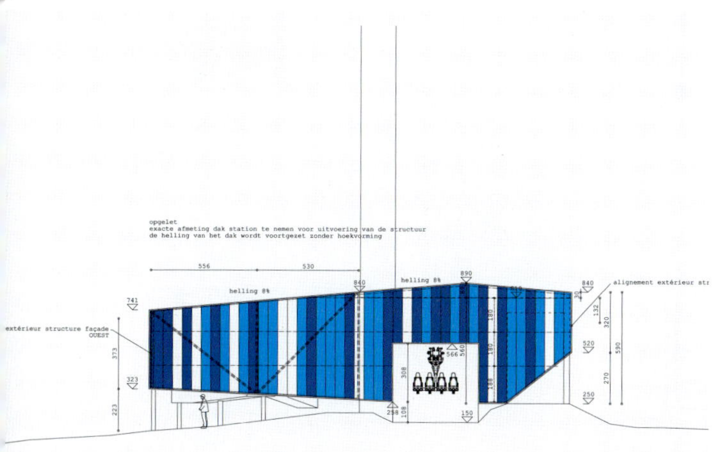

11

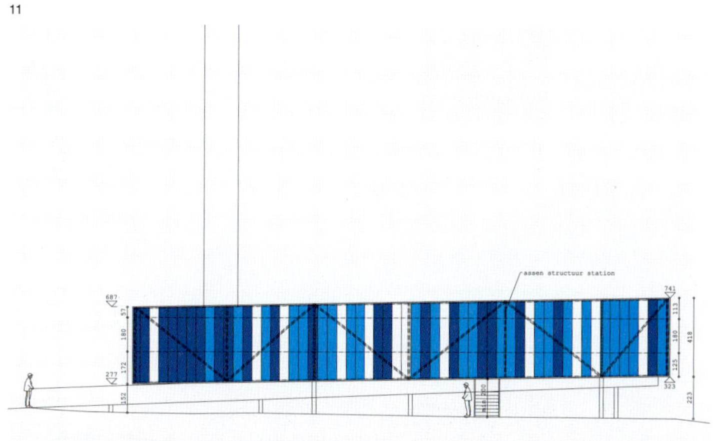

7
onstruction site

08–11
execution drawings, clockwise from upper left: west, north, east, south elevation

0 1 2 5 10

BPS22	extension and redevelopment of a museum	2006	Charleroi	in collaboration with Matador

01

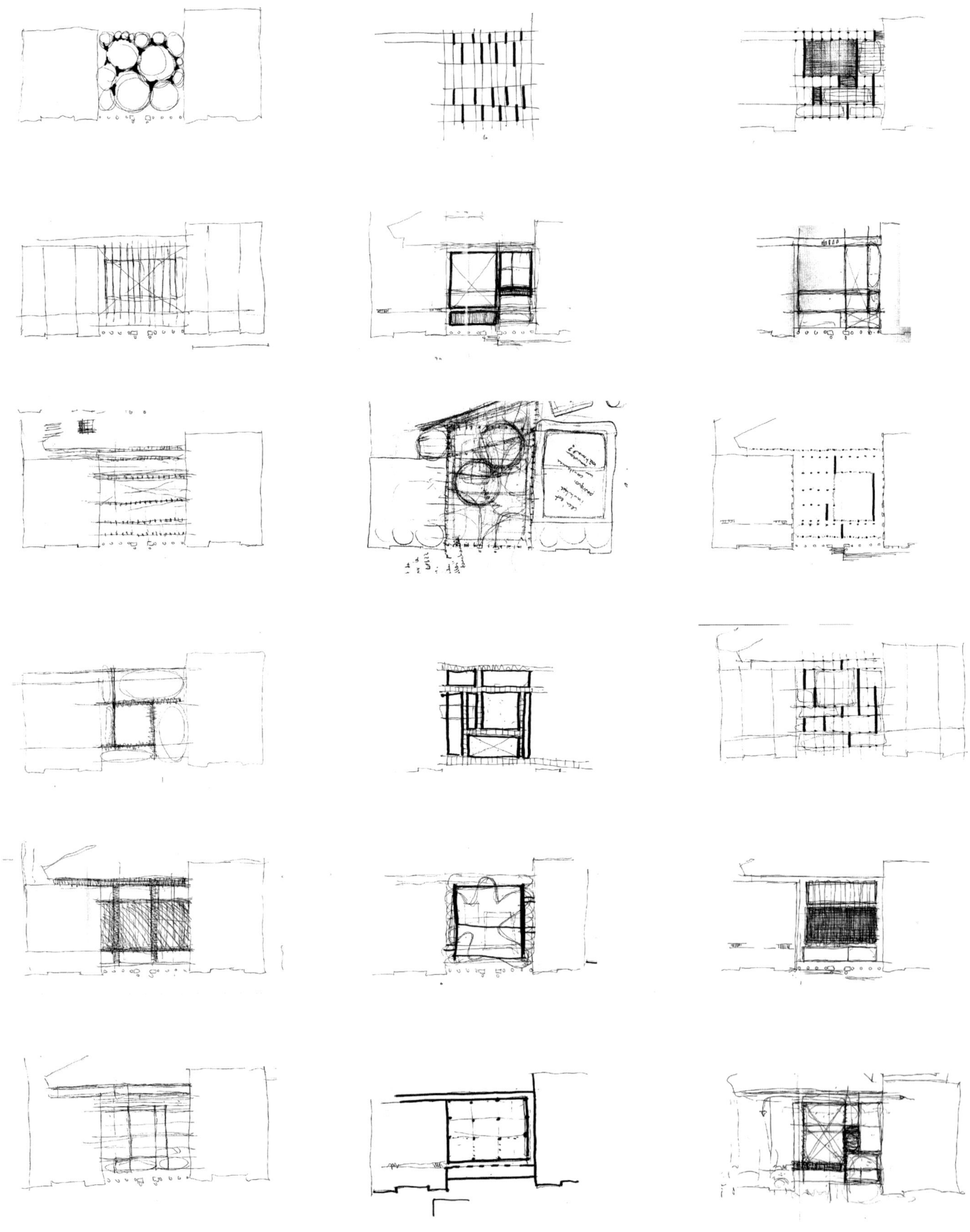

The competition brief for the refurbishment of the BPS22 contemporary art museum addressed only the central building and the left wing of the eclectic nineteenth-century Université du Travail. The proposal was to demolish the blind central volume behind the monumental colonnade and to occupy the entire plot with an open floor plan covered by sheds linking both wings. This was the first in a series of projects to explore the autonomy of form and geometric plan systems.

02

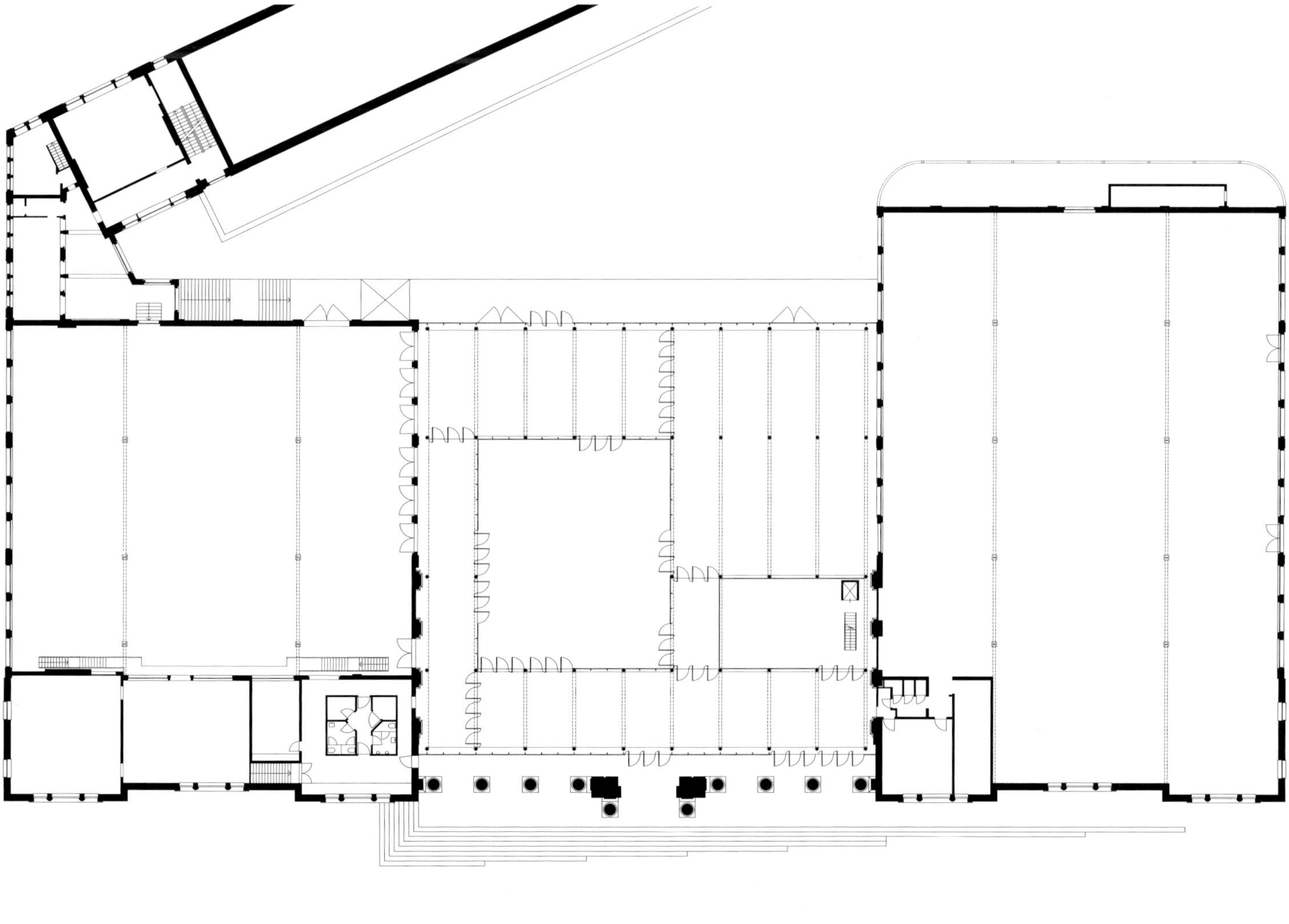

01
plan experiments

02
proposed intervention seen through existing colonnade

PHILIPPEVILLE | **construction of a school kitchen and restaurant** | **2008** | **Philippeville** | **in collaboration with Artgineering**

01

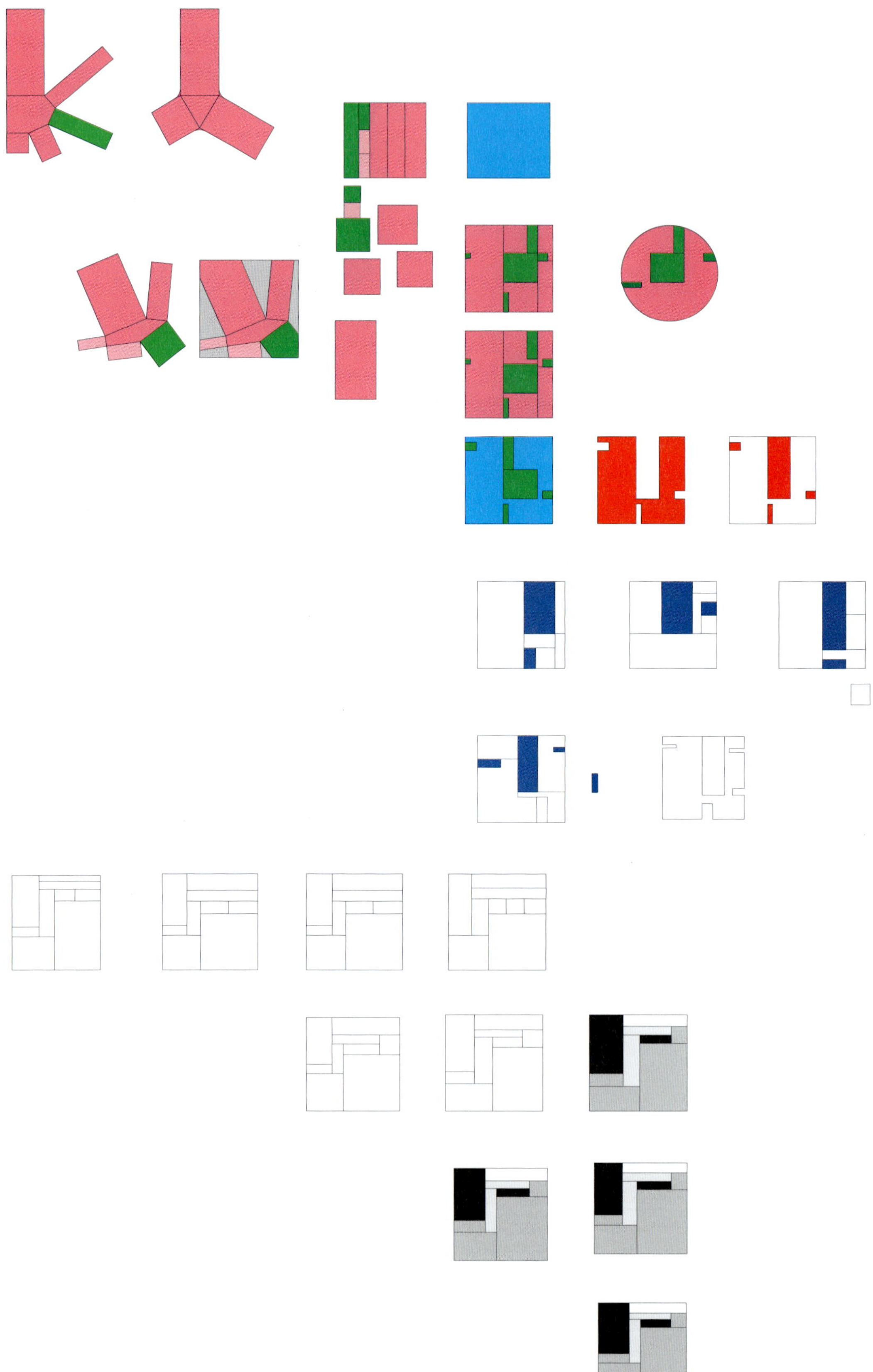

The school restaurant is located at the geometric centre of the campus. A study of the floor plan led to a square isotropic footprint opening up towards the site on the entire periphery of the building. The layout of the spaces resembles a mathematical perfect square dissection. Each room is a different rectangle. With the exception of the kitchen ensemble, the building is the smallest rectangular collection of rooms (in this case, a square). The entrance canopy and the central circulation hall are covered with glass. Truncated pyramids cover the three main spaces.

02

03

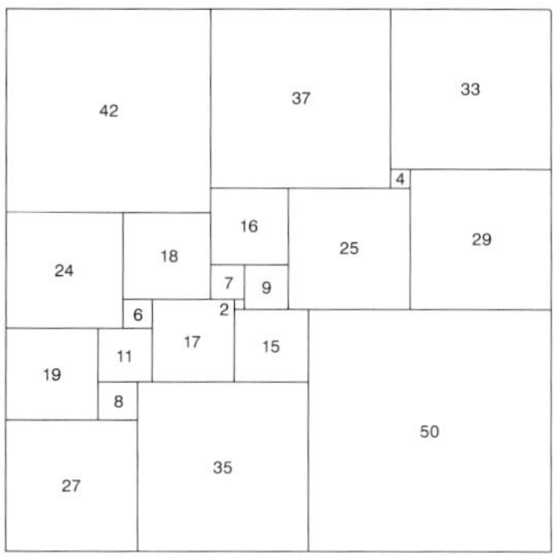

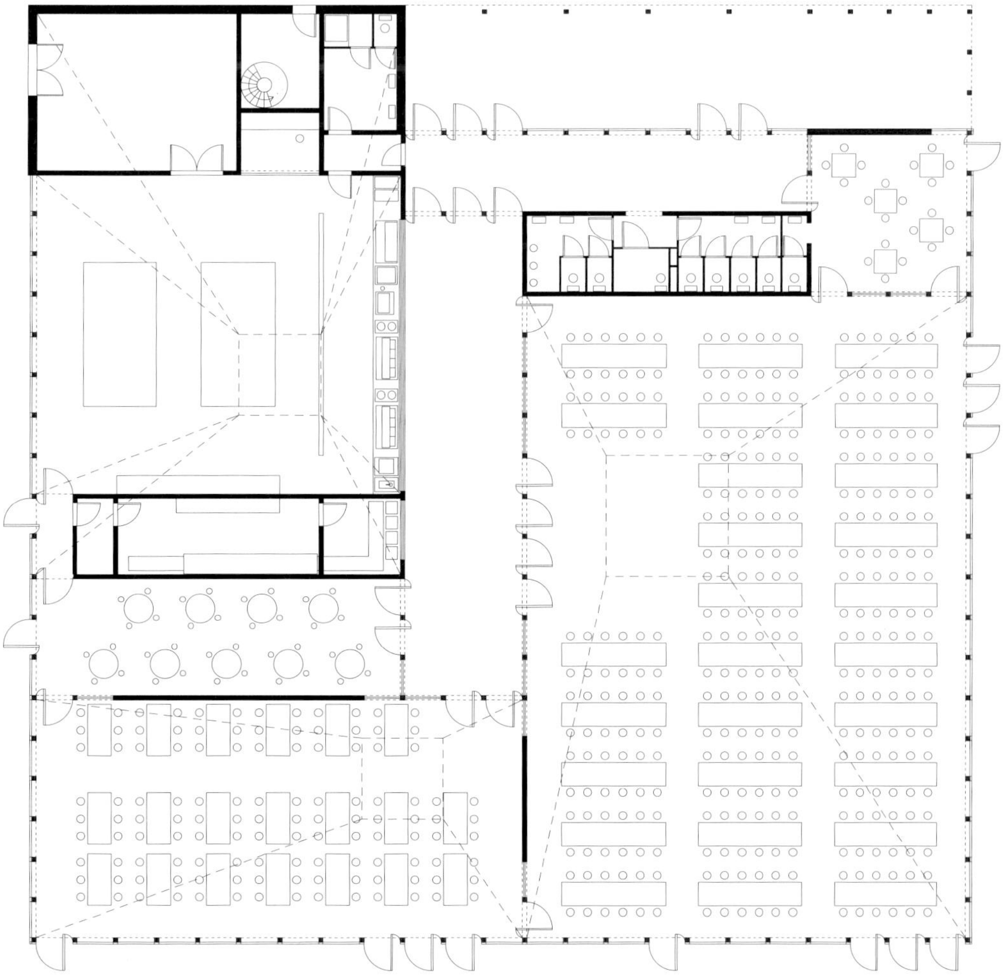

01
plan design process

02
scale model of
the roof composition

03
lowest order perfect
square dissection

0 1 2 5

01

02

03

CARRÉ | retractile covering of a historic courtyard | 2008–14 | Mons | in collaboration with Ney & Partners

04

05

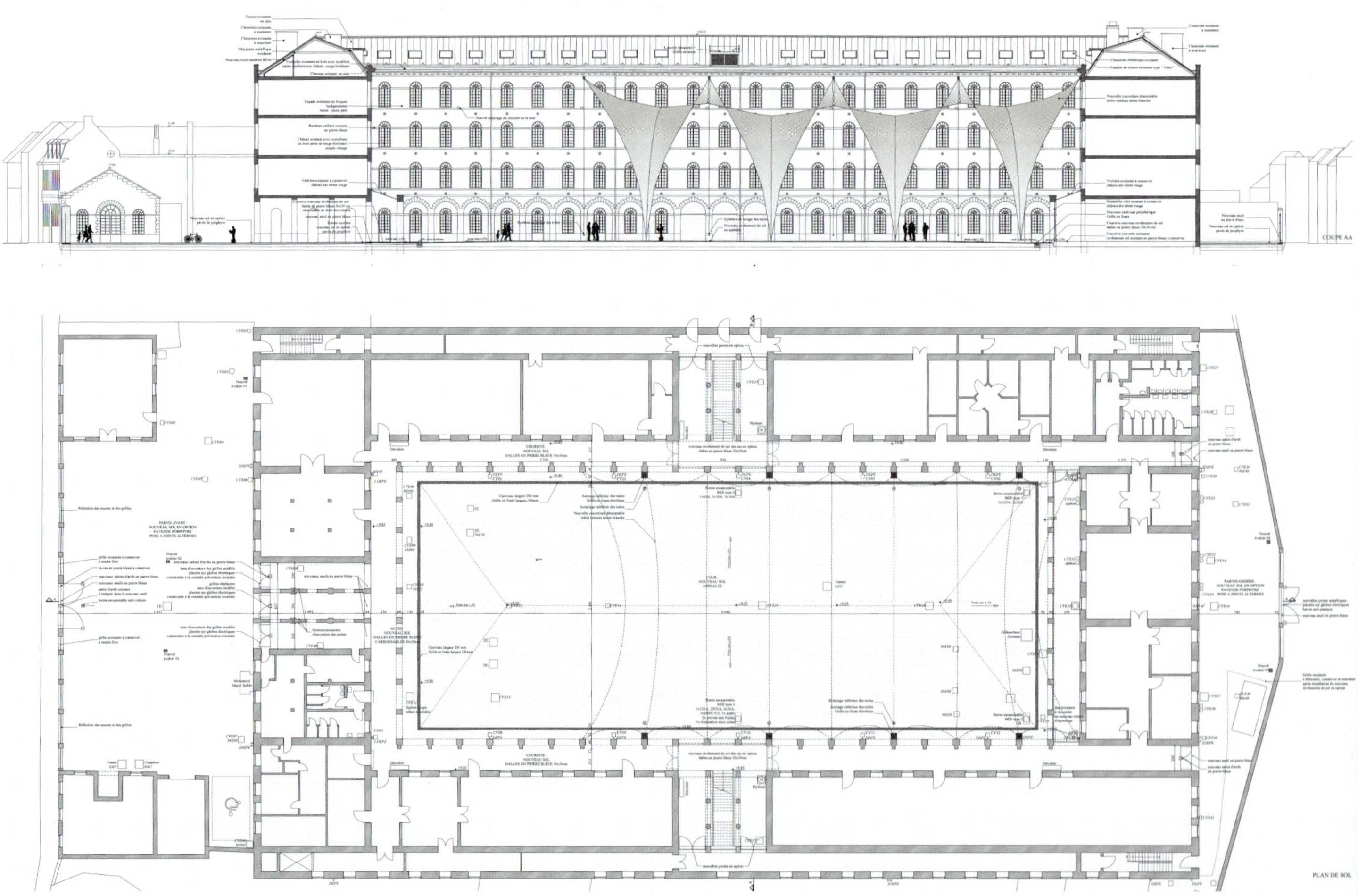

The military barracks are home to an art school, the local television station and the offices of Le Manège, which ran operations for Mons 2015, European Capital of Culture. The retractable membrane roof shelters the yearly *Festival au Carré* and other summer events. Structural anchor points were realized on the floor and below the cornice. A cable system makes it possible to stretch and tighten the membranes without a crane. The repetitive vaulted geometry echoes the arched architecture. The playful painting byJean-Luc Moerman lightens the pragmatic asphalt flooring of the military courtyard.

see p. 234–239

06

07

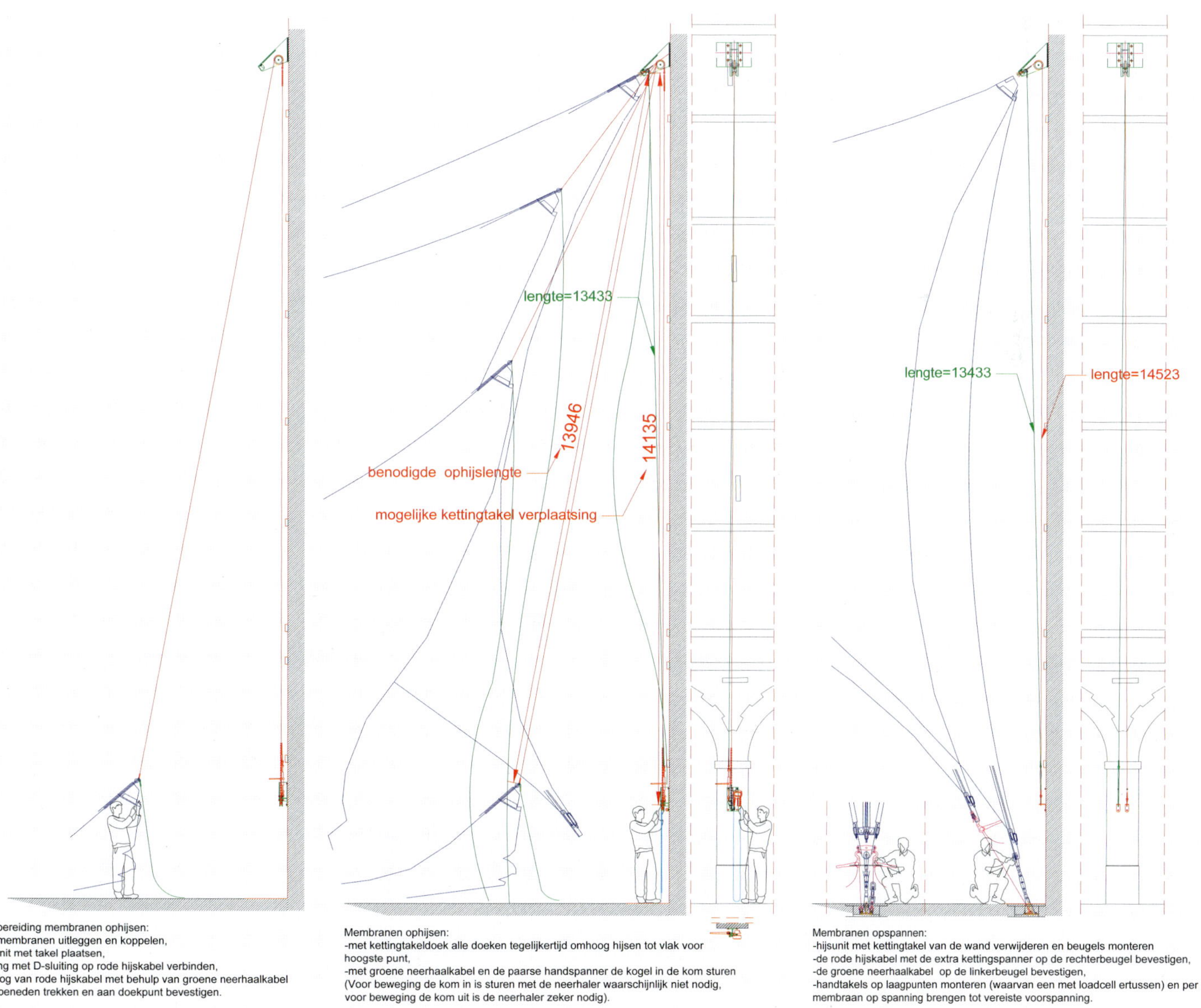

01–03
construction site (2013, 2014, 2014)

04
one of three scale models made for the feasibility study (2009)

05
ground floor plan and section, building permit phase (2013)

06
situation plan, city of Mons

07
assembly scheme by the contractor, Veldeman (2014)

PÉRONNES | **redevelopment and renovation of a nautical and sports centre** | **2009–ongoing** | **Péronnes-lez-Antoing** | **in collaboration with Artgineering**

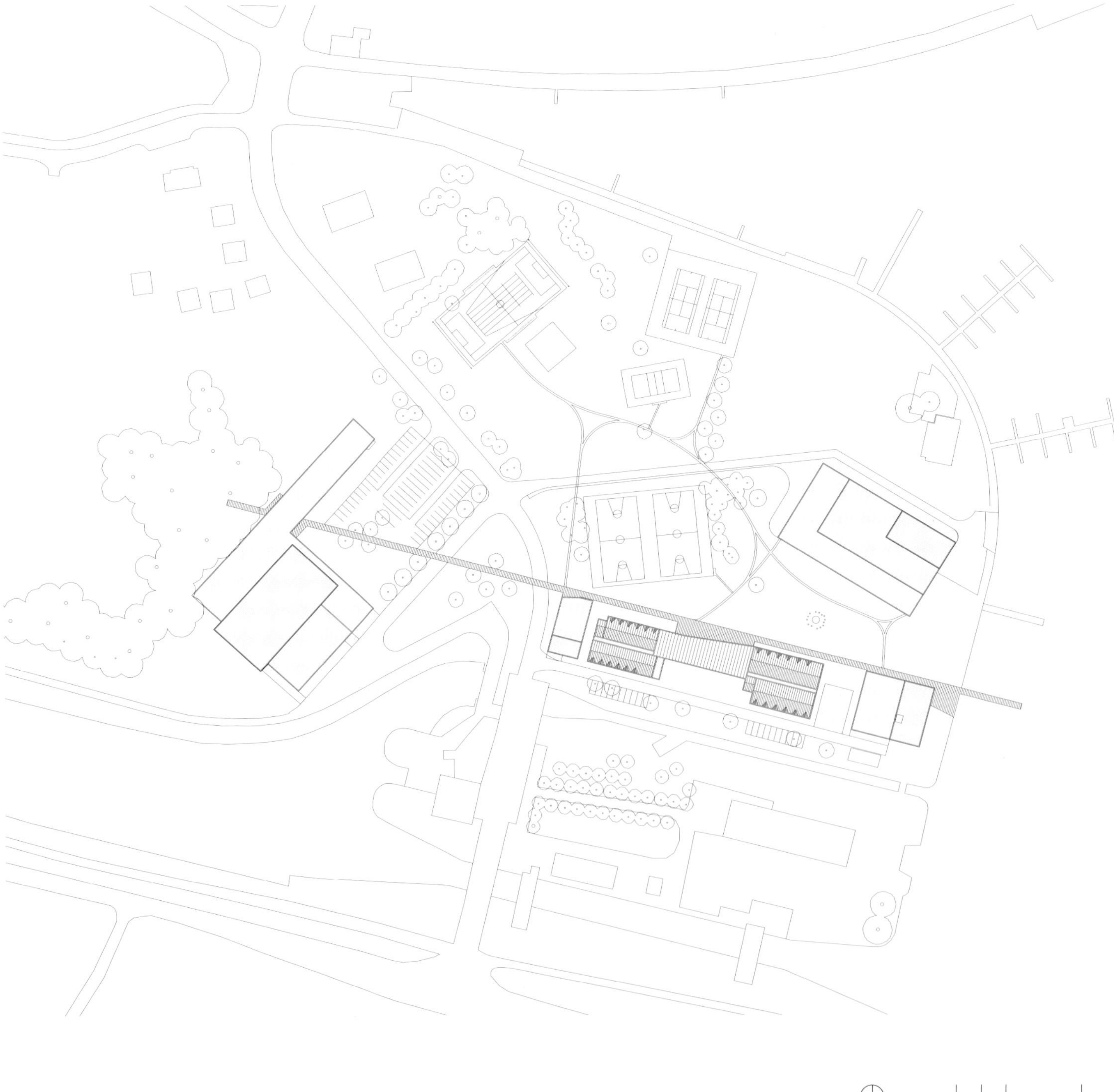

01

A long jetty inscribes the open-air sports centre and sailing school in its fluvial context. It links the sports hall and the boarding school complex. It opens up towards a landscape punctuated with sports fields and a sailing workshop. Facing the lake, this workshop is a concrete, wood and steel structure clad with aluminium. The cantilevering concrete structure of the boarding school complex creates low, continuous openings that intensify the panoramic visual relation to the water and the landscape. The concrete blocks and lintels of the façades echo the existing buildings.

see p. 226–233

02

03

01–03
boarding school during works (2017), © Delphine Mathy

05

04

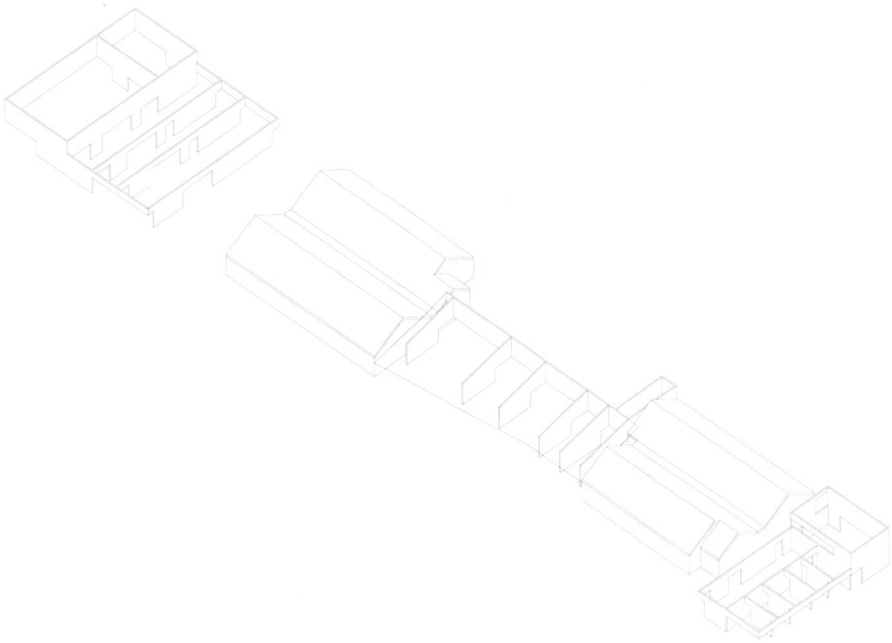

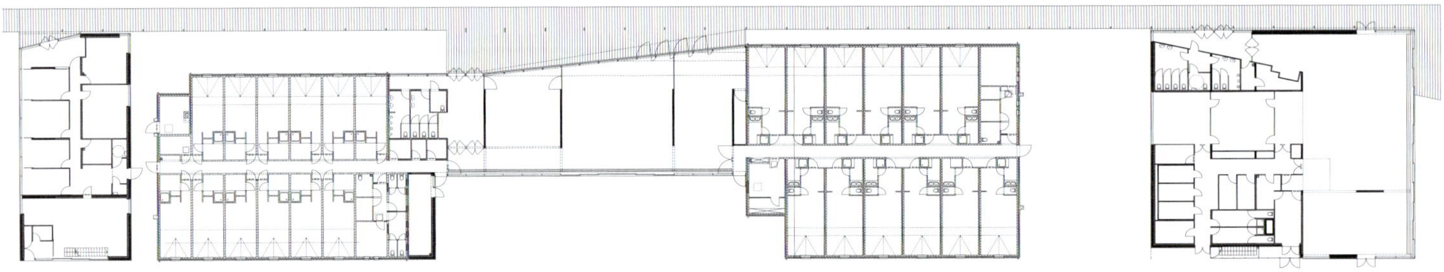

boarding school complex
south elevation / janitor's house dormitories foyer dormitories restaurant

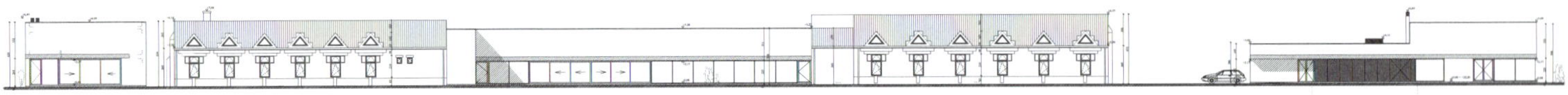

north elevation / restaurant dormitories foyer dormitories administration

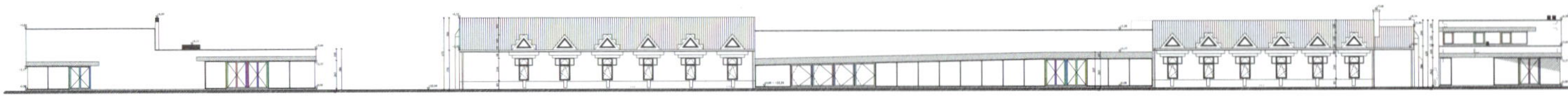

west elevation / restaurant

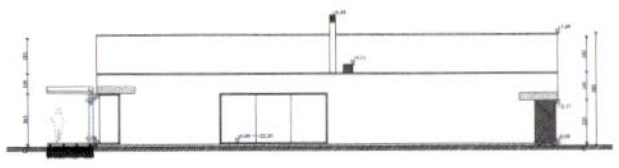

east elevation / restaurant

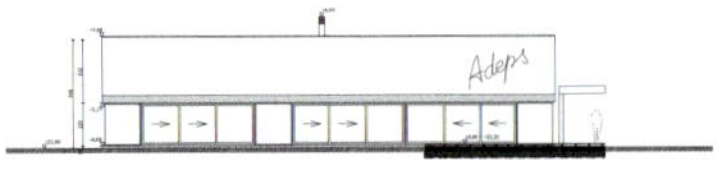

west elevation / administration and janitor's house

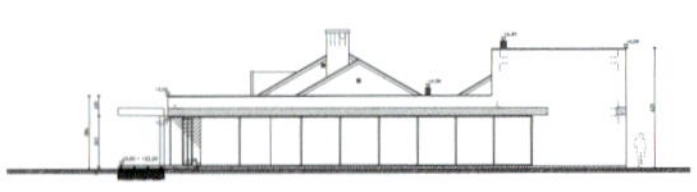

east elevation / administration and janitor's house

0 2 5 10

06

07

04
axonometric view of
the primary structure

05–06
construction site (2017),
construction site (2016)

07
construction site (2017),
© Delphine Mathy

08

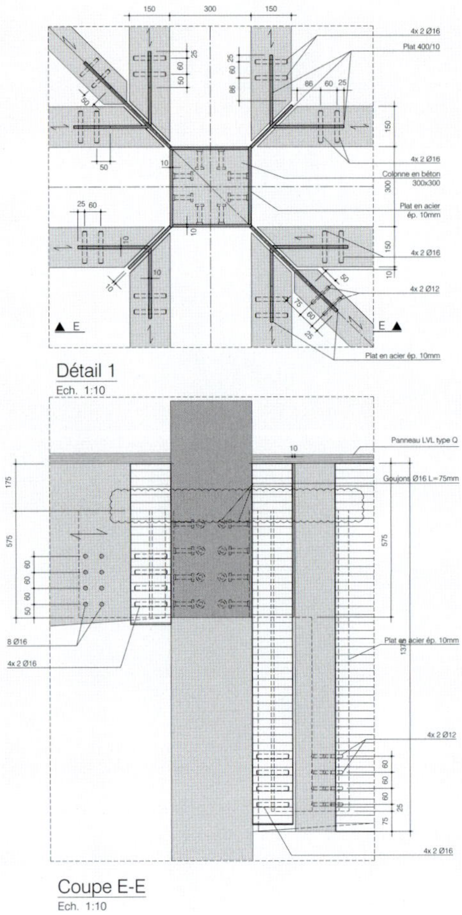
4x 2 Ø16
Plat 400/10
Colonne en béton 300x300
Plat en acier ép. 10mm
4x 2 Ø12
Plat en acier ép. 10mm
Détail 1
Ech. 1:10
Panneau LVL type Q
Goujons Ø16 L=75mm
8 Ø16
Coupe E-E
Ech. 1:10

09

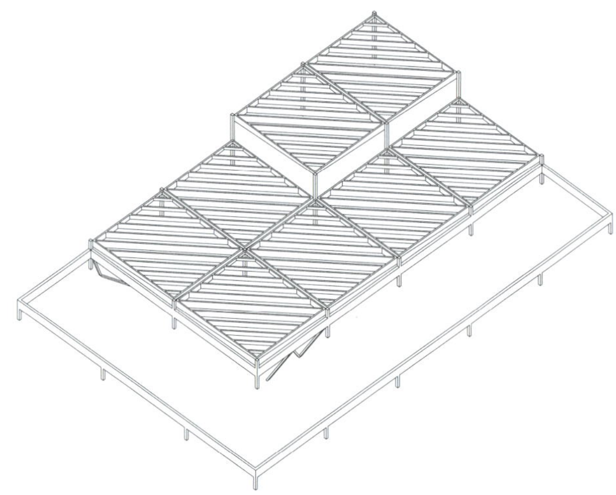

10

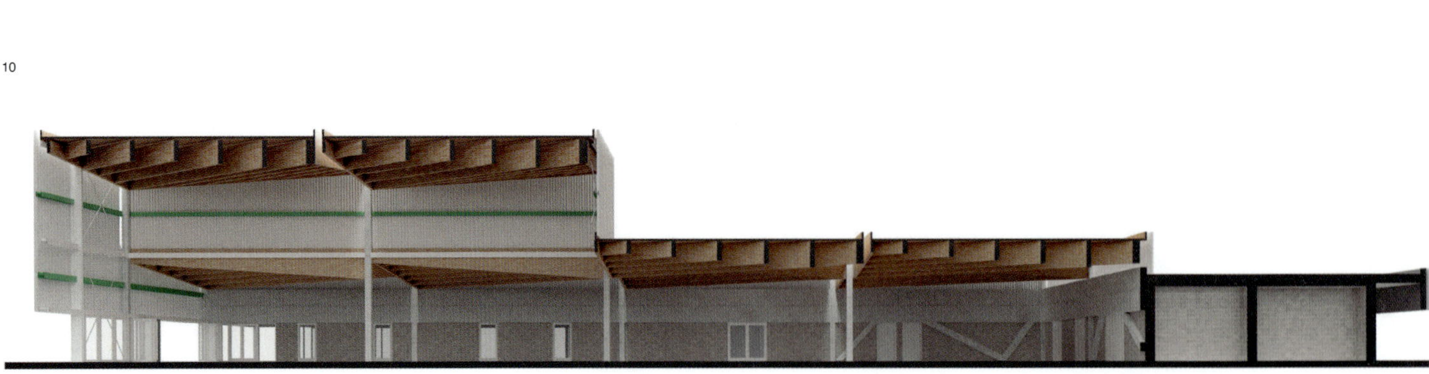

11

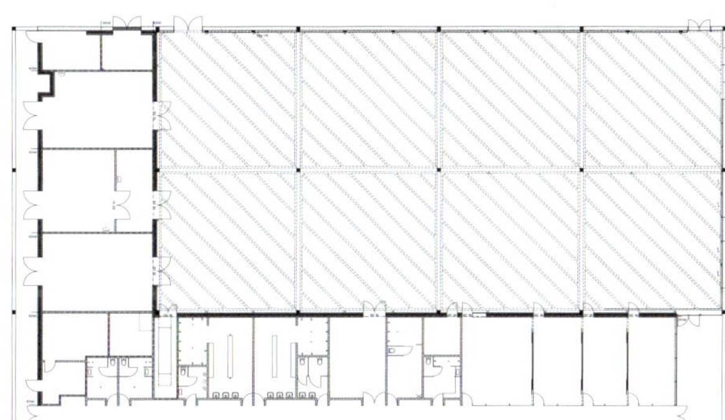

sailing workshop
north east elevation

south west elevation

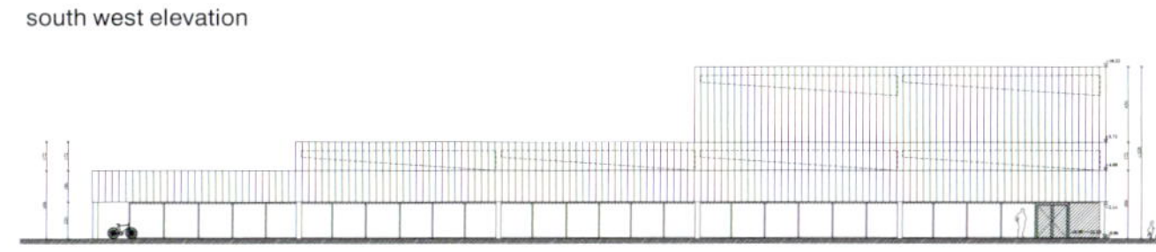

north west elevation

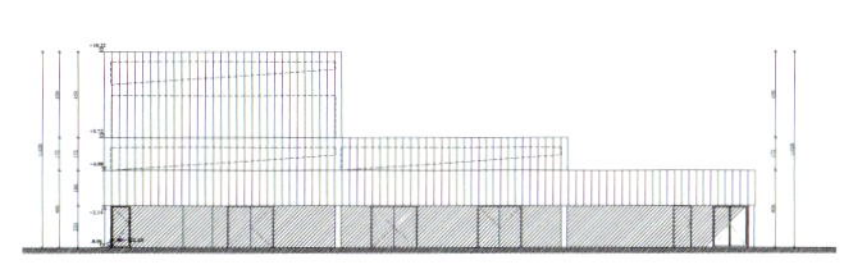

south east elevation

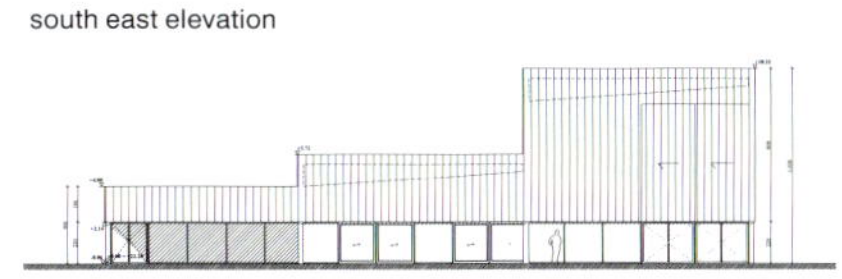

08
execution drawing of the junction between columns and beams (2011) by Ney & Partners

09
axonometric view of the primary structure

10
section of the sailing workshop (2022)

11
render of the sailing workshop (2012)

0 2 5 10

01

02

03

KRIEKELAAR **renovation of a theatre hall** **2013–15** **Schaerbeek, Brussels**

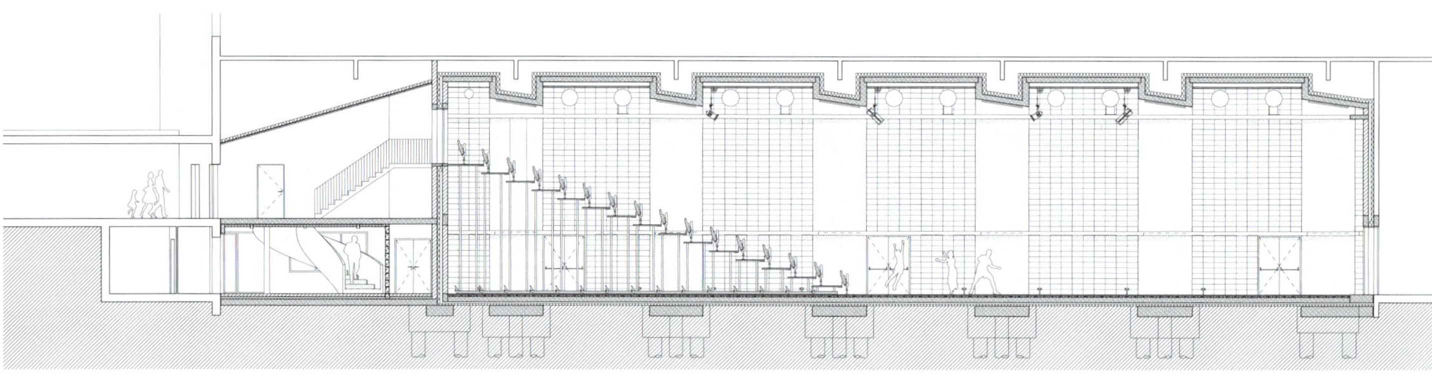

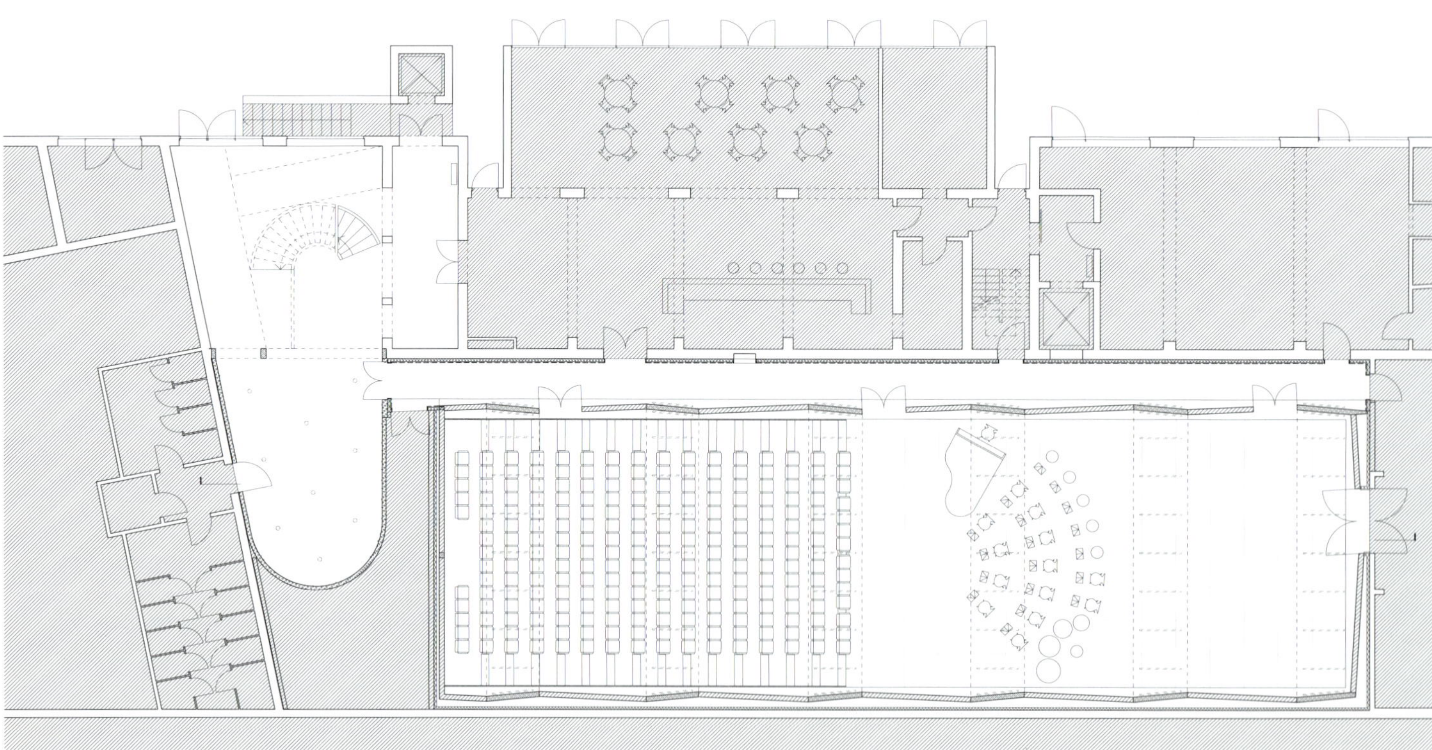

04

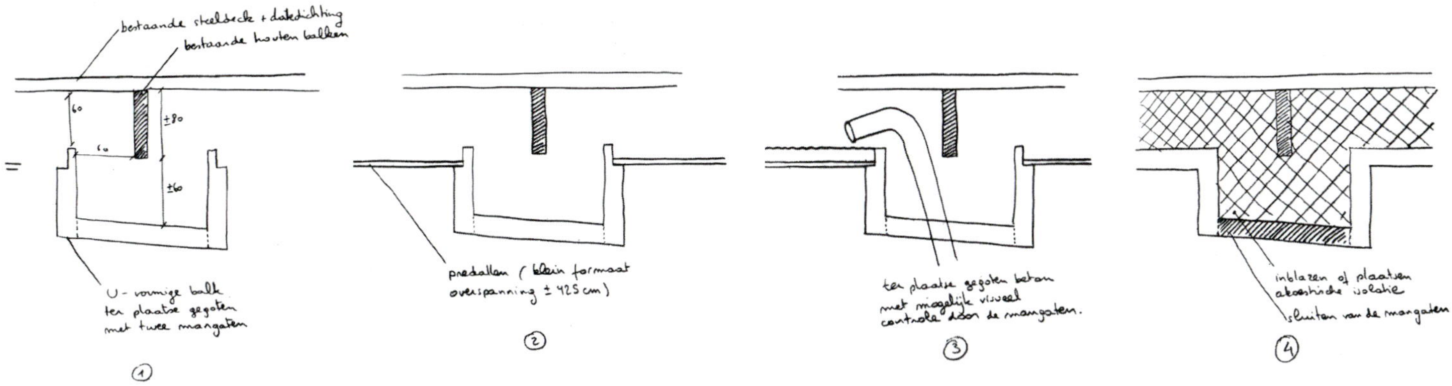

A concrete box-in-box is integrated in the main hall of community centre De Kriekelaar for acoustic reasons related to the neighbourhood. In the margins around the new hall, a new foyer in apparent ceramic blocks has been created along with a spiral staircase and a longitudinal circulation clad with stained lumber.

The construction of the hall inside the existing building is at the heart of the architectural attitude. Concrete walls, beams and infills of massive blocks create a folded composition ensuring acoustic insulation, internal comfort, constructive feasibility and architectural identity.
see p. 220–225

05

01–03
construction site (2014, 2015, 2015)

04
construction principles for the ceiling, competition phase (2013)

05
construction site (2015)

01

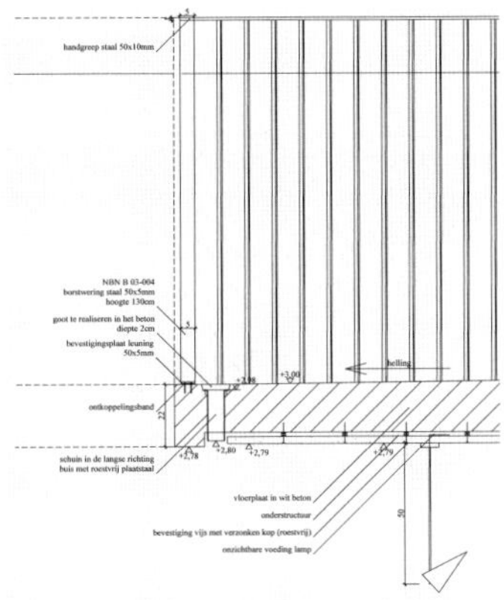

02

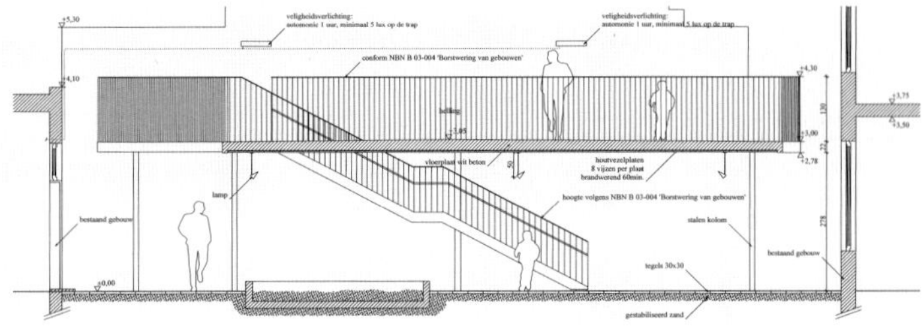

PRINS DRIES **construction of a walkable canopy for a kindergarten** **2013–14** **Antwerp**

03

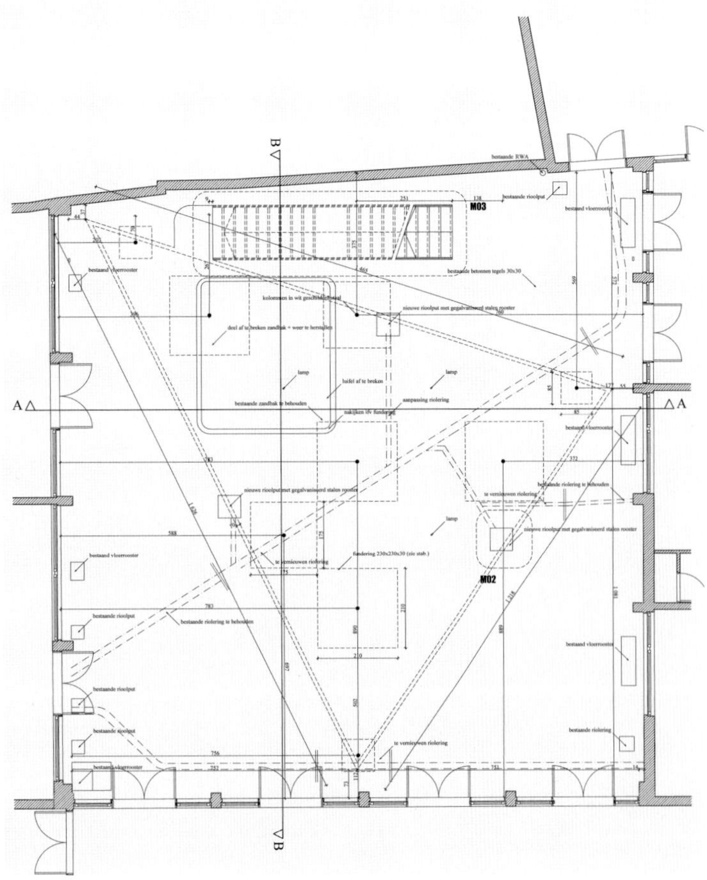

04

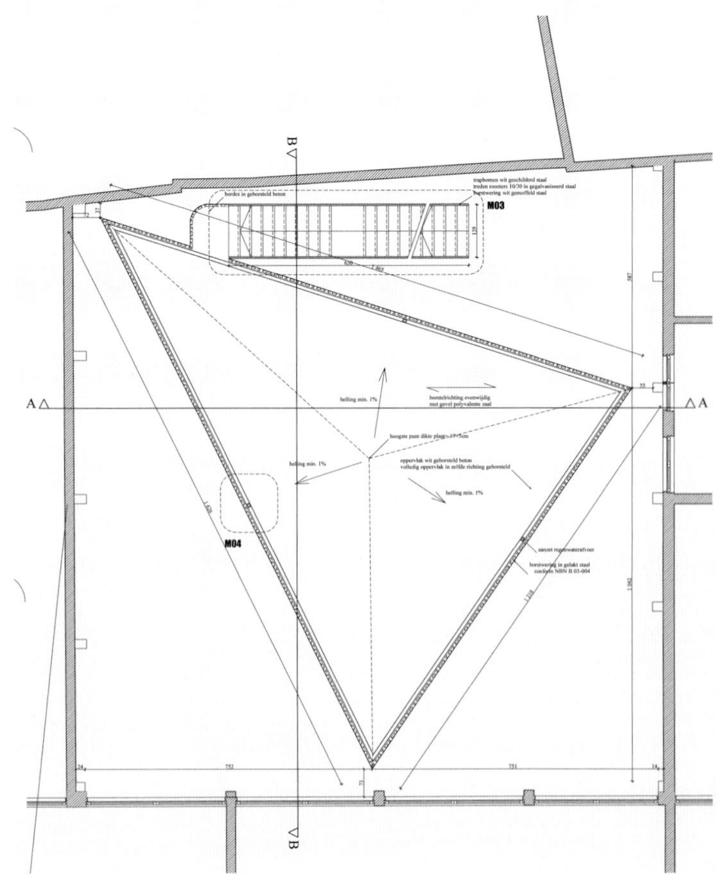

0 1 2 5

05

06

A new platform extends the available surface of the central playground of this small kindergarten in a dense neighbourhood in Antwerp while it retains the sandpit. A morphological examination led to a triangular shape, defined according to the existing architecture and entrances. Beyond the formal autonomy and playful character, the triangle liberates the surrounding façades and allows natural light to penetrate everywhere. A grid of steel columns supporting a thin concrete slab appeared to be the most efficient solution in regard to the restrained budget and time available.

see p. 218–219

07

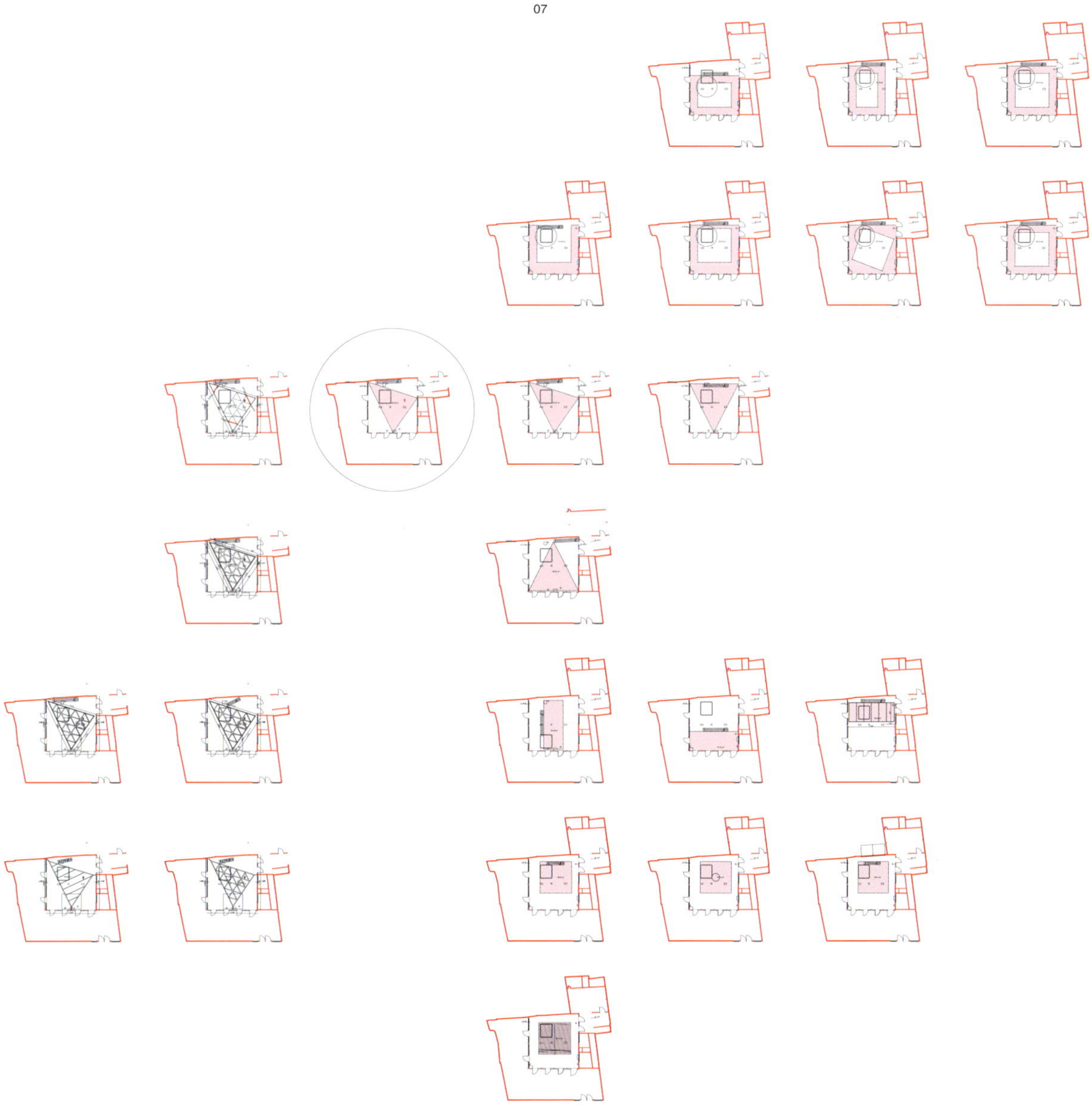

01–04
execution drawings, railing detail, section, ground floor plan, level +1 (2014)

05
preliminary design (2014)

06
selective demolition (2014)

07
plan experiments, preliminary design (2013)

01

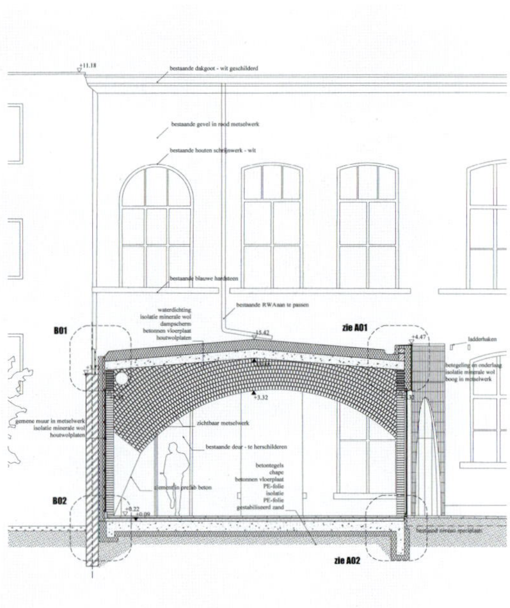

BREDA **extension and refurbishment of a school** **2013–20** **Antwerp**

02

03

04

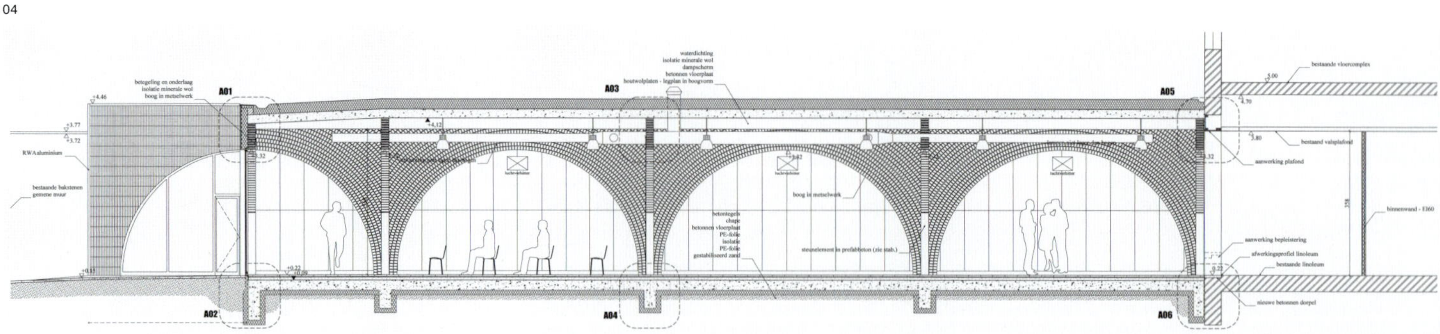

0 1 2 5

05

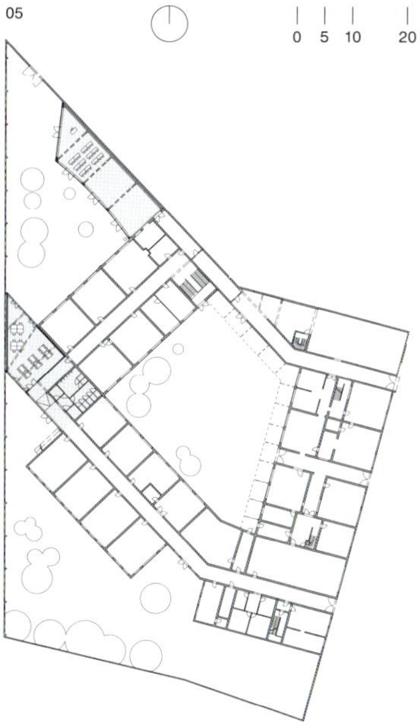

06

Besides a series of local upgrades in the vocational secondary school on Bredastraat in Antwerp, two new workshops were realized when a new tram line redefined the back edge of the plot. First, a masonry workshop, soon to become a bike repair centre, was marked by a series of structural brick arches. The slightly curved façade is isolated and clad with white ceramic tiles. Second, the textile classroom, soon to become a bakery kitchen, is roofed with variable, sloping concrete beams that adapt to the irregular geometry of the spot, between a corner of the building and the new tram line.

see p. 212–219

07

08

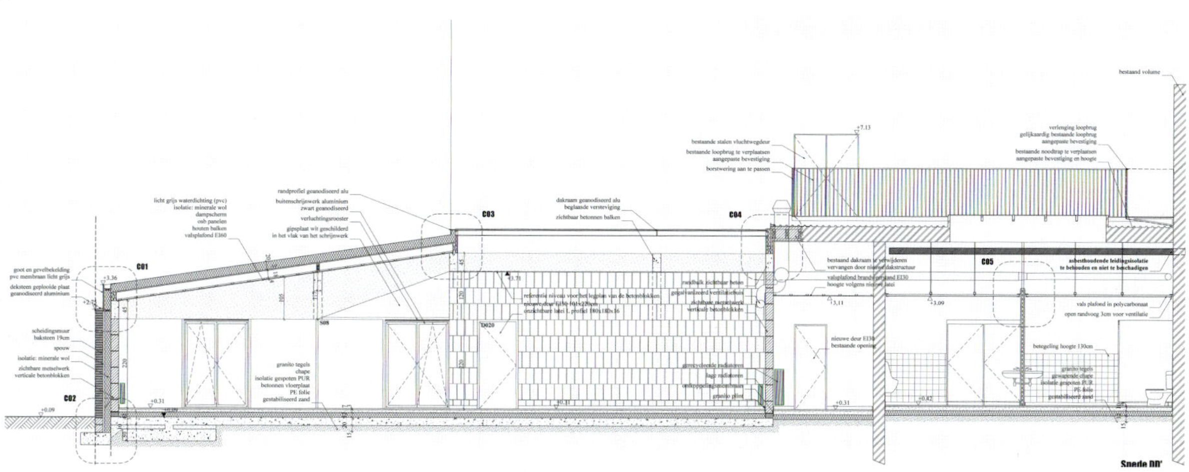

01, 04
execution drawing,
masonry workshop (2014)

02–03
construction site,
masonry workshop (2016)

05
situation plan indicating
masonry workshop (north)
and textile workshop

06–07
construction site, textile workshop
(2019) © Arvi Anderson (AgwA)

08
execution drawing,
textile workshop (2014)

section aa'

section bb'

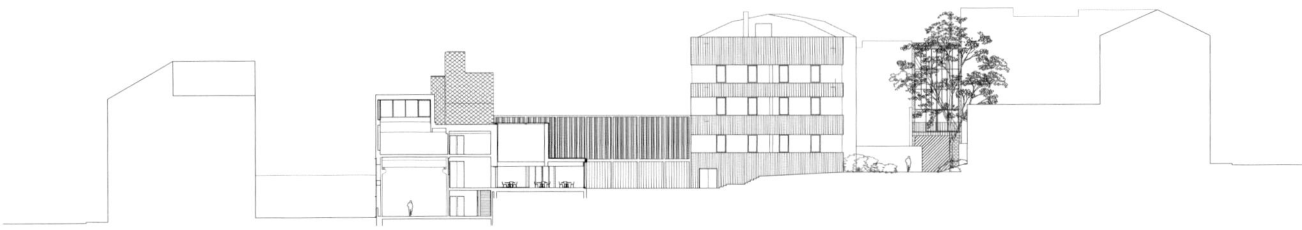

ECAM | **transformation of a former engineering school into a park, sports complex, kindergarten and youth facilities** | **2014–22** | **Saint-Gilles, Brussels**

01

02

The former École Centrale des Arts et Métiers (ECAM) comprises a series of heterogeneous buildings in a dense city block between two streets. The demolition of a town house on Rue Théodore Verhaegen creates a shortcut leading to a park at the heart of the site. The structure ensuring the stability of the adjacent buildings is covered with simple glazing, offering an informal, unconditioned platform for the neighbourhood. The old school building is converted into a kindergarten. Its extension is the cornerstone of the park. The steel roof structure of a new sports field separates the garden of the kindergarten from the park. The 1980s workshops are reused as a sports centre. A cafeteria articulates the sports activities with the park. The long volume along Rue du Tir that closes the site was converted into multifunctional spaces, with two additional entrances to the park.

see p. 198–211

03

01
construction site, view of the sports hall (2020), © Séverin Malaud

02
void in the city block: plan of the park, competition phase (2014)

03
scale model made for the *Operational Aesthetics* exhibition at CIVA, Brussels (2018), © Delphine Mathy

04

05

06

07

08

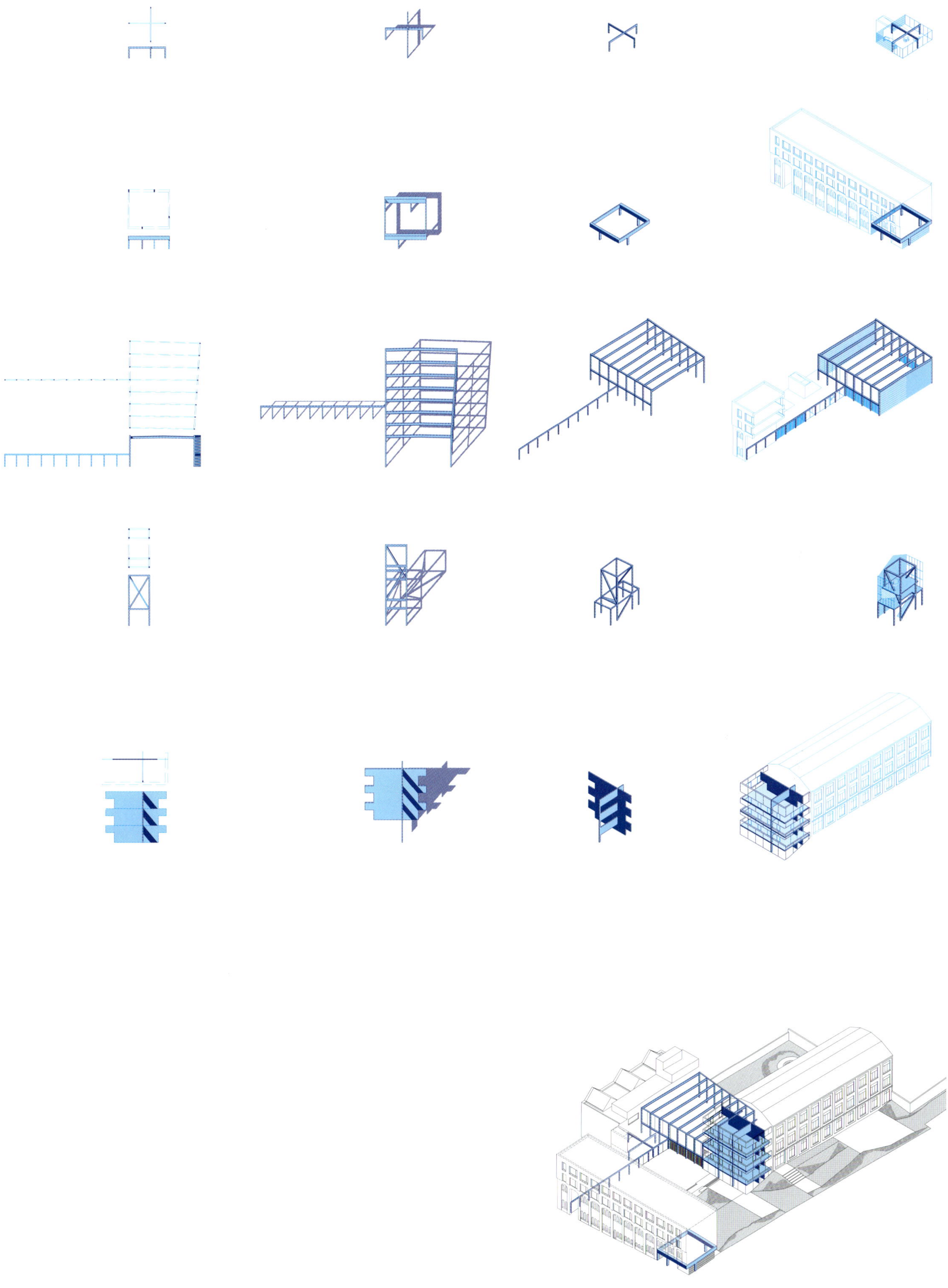

04–07
construction site, (04) sports hall (2020), (05) kindergarten extension (2020), (06) park entrance and ateliers (2021), (07) cafeteria (2020), © Séverin Malaud

08
orthogonal projections of the primary structures, made for the inaugural lecture at ULiège by Benoît Vandenbulcke

09

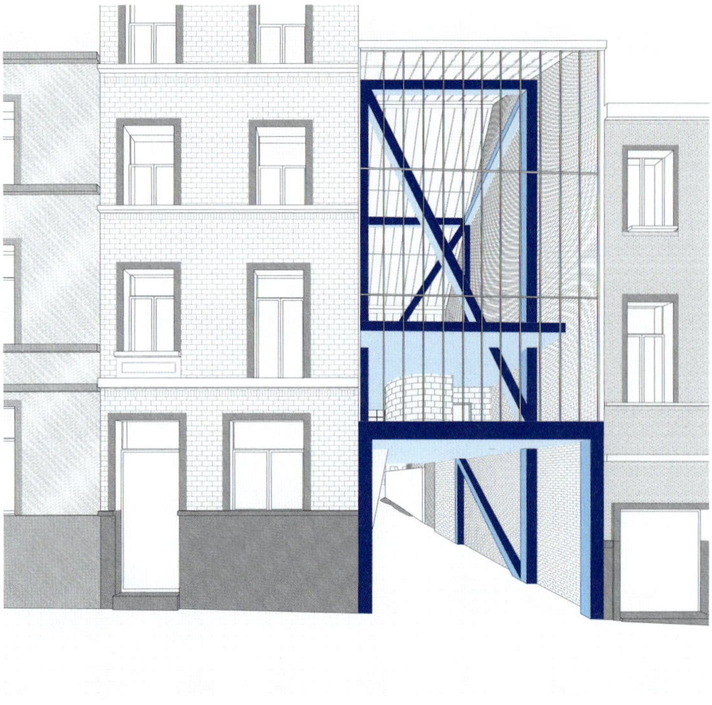

10

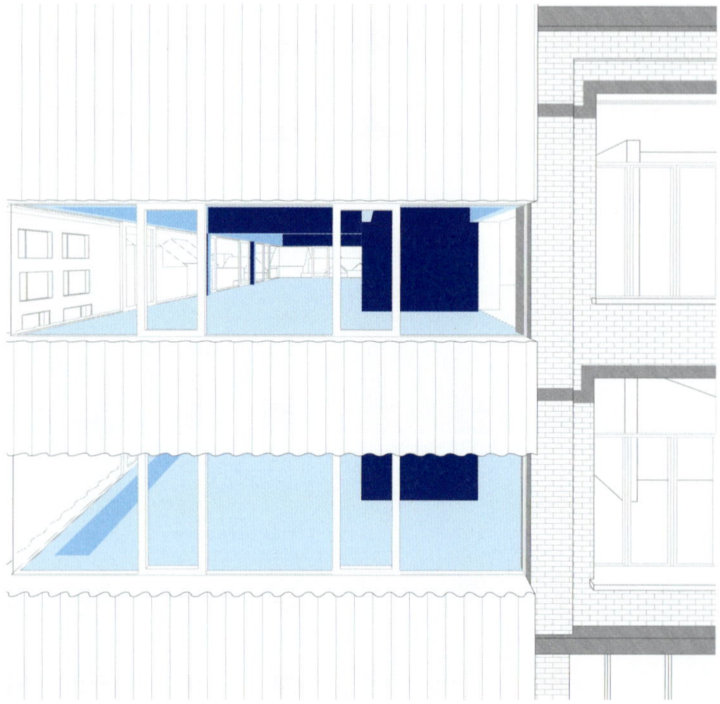

11

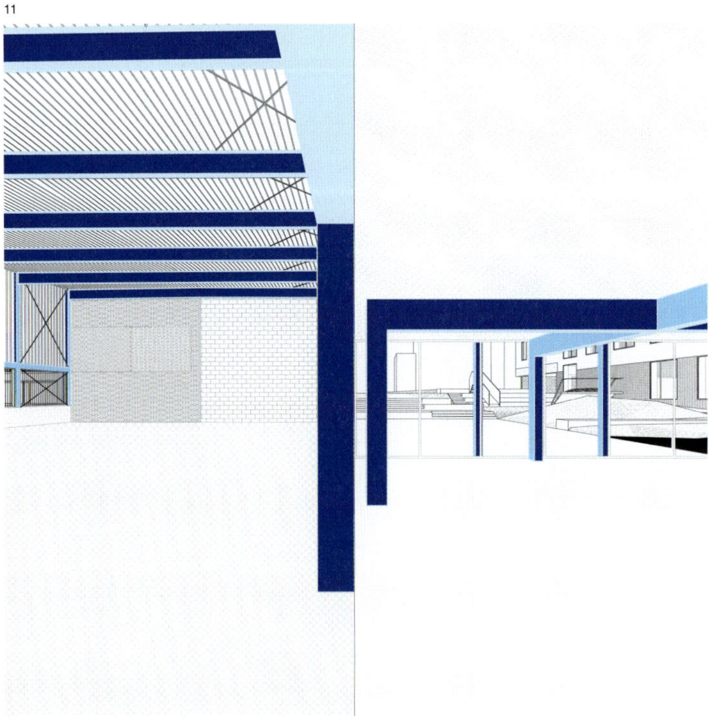

12

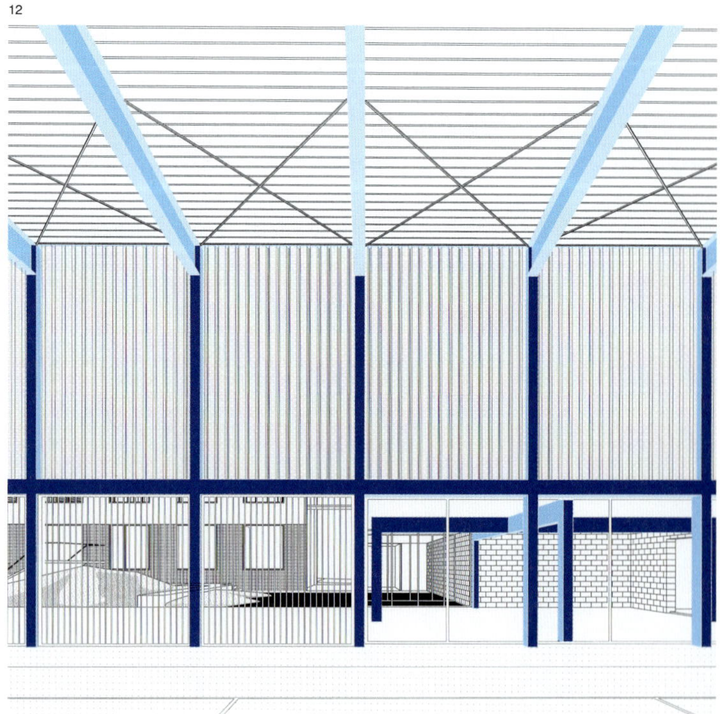

13

14

09–12
perspective drawings of the primary structures, (09) park entrance and ateliers, (10) kindergarten extension, (11) sports hall and (12) cafeteria, made for the inaugural lecture at ULiège by Benoît Vandenbulcke (2017)

13–14
construction site, demolition phase (top) (2018), construction phase (2020), © Séverin Malaud

15

16

17

18

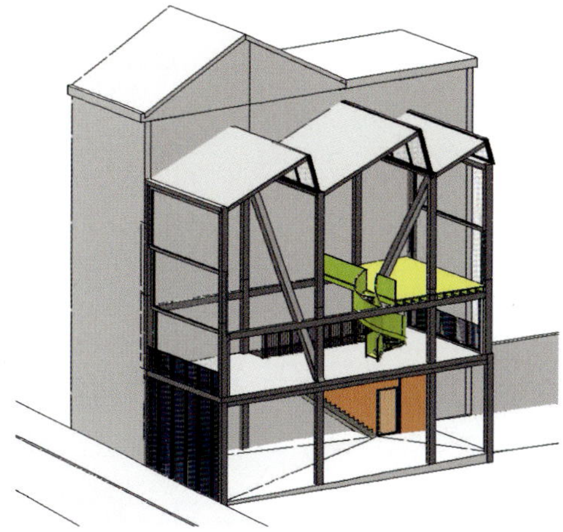

19

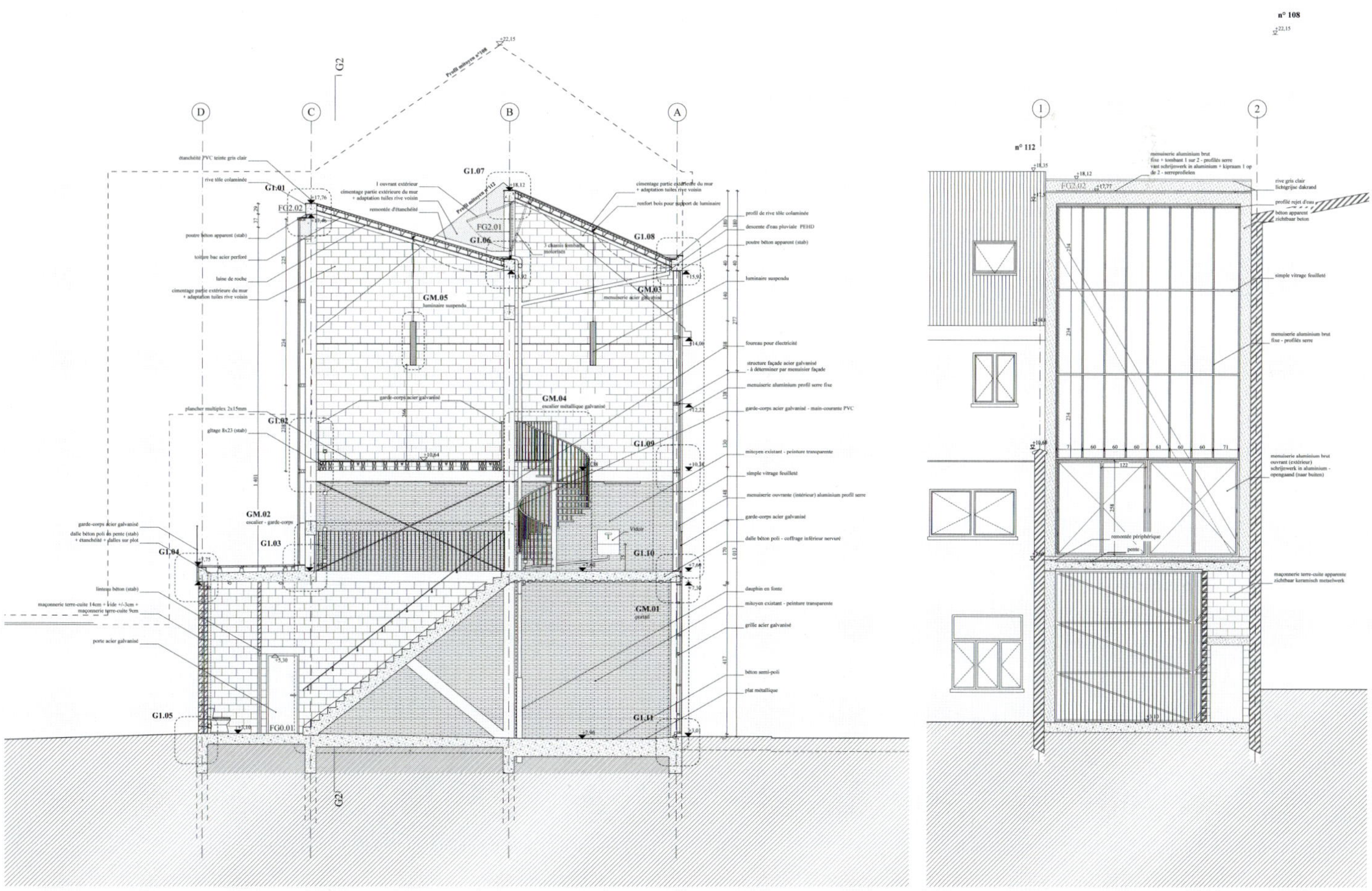

15–17
construction site, park entrance and ateliers (2021), © Séverin Malaud

18
axonometric view, building permit phase (2015)

19
execution drawing (2019)

0 1 2 5

01

CHAPEX+CHAPCO	renovation of an exhibition centre	2015–ongoing	Charleroi	in collaboration with architecten jan de vylder inge vinck

02

03

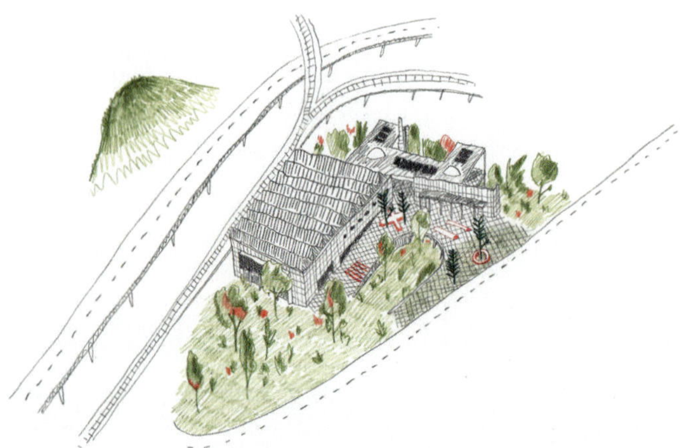

06

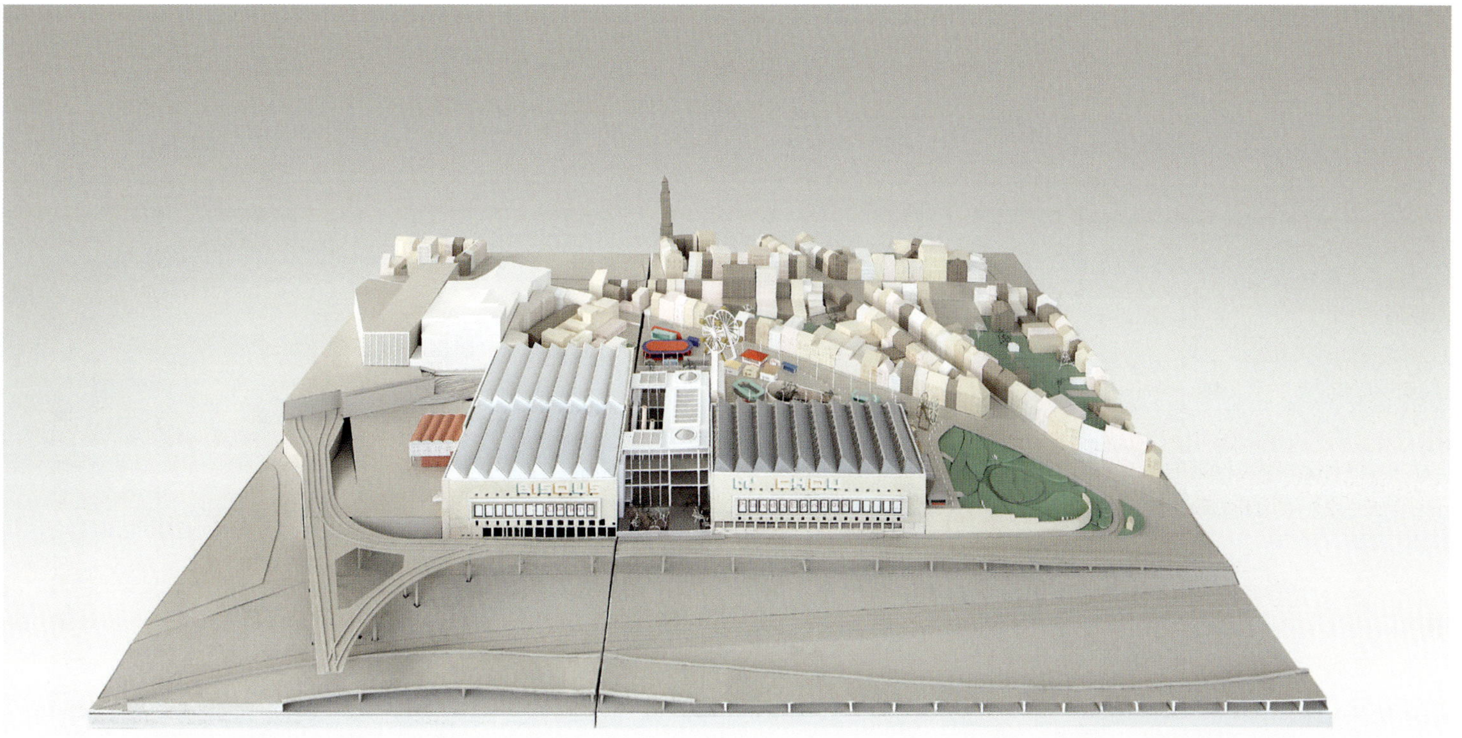

The very low budget available to restructure this huge venue for fairs and shows (CHAPEX) built in 1954 on the edge of the city centre of Charleroi made it necessary to keep most of the original structures. The façades of the central 'Halls d'honneur' were removed to transform these halls into a covered outdoor space characterized by monumental staircases and the slopes of the former slag heap, connecting the street below with the city centre.

On one side of the garden, three halls are used as car parks or as potential non-climatized extensions of the exhibition spaces. On the other, three stacked exhibition halls are connected by an escalator to the garden. The upper floor remains non-climatized. A fully equipped 'black box' is integrated in the lower floor. In 2021, during construction, additional funding made it possible to integrate congress facilities (CHAPCO) on the intermediate floor, with a longitudinal foyer opening up the building towards the central garden. The surroundings will be converted in an urban nature reserve.

see p. 184–197

04

05

01
archive photo during construction phase (c. 1953), © Archives of the City of Charleroi

02–05
drawings made during the feasability study of the congress facility (2020)

06
model preliminary phase (2017), © Filip Dujardin

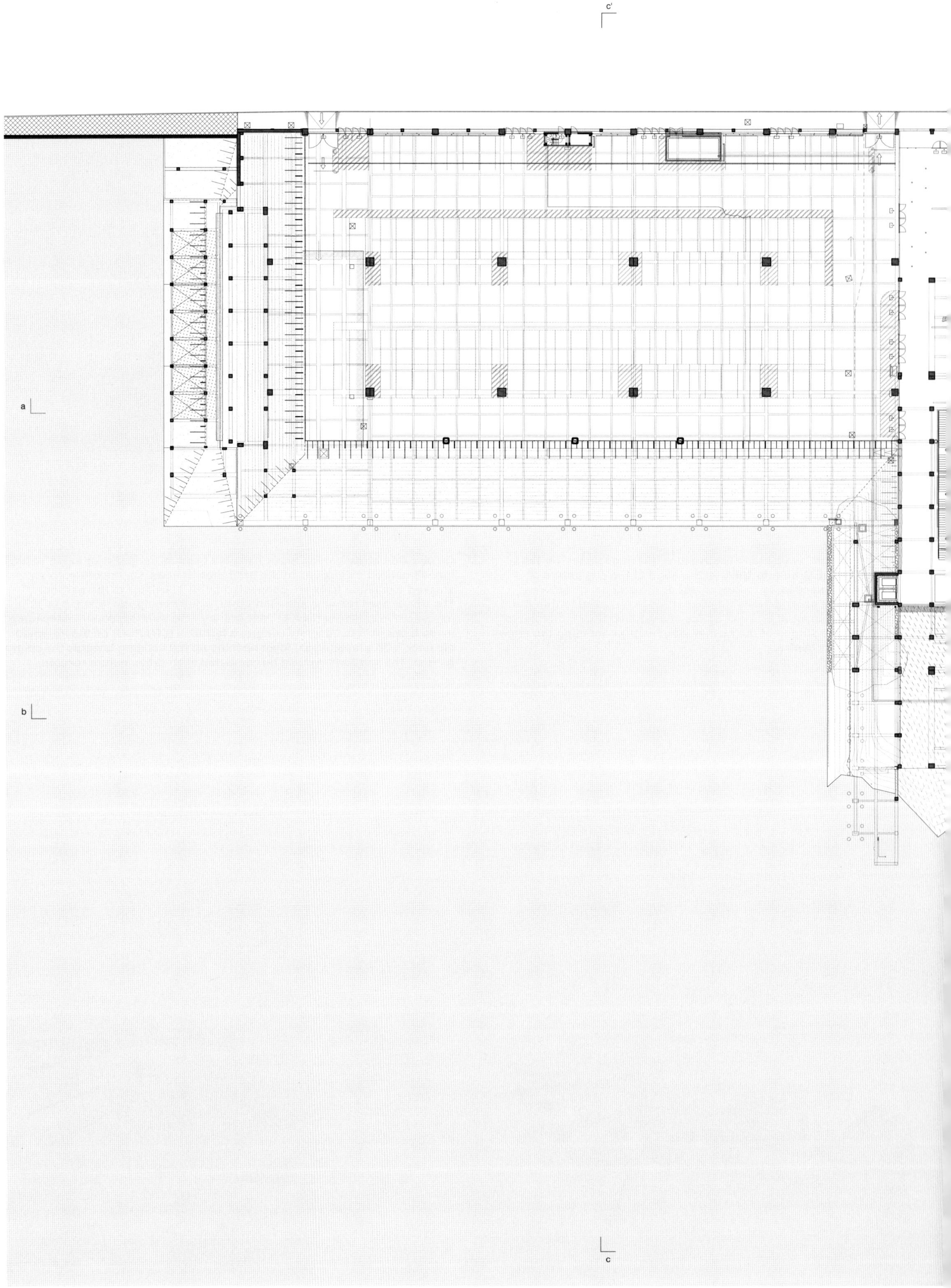
c'
a
b
c

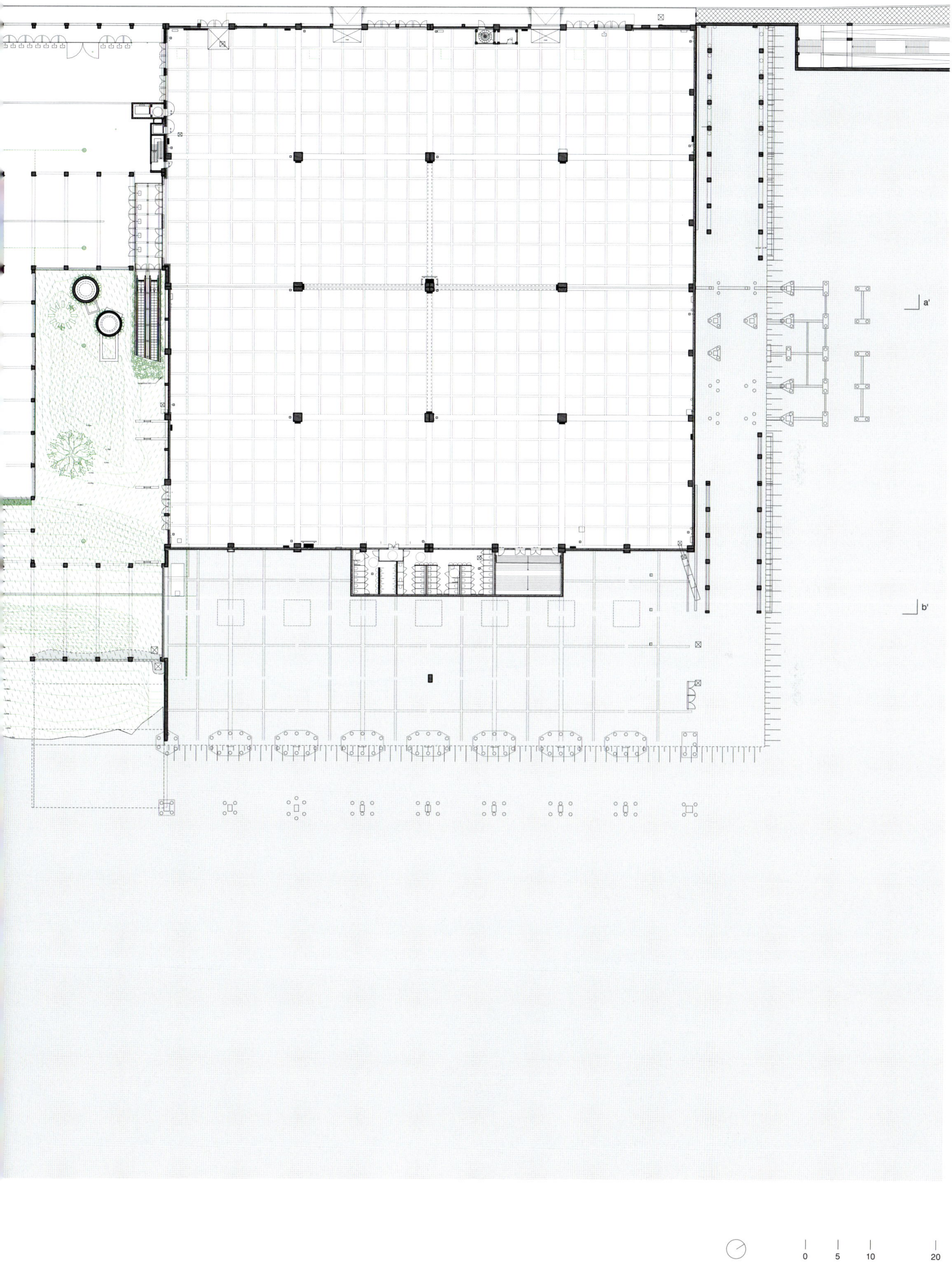
a'
b'
0
5
10
20

level -1, Square Octave Pinckers

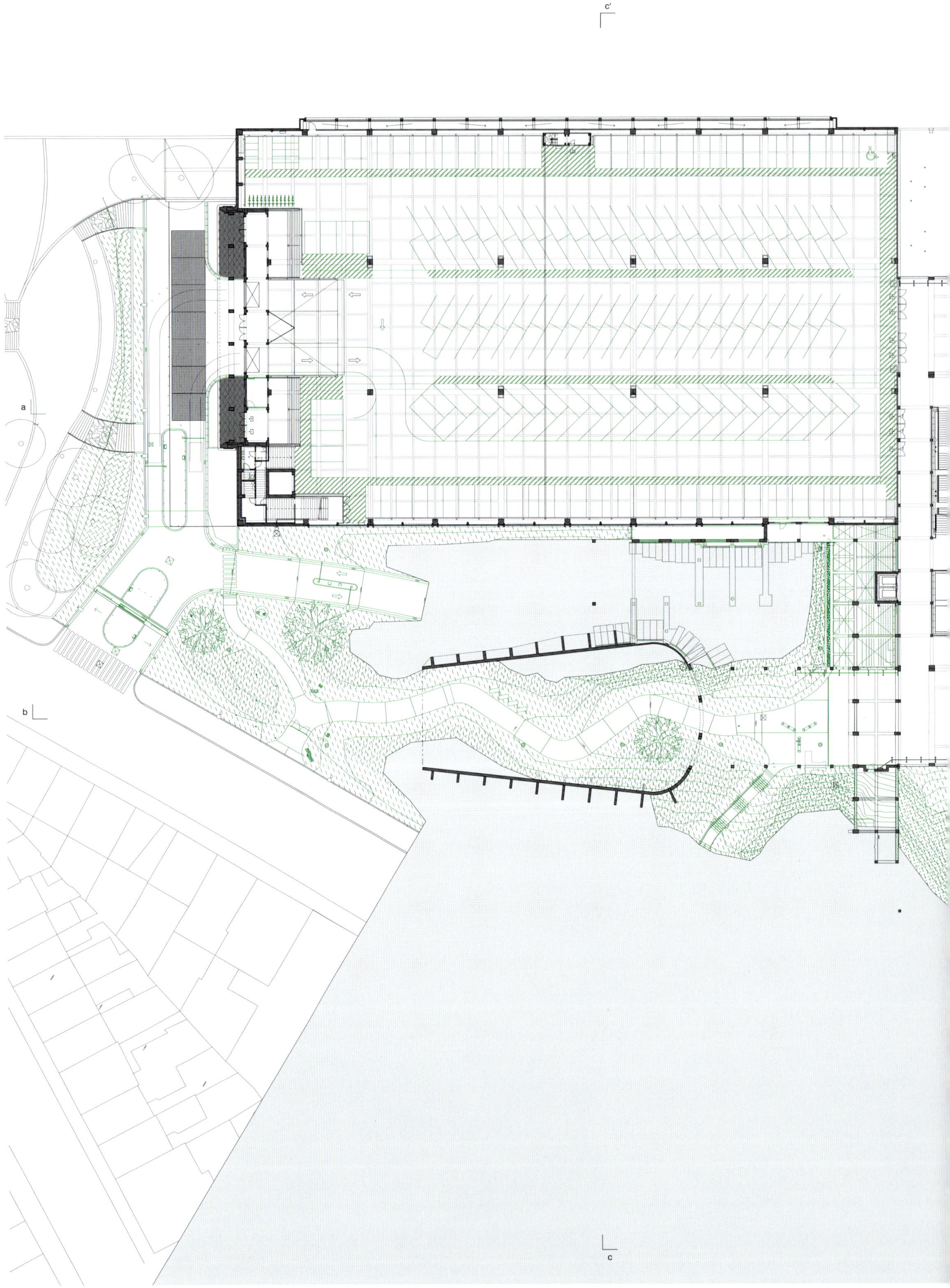

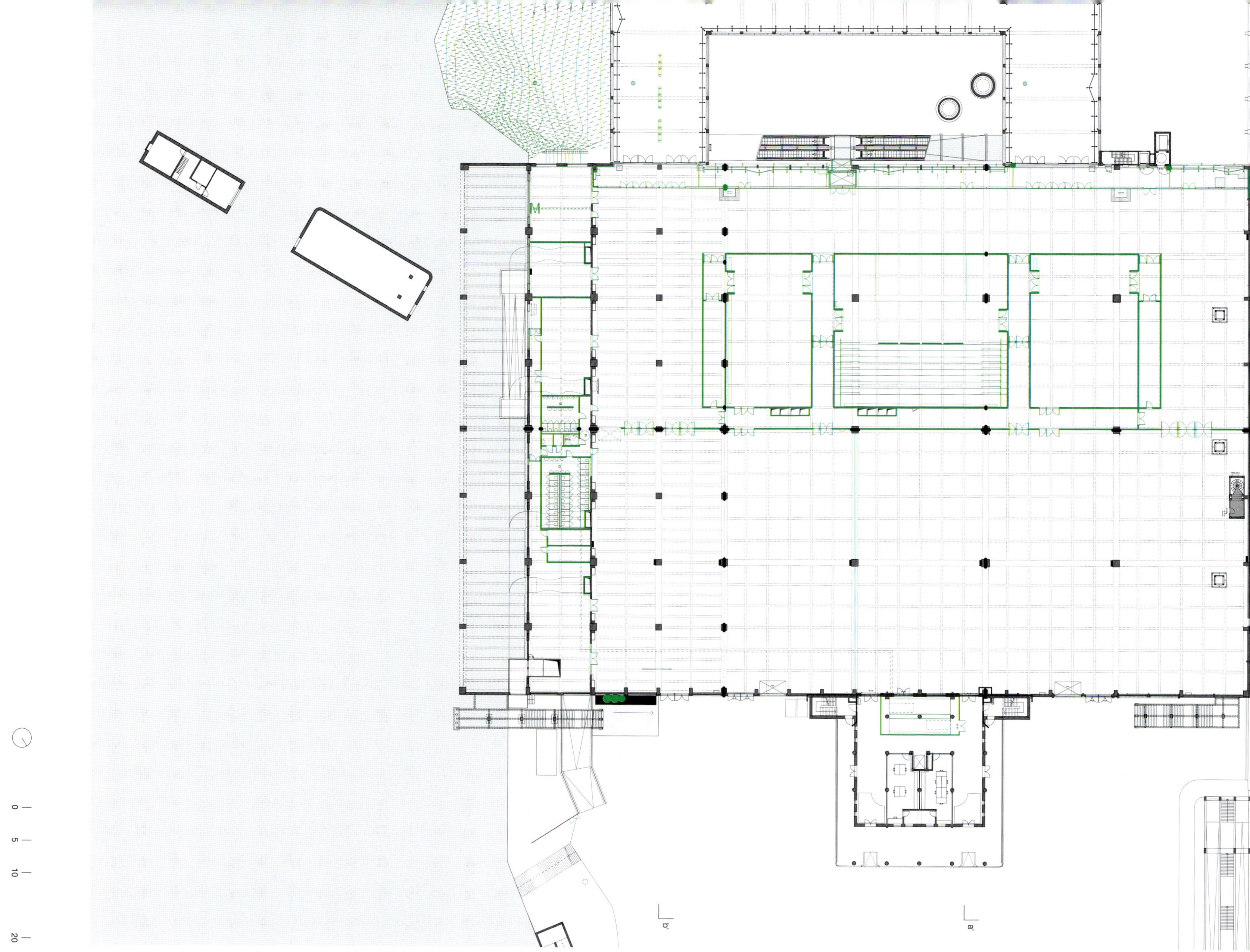
M
b'
a'
0
5
10
20

ground floor plan, Boulevard de l'Europe

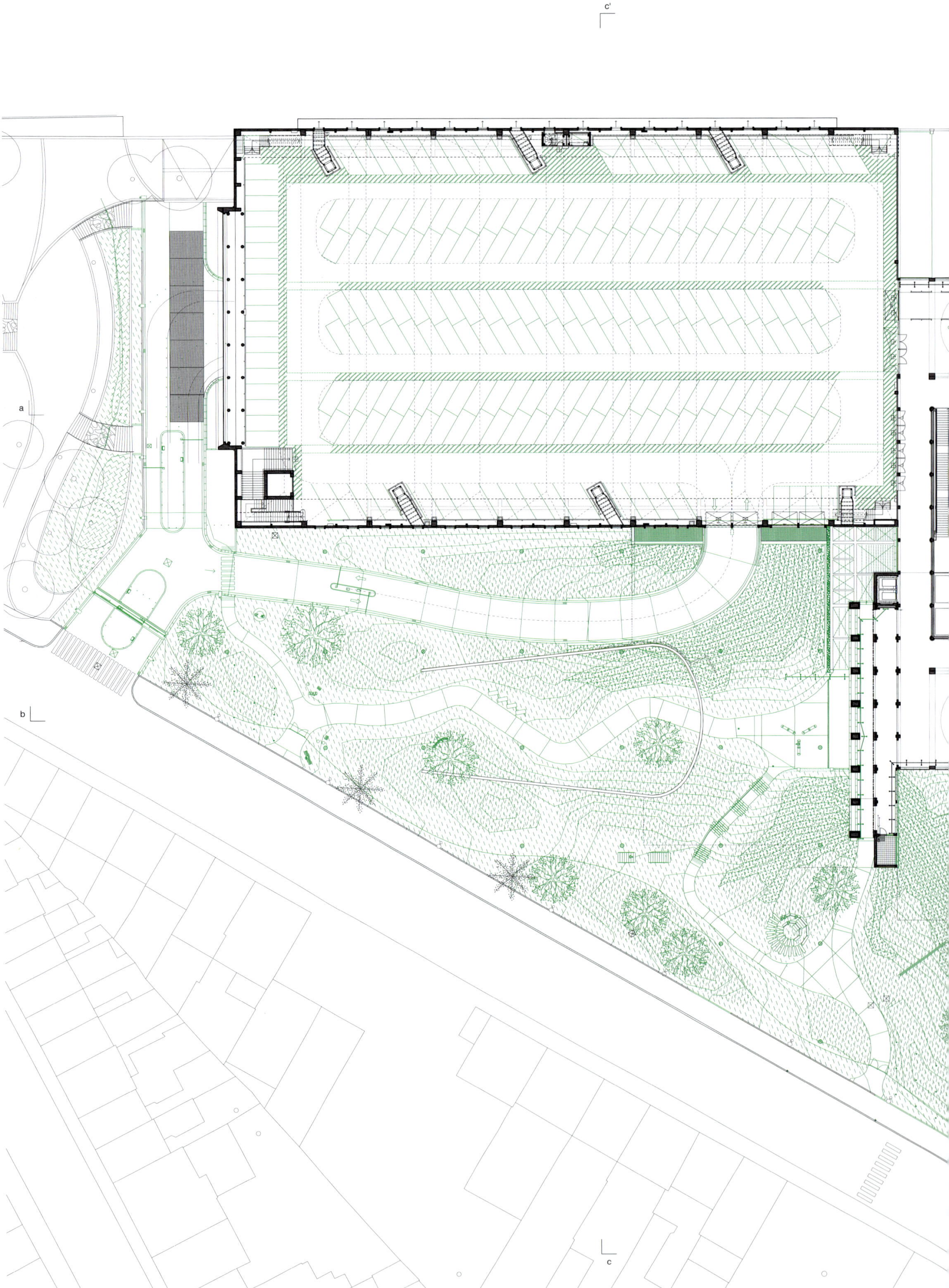

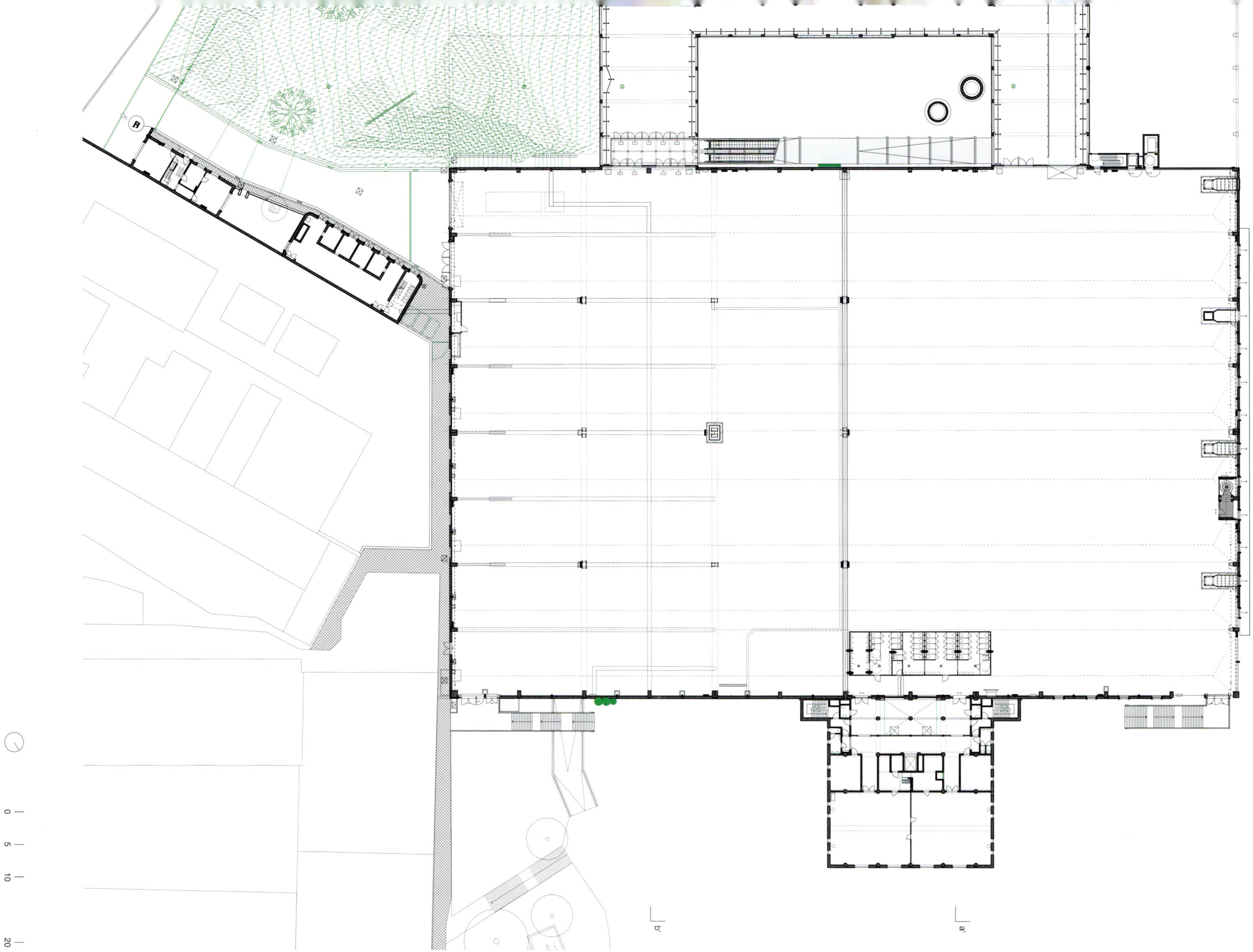
a'
b'
R
0
5
10
20

section aa'

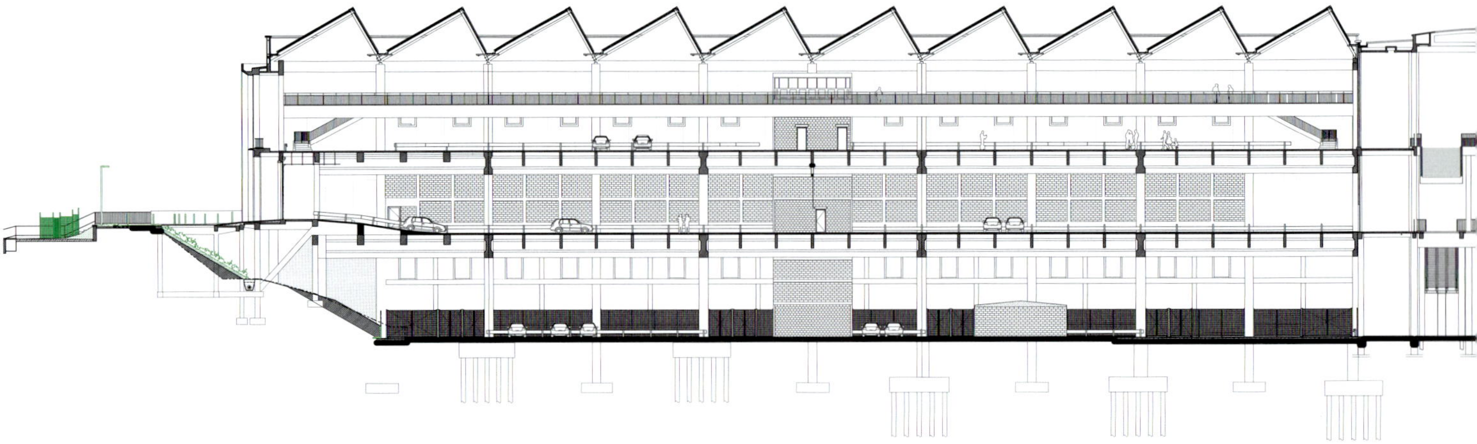

section bb'

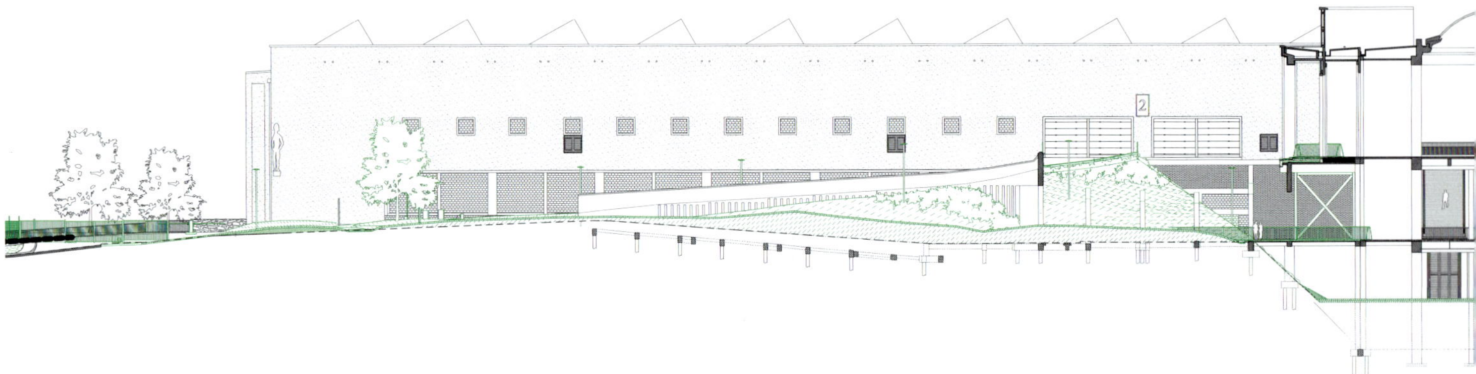

section cc'

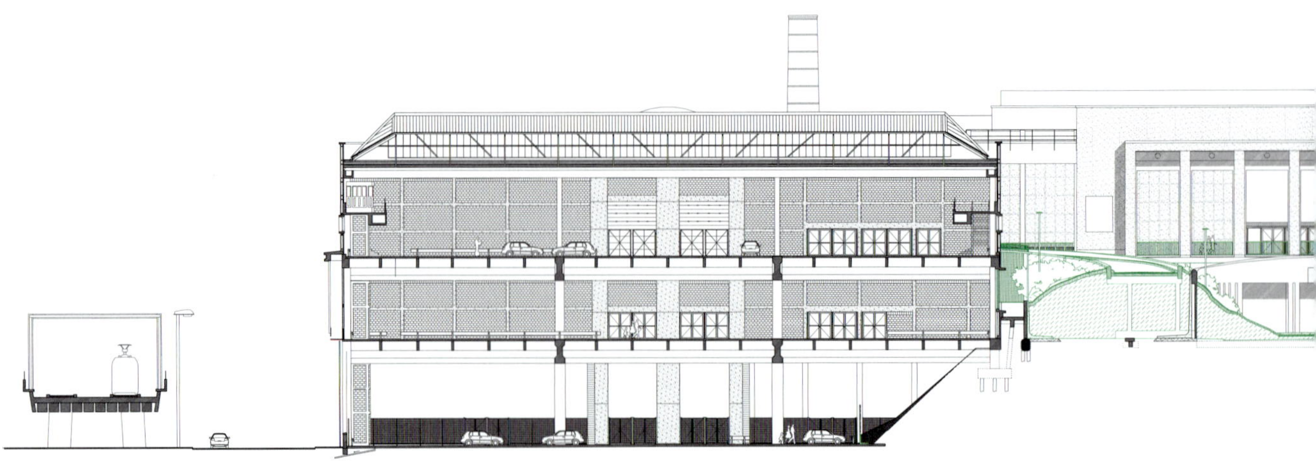

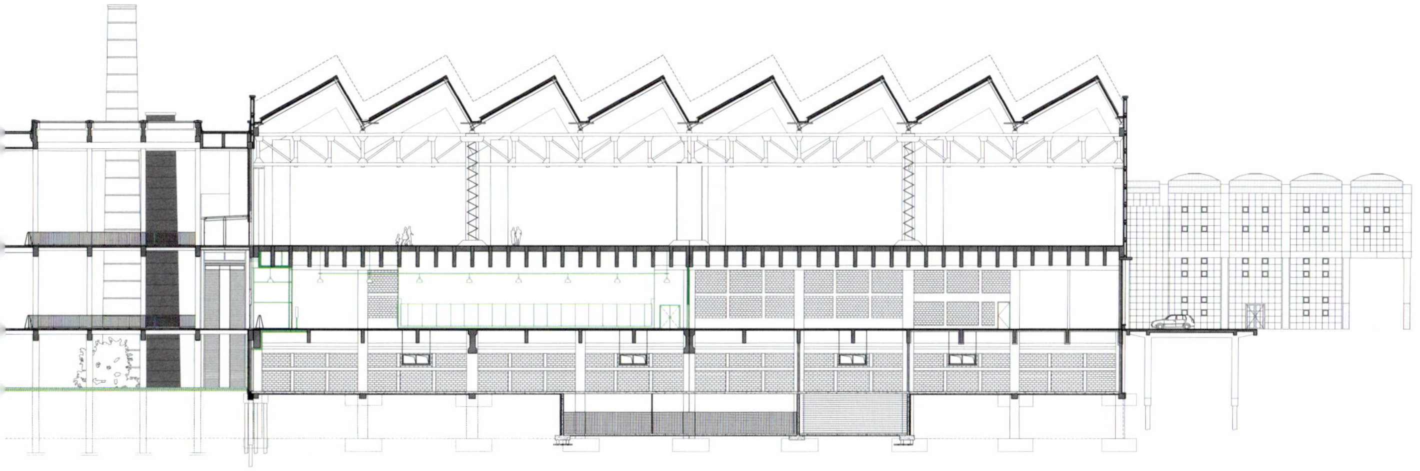

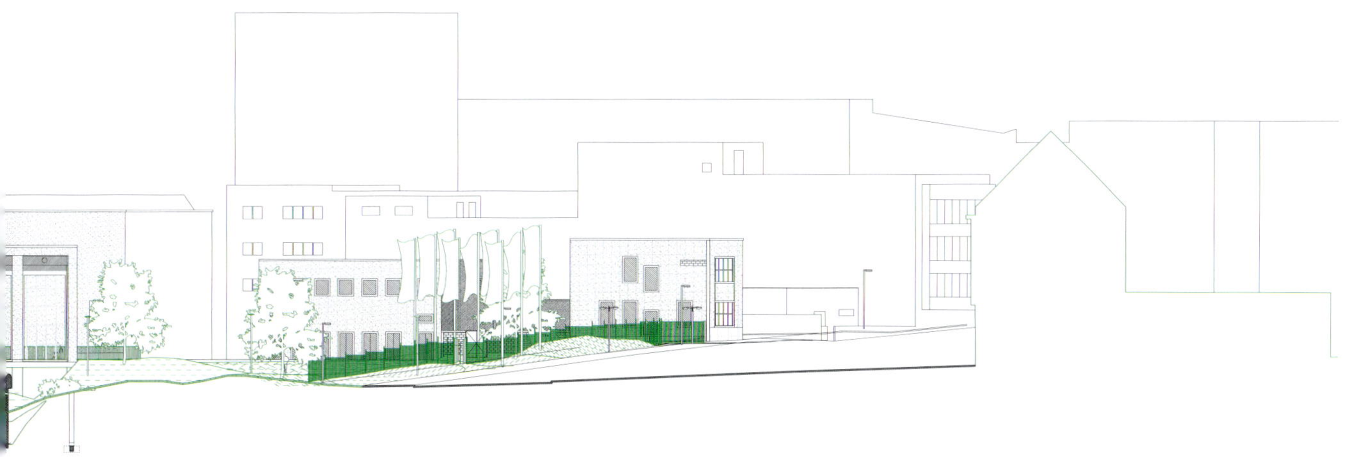

0 5 10 20

07

08

09

10

11

07–08
preliminary design (2017),
© Filip Dujardin

09–10
preliminary design,
congress facility (2021)

11
construction site (2021),
© Filip Dujardin

01

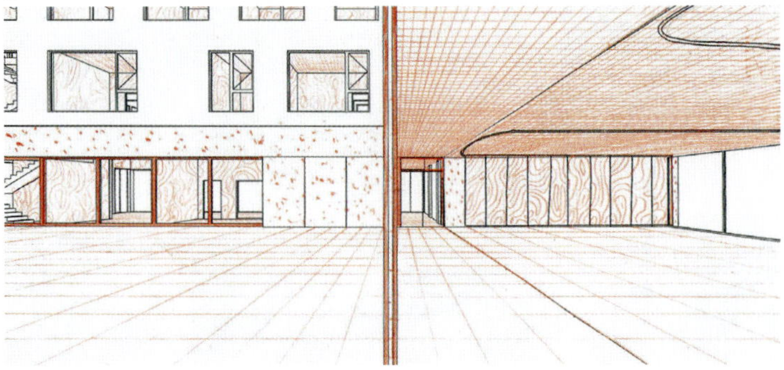

02

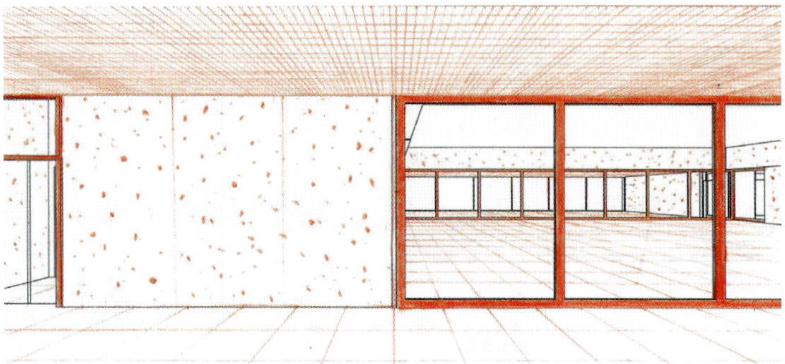

EMBASSY | **construction of an embassy** | **2015–ongoing** | **Beijing, China** | **in collaboration with GeJianZhu, ZhongZhu**

03

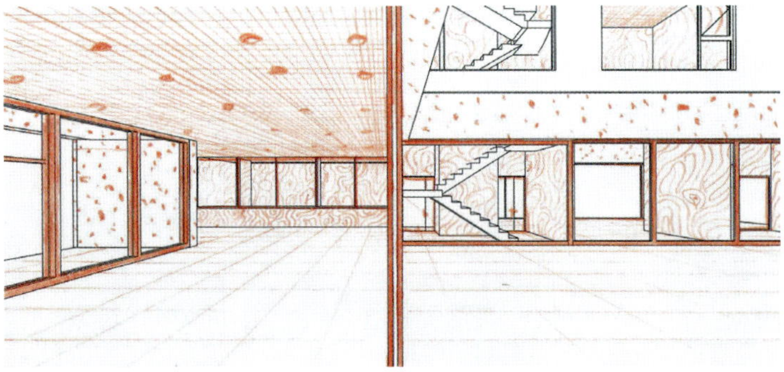

04

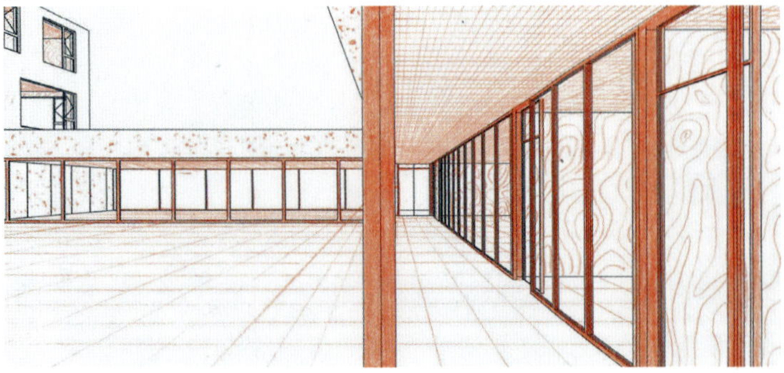

05

06

07

08

The embassy of Belgium in China unfolds around a central courtyard reminiscent of farm typologies punctuating the Belgian landscape and Chinese *siheyuan* courtyard houses. The ground floor, created with recycled materials from the former embassy, contains spaces accessible to the public. The upper levels, housing the offices, are made in wood. Although wood architecture is historically embedded in Chinese culture, this craftsmanship was lost over the last century. The project is at once a strictly functional machine, a vitrine for know-how and traditions, and a semiotic millefeuille.

09

01–04
perspective drawings around the central courtyard, preliminary design (2017)

05–06
construction site (2022)

07
preliminary design (2017)

08
façade study, preliminary design (2017), © Delphine Mathy

09
perspective section, preliminary design (2016)

10

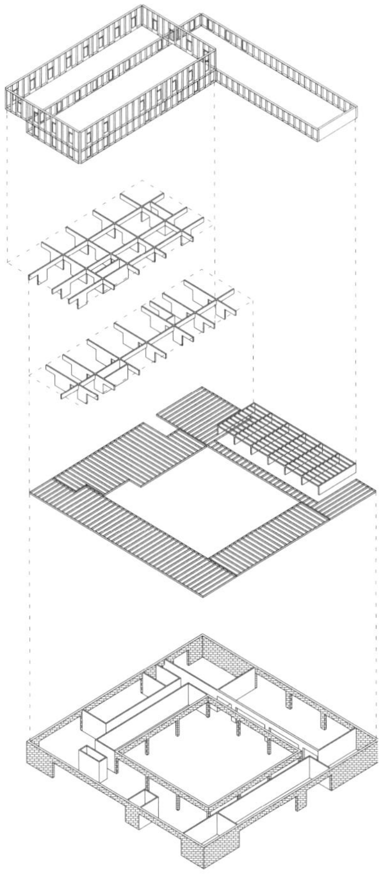

11

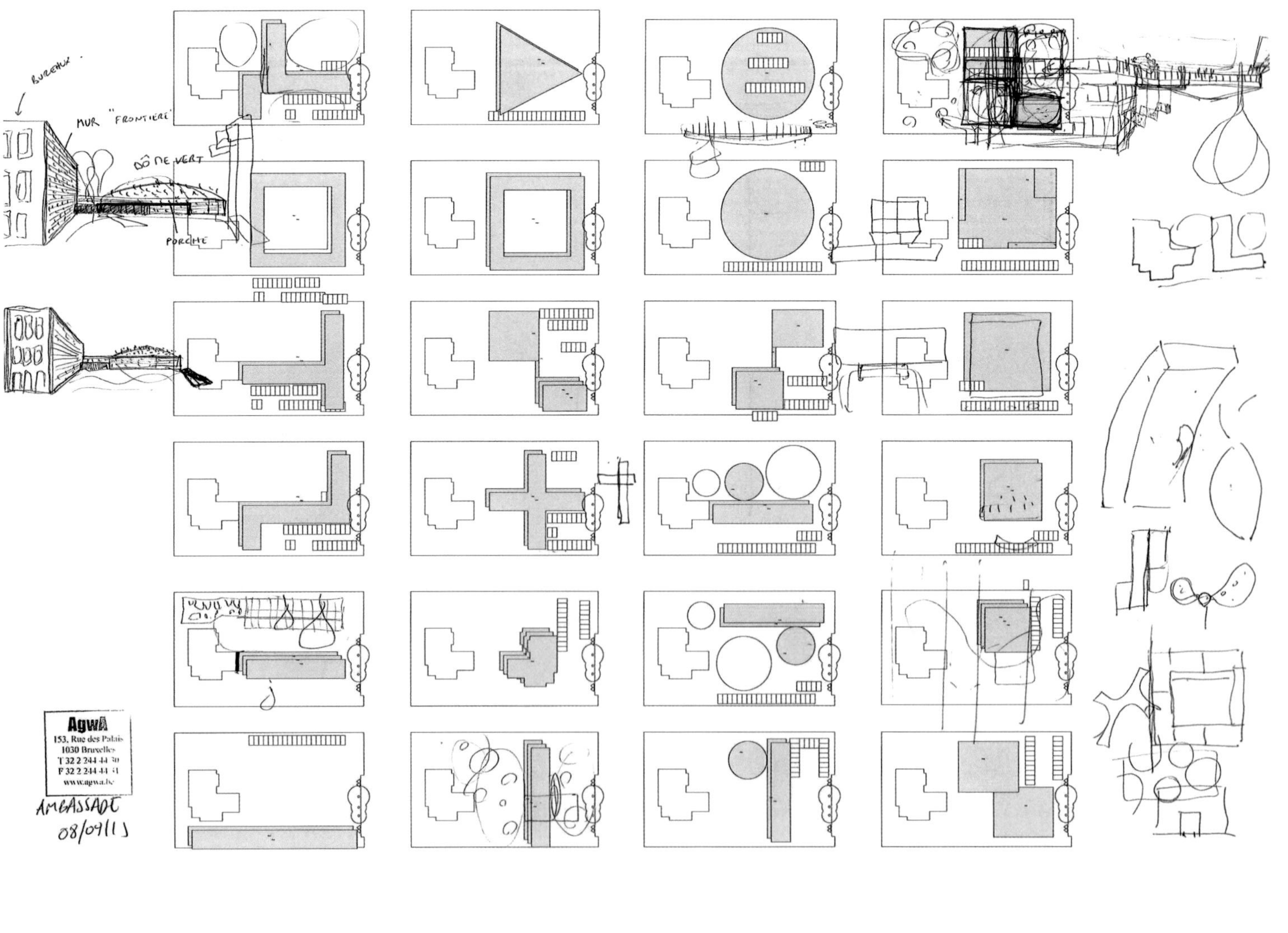
BUREAUX
MUR "FRONTIÈRE"
DÔME VERT
PORCHE
AgwA
153, Rue des Palais
1030 Bruxelles
T 32 2 244 44 30
F 32 2 244 44 31
www.agwa.be
AMBASSADE
08/04/11

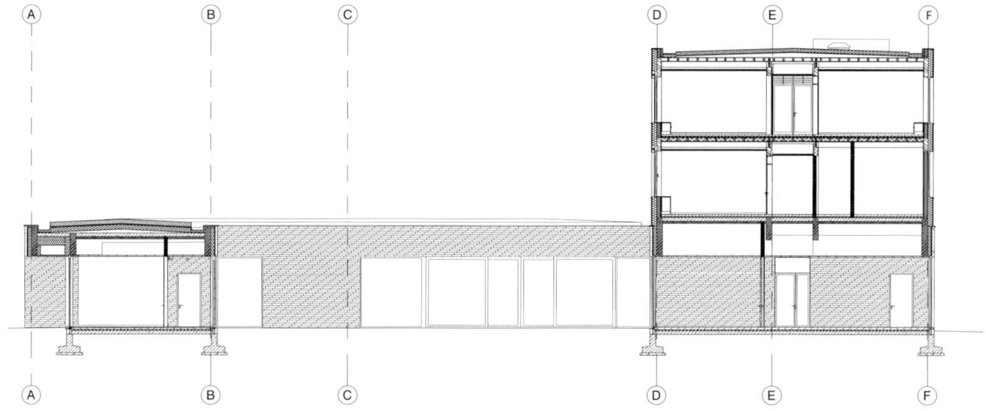

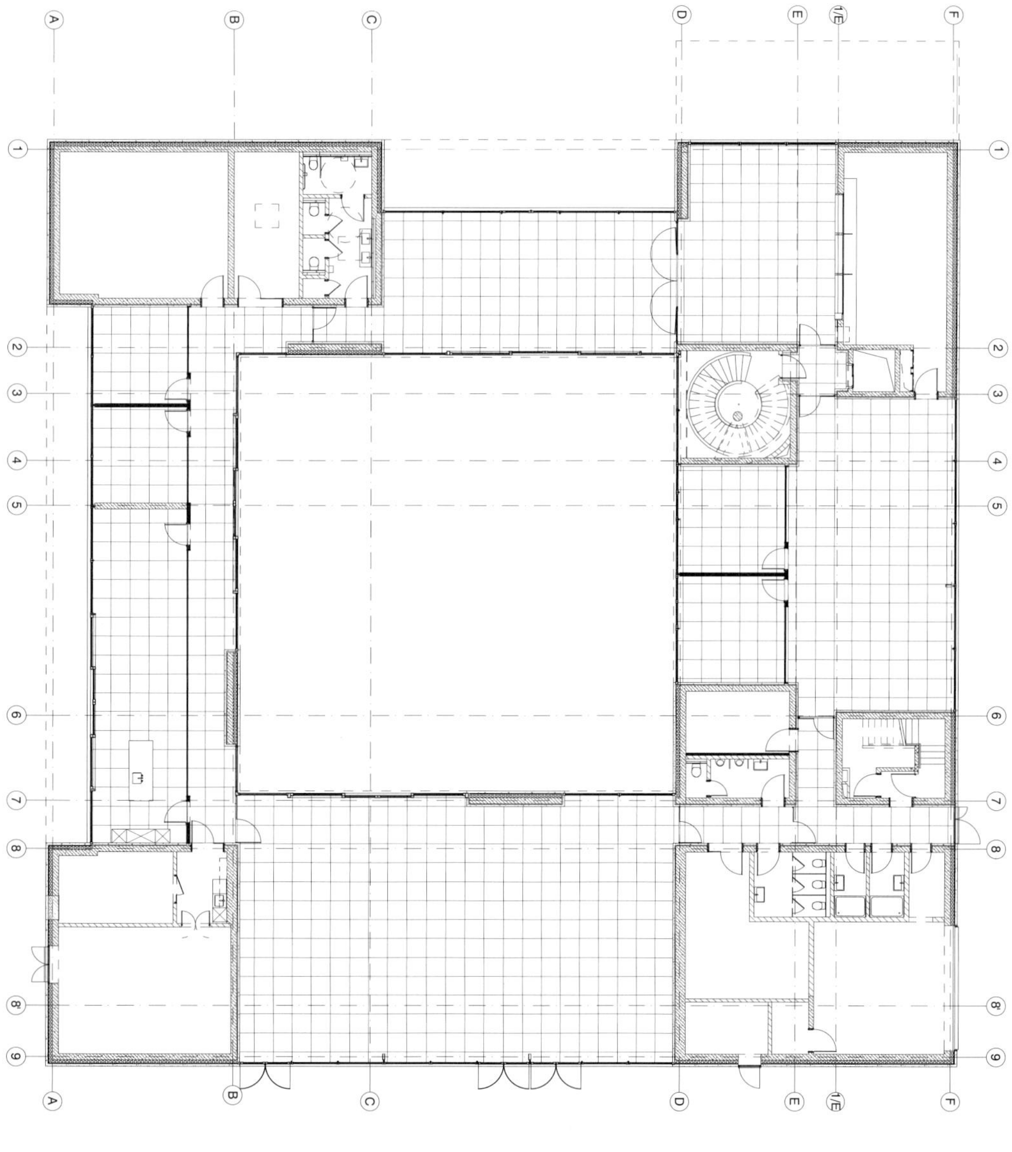

10
axonometric view of structural elements, competition phase (2015)

11
plan experiments (2015)

0 1 2 5

level +3

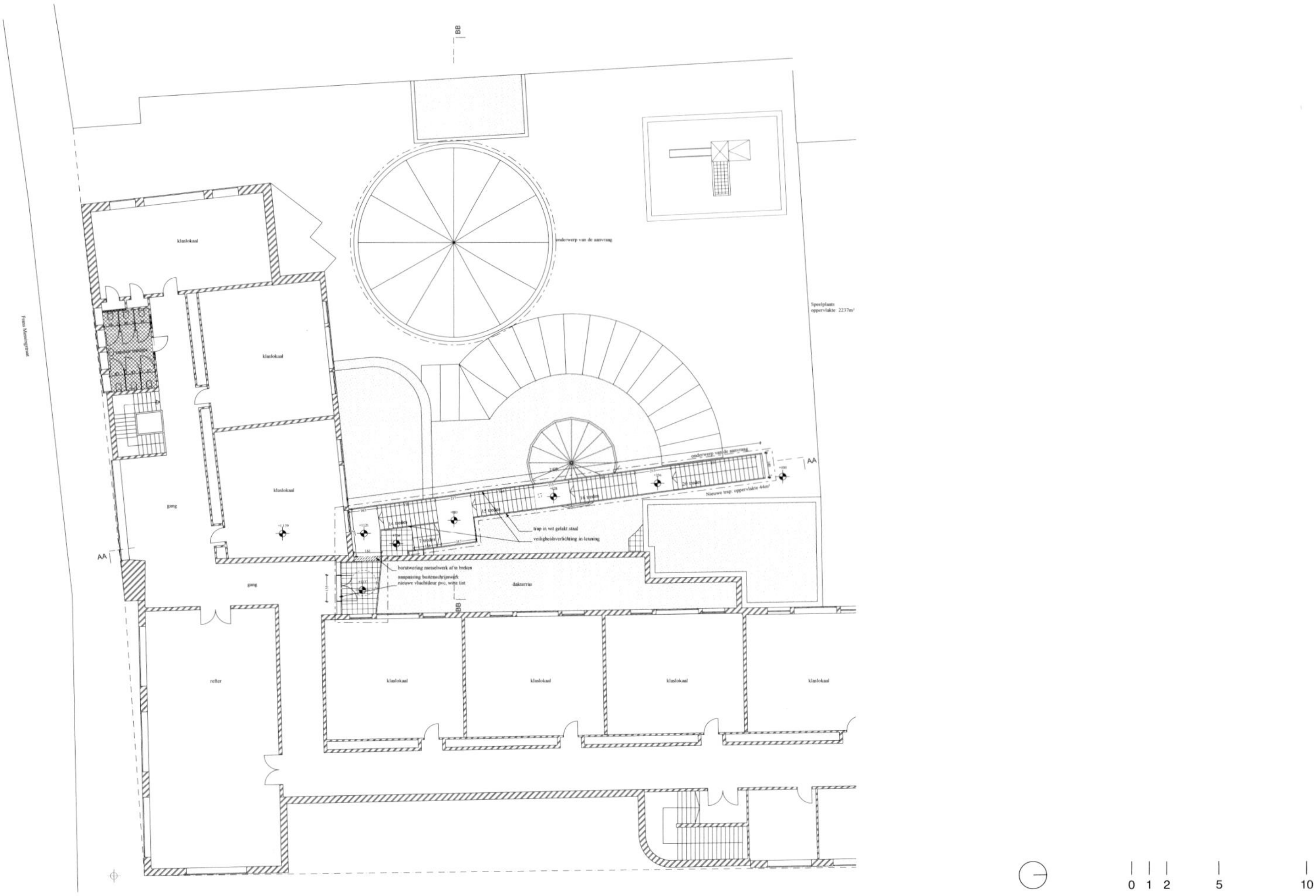

BARONNEKE | **construction of a canopy for a kindergarten** | **2015–20** | **Antwerp**

01

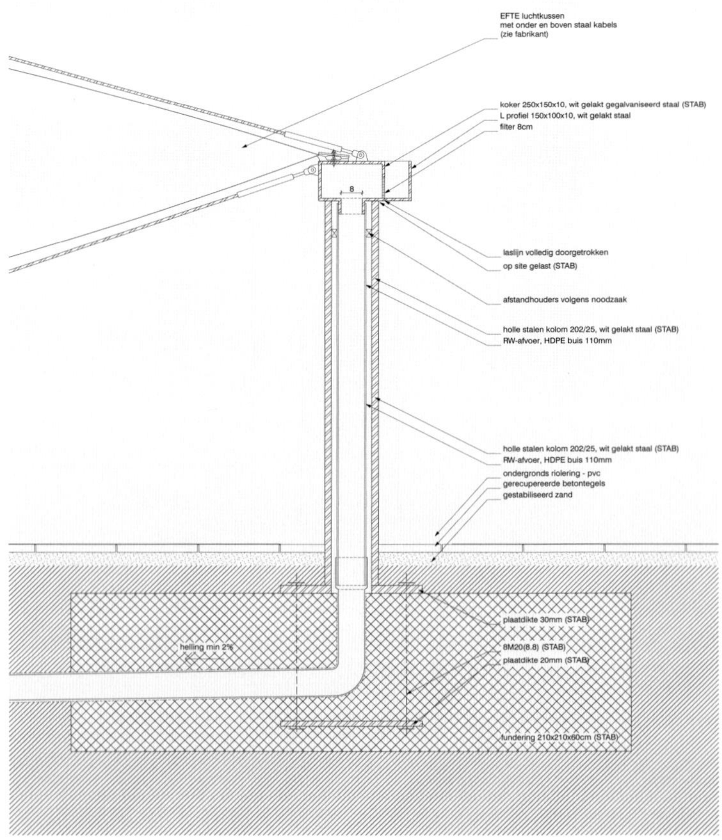

02

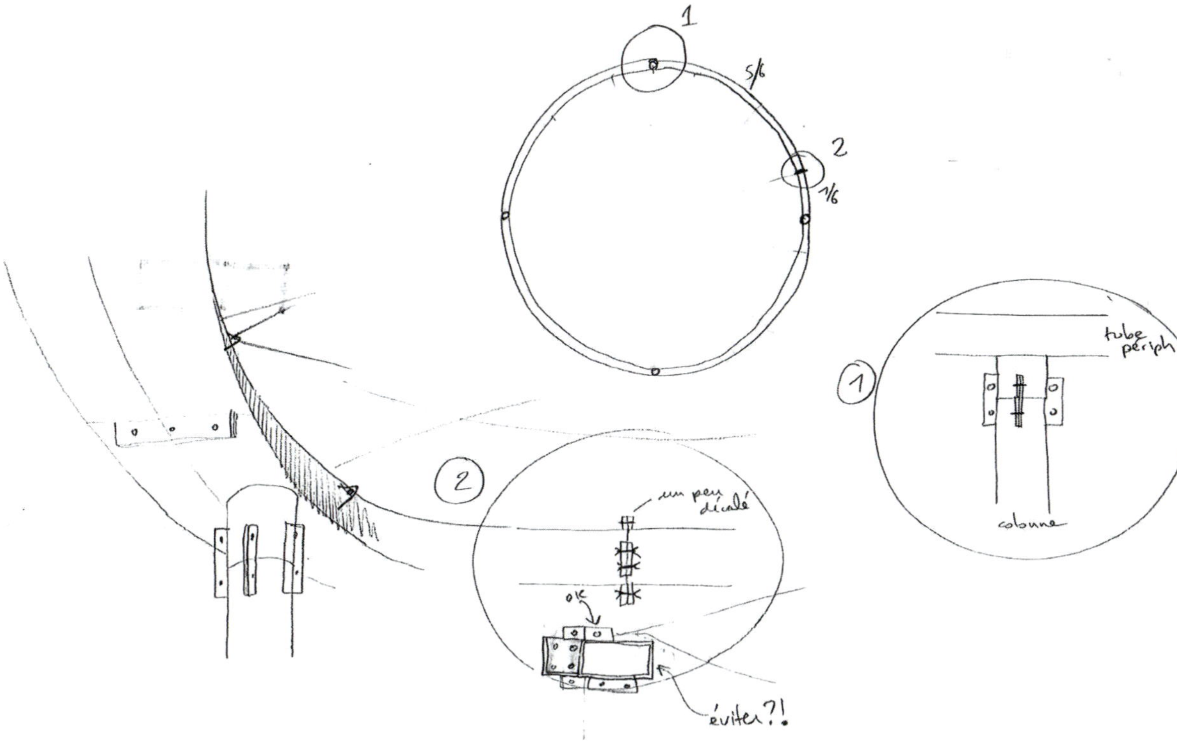

The steel structures of a new emergency exit staircase and a shelter for the playground were the main interventions in this upgrade of the Baronneke school in Antwerp. The shelter is a steel ring resting on four columns, spanning the space between the two wings of the kindergarten with a single transparent ETFE cushion.

The spectacular staircase unfolds over four levels, with a single intermediary support point piercing the roof of the foyer of the cultural centre housed in the same building. The straightforward steel structure varies according to the contextual constraints.

see p. 180–183

03

04

01
detail section of the canopy, execution phase (2017)

02
details of steel joints and articulations, execution phase (2017)

03–04
construction site (2019)

05

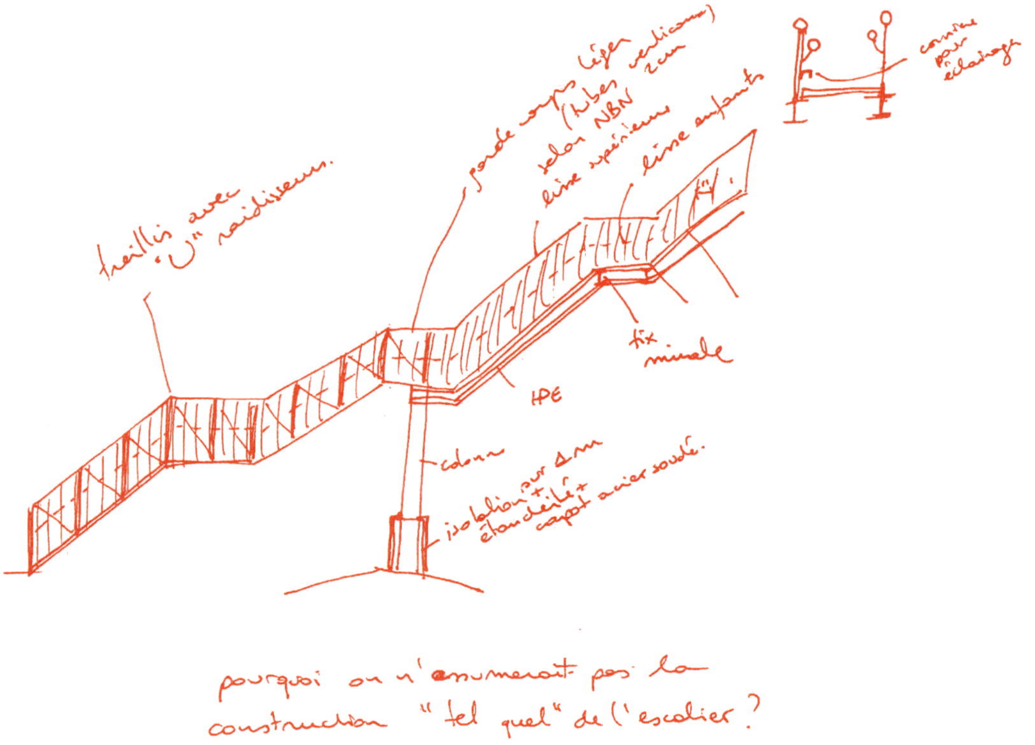
treillis avec "U" raidisseurs.
HPE
colonne
fix murale
pourquoi on n'assumerait pas la construction "tel quel" de l'escalier ?

06

07

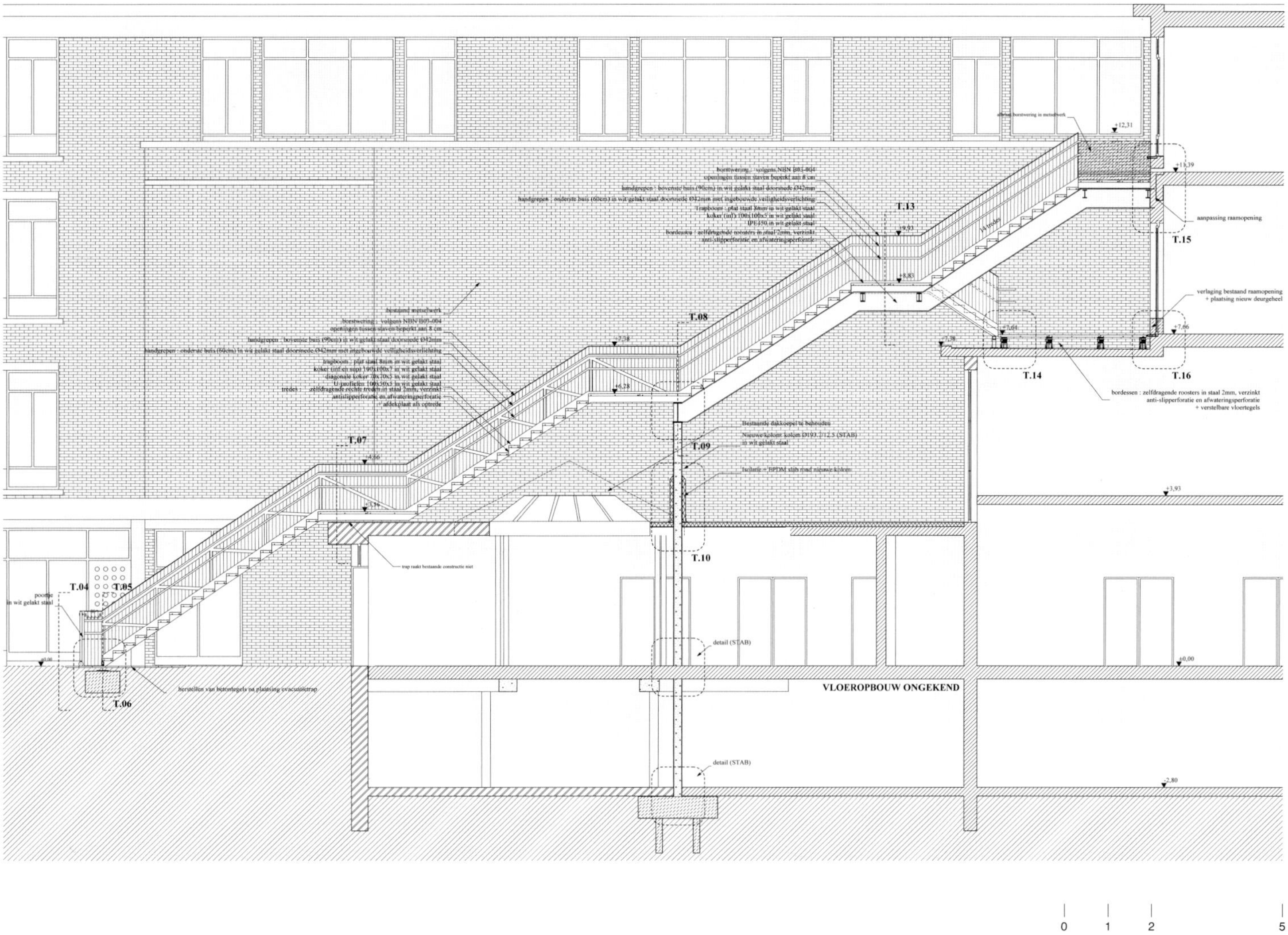

05
structural elements,
execution phase (2017)

06–07
construction site (2019)

08
section of the new stairs,
execution phase (2017)

01

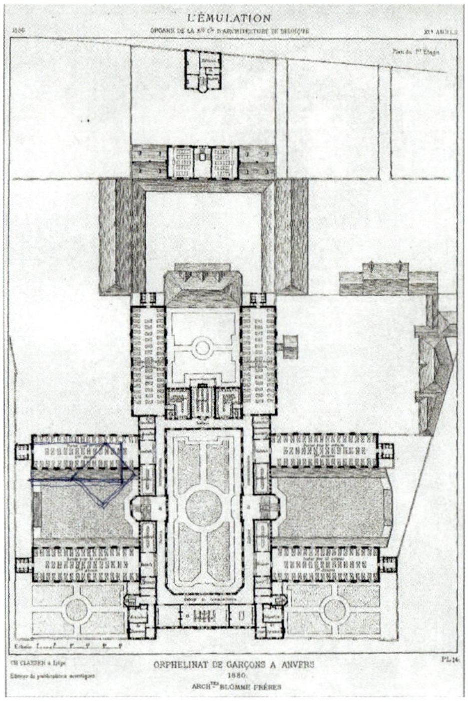

02

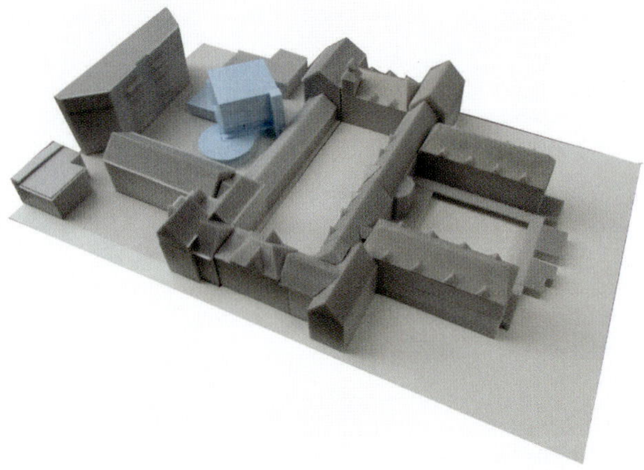

DURLET **extension of a secondary school** **2016–19** **Antwerp**

04

04

Three wings of the neo-Flemish Renaissance building from the nineteenth century were rebuilt in the 1960s. The city of Antwerp wished to reconstruct the fourth wing following the initial plan, but new adjacent buildings called for a different approach.

The ground floor follows the general plan of the existing ensemble. The upper floors were placed in an autonomous prismatic volume, rotated 53° from its base, reducing the density of the site by opening up diagonal views. The façades were executed in white concrete blocks with prefabricated concrete elements, integrating the construction into the mineral context of the surrounding brick buildings.

see p. 172–179

05

01
drawing of the project on archive plan published in *L'Émulation* (1886)

02, 03, 05
volumetric study, sketch design (2016)

04
construction phase (2018), © Séverin Malaud

06

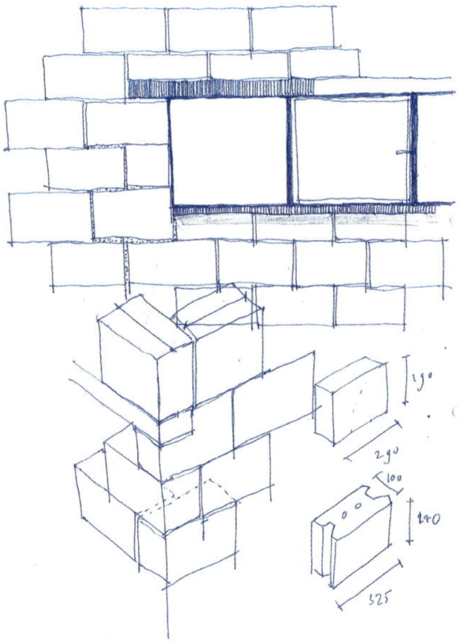

07

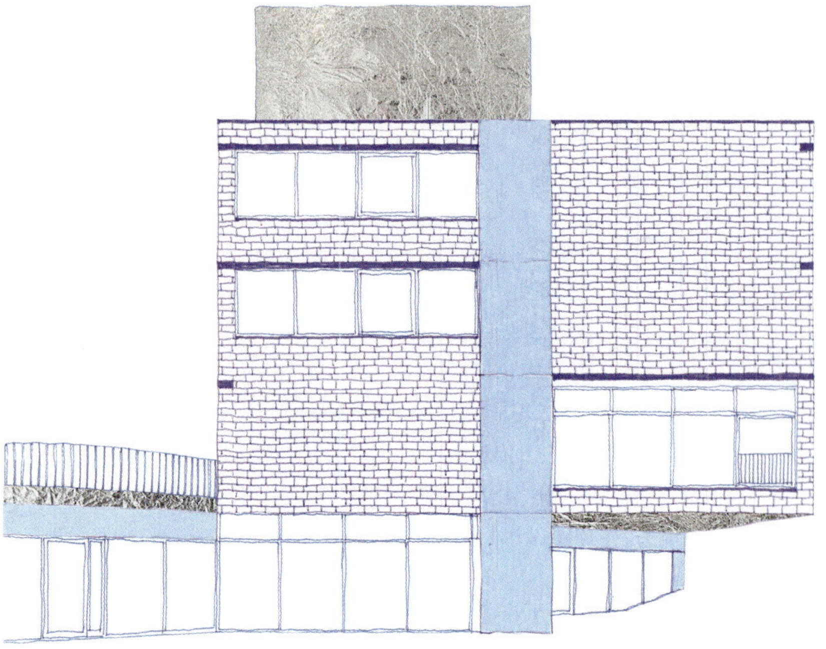

08

level +4

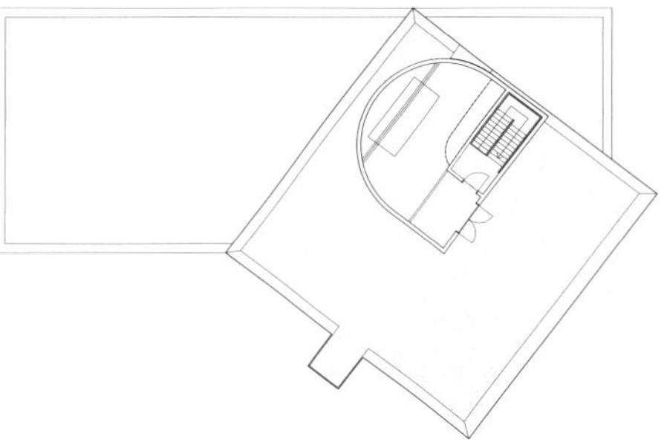

level +3

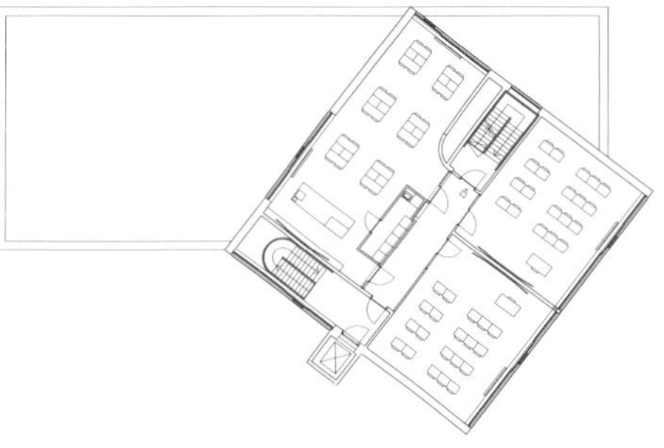

level +2

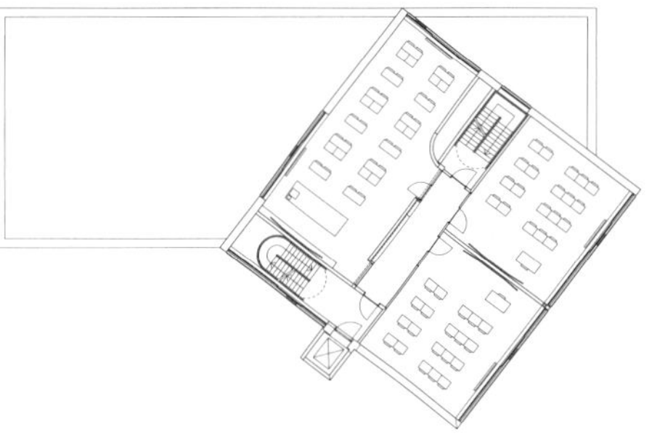

level +1

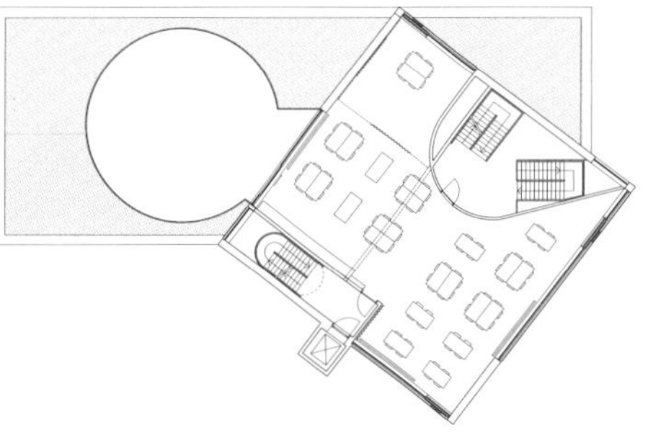

ground floor plan

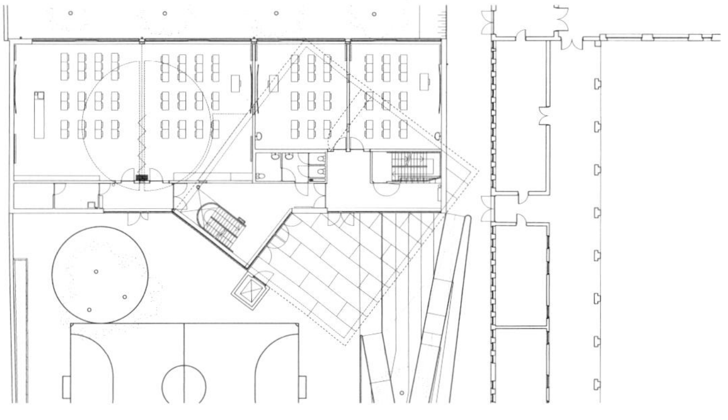

06–07
façade study, building permit phase (2016)

08
construction phase (2018), © Séverin Malaud

0 1 2 5 10

09

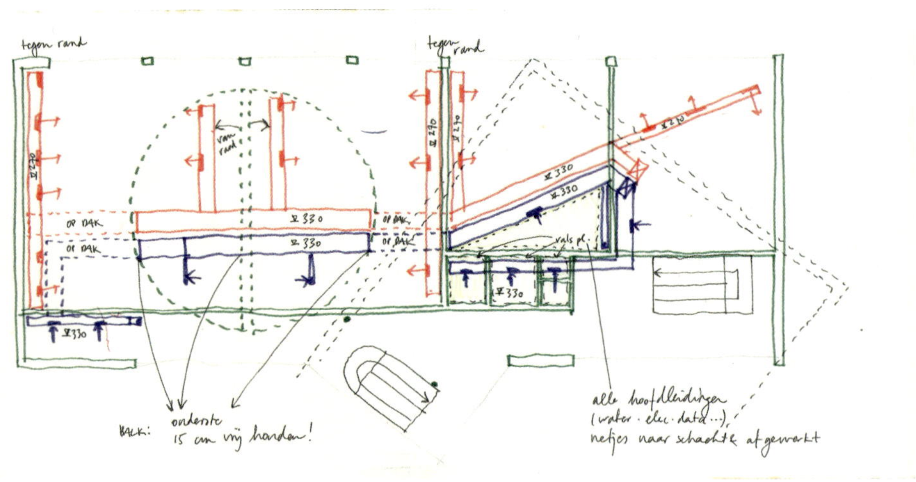
tegen rand
tegen rand
02 DAK
01 DAK
vals pl.
BALK: onderste 15 cm vrij houden!
alle hoofdleidingen (water - elec - data...) netjes naar schachte afgewerkt

10

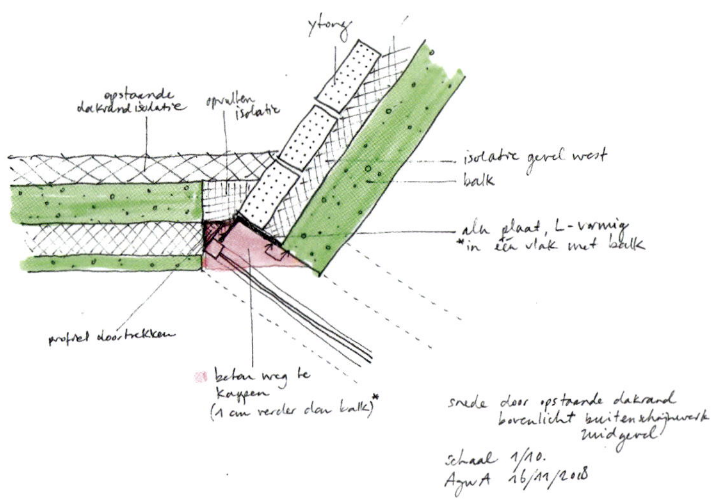
ytong
opstaande dakrand isolatie
opvullen isolatie
isolatie gevel west
balk
alu plaat, L-vormig
*in één vlak met balk
profiel doortrekken
beton weg te kappen (1 cm verder dan balk)*
snede door opstaande dakrand bovenlicht buitenschrijnwerk zuidgevel
schaal 1/10.
AgwA 16/11/2018

11

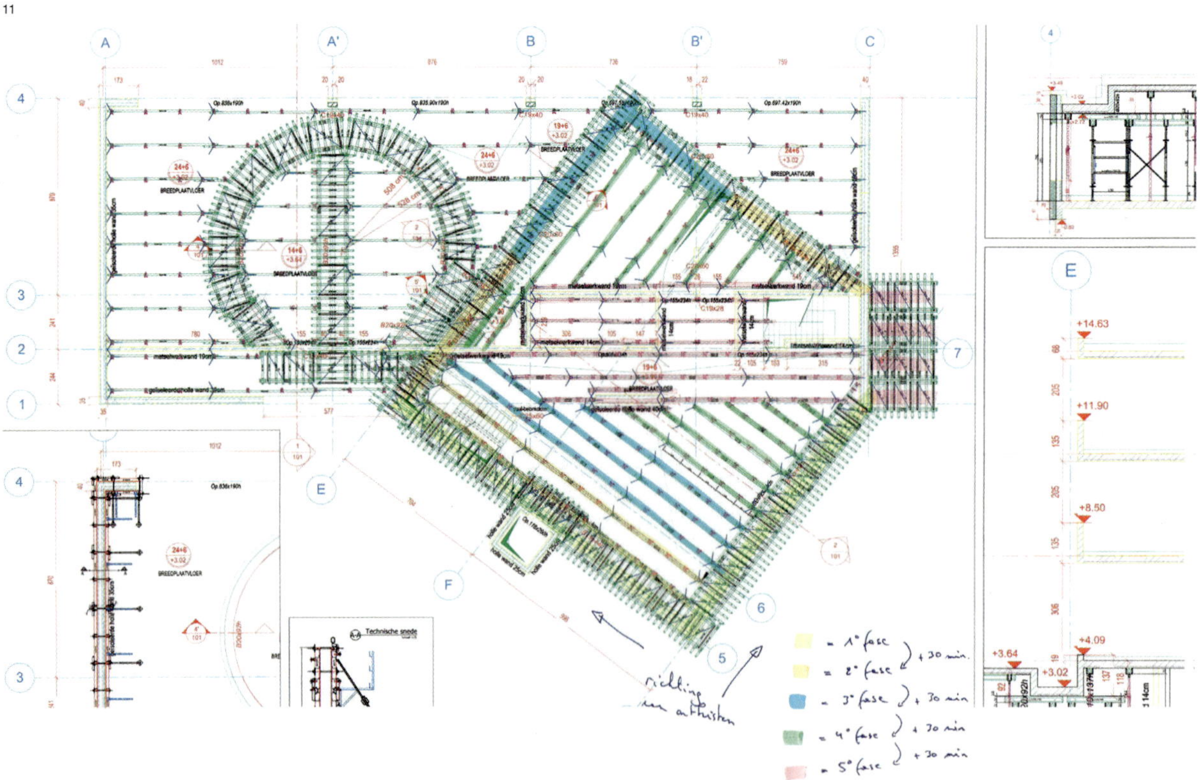
A
A'
B
B'
C
E
F
BREEDPLAATVLOER
Technische snede
+14.63
+11.90
+8.50
+4.09
+3.64
+3.02
= 1° fase
= 2° fase
= 3° fase
= 4° fase
= 5° fase
+ 30 min

09
sketch integration of ventilation and technical elements in respect to primary structure (2017)

10
drawing of the corner of the upper floors and the socle, construction phase (2017)

11
scaffolding plan by the contractor, Gillion Bouw (2018), sketch: Bram Van Asch (project leader)

12
construction phase (2019), © Arvi Anderson (AgwA)

13

14

15

16

17

18

19

13–14
ground floor classrooms, first floor open learning centre, construction phase (2018), © Séverin Malaud

15–17
renders, execution phase (2017)

18–19
drawings of interior spaces and materials, execution phase (2017)

01

WANDRE	extension of a community hall, library and park	2016–ongoing	Liège	in collaboration with S2JD

02

03

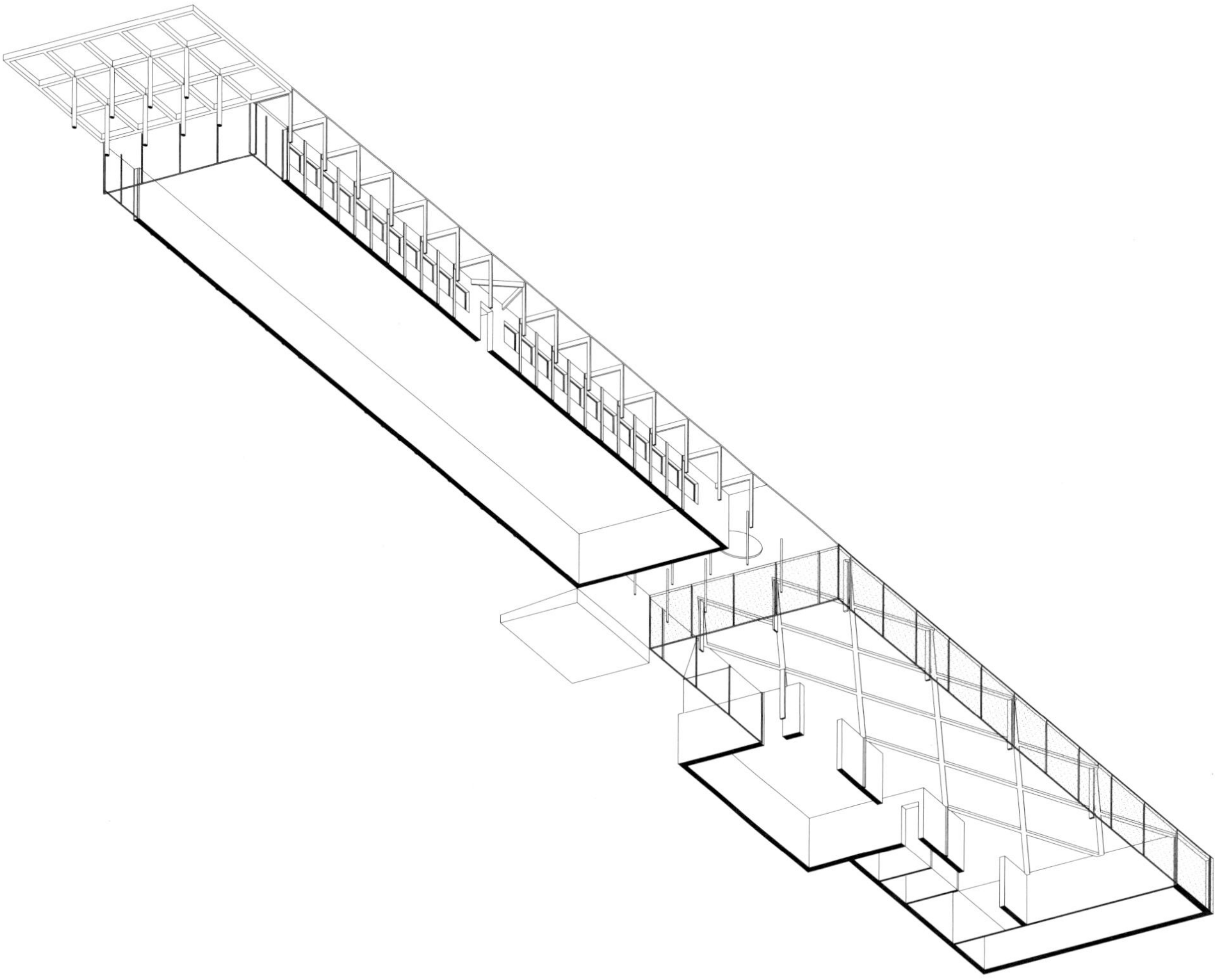

The former nineteenth-century city hall and the modular library renovated in the 1990s were preserved in this project for a municipal centre in Wandre. This made possible its contextual anchoring. A new structure on the ground floor brings both buildings together. The ensemble integrates a youth centre, multipurpose hall, police station and library, all connected with a circulation porch facing the park. The linear steel structure projects a clear front, clarifies the identity of the whole and distributes the circulation between park and city.

04

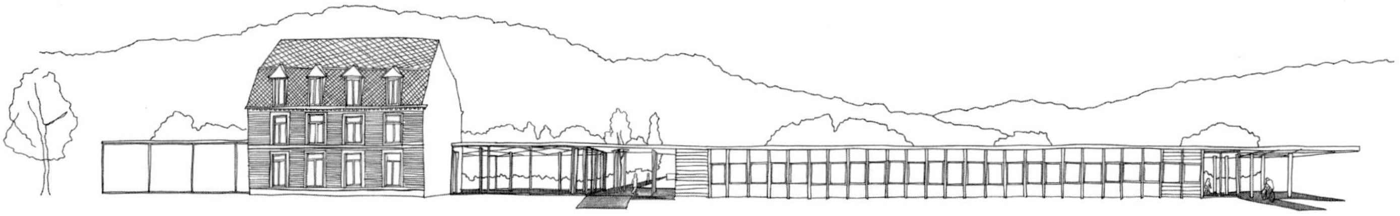

01
view from the park, competition phase (2016)

02
view of the existing situation from the street (2022)

03
axonometry of the primary structures, competition phase (2016)

04
street façade, competition phase (2016)

05

06

07

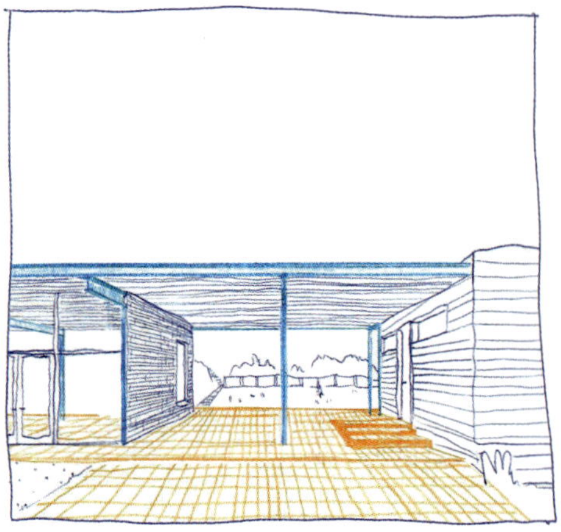

11

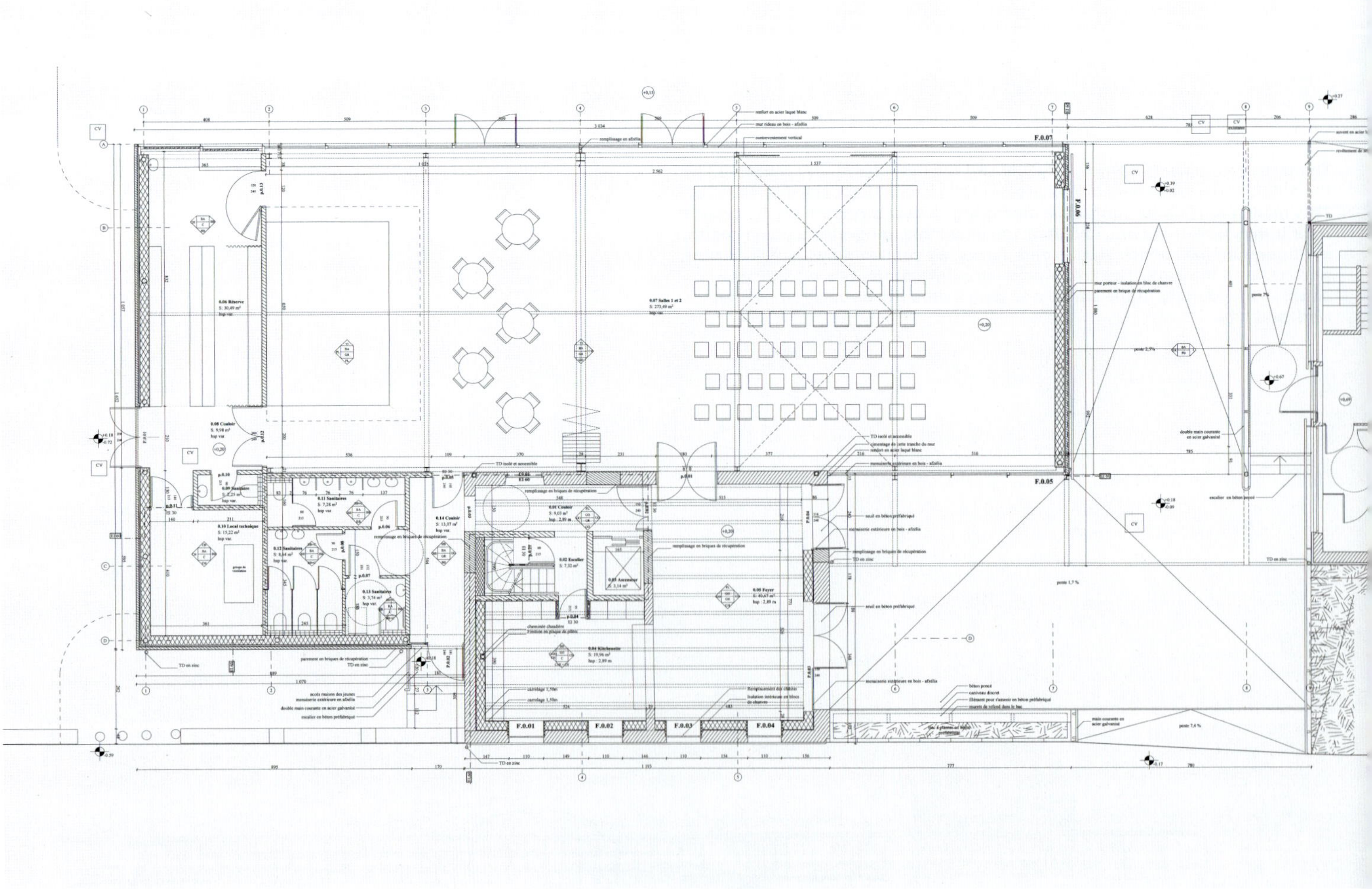

08

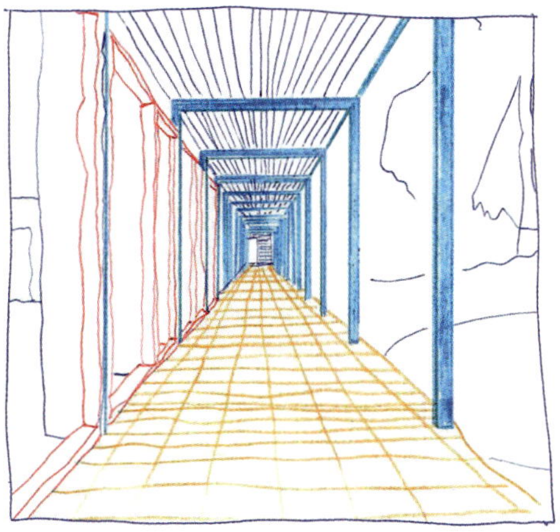

09

10

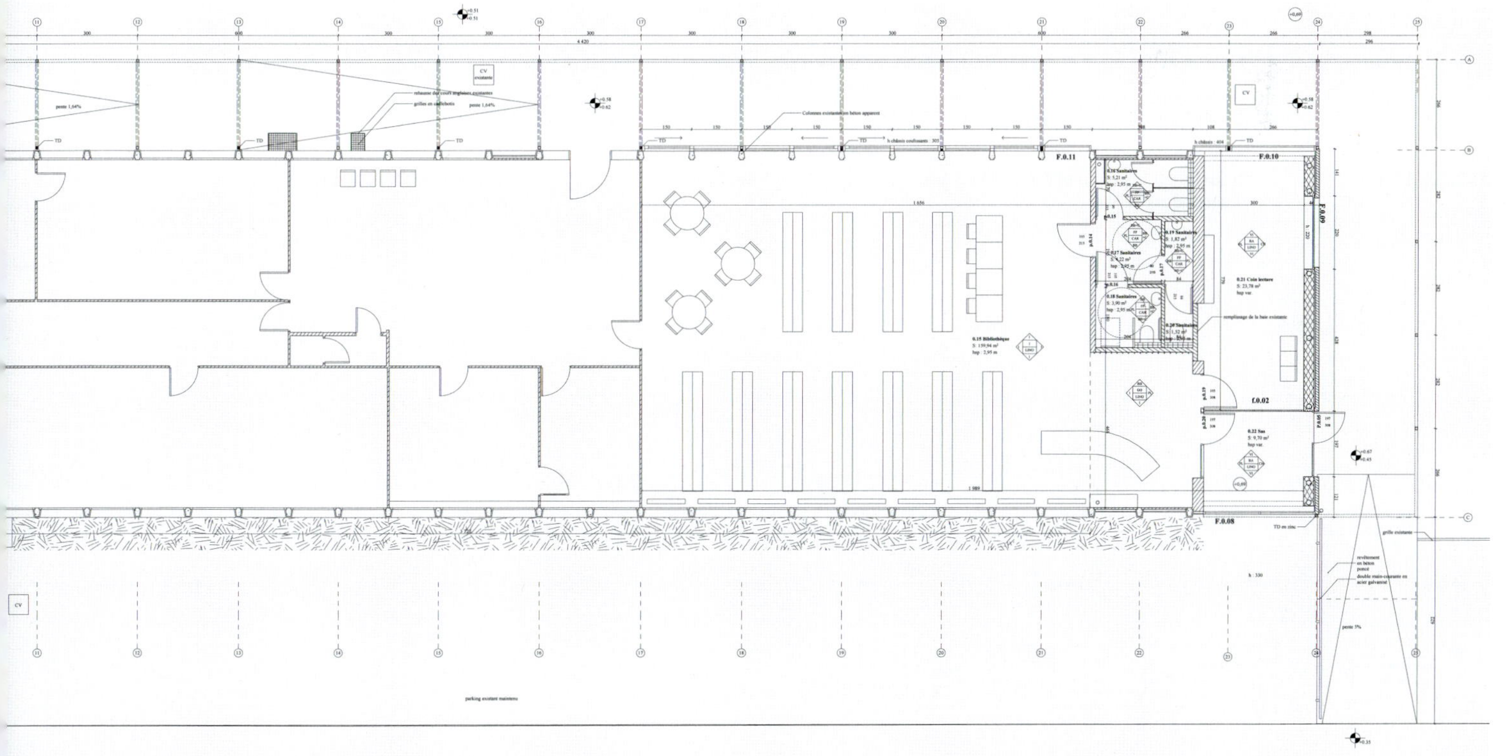

05–10
sequence of spaces, (05) multipurpose hall, (06) cafeteria in existing building, (07) canopy entrance, (08) canopy gallery adjoining the library, (09) library, (10) canopy over bicycle parking area, preliminary design (2019)

11
ground floor plan, execution phase (2021)

0 1 2 5

01

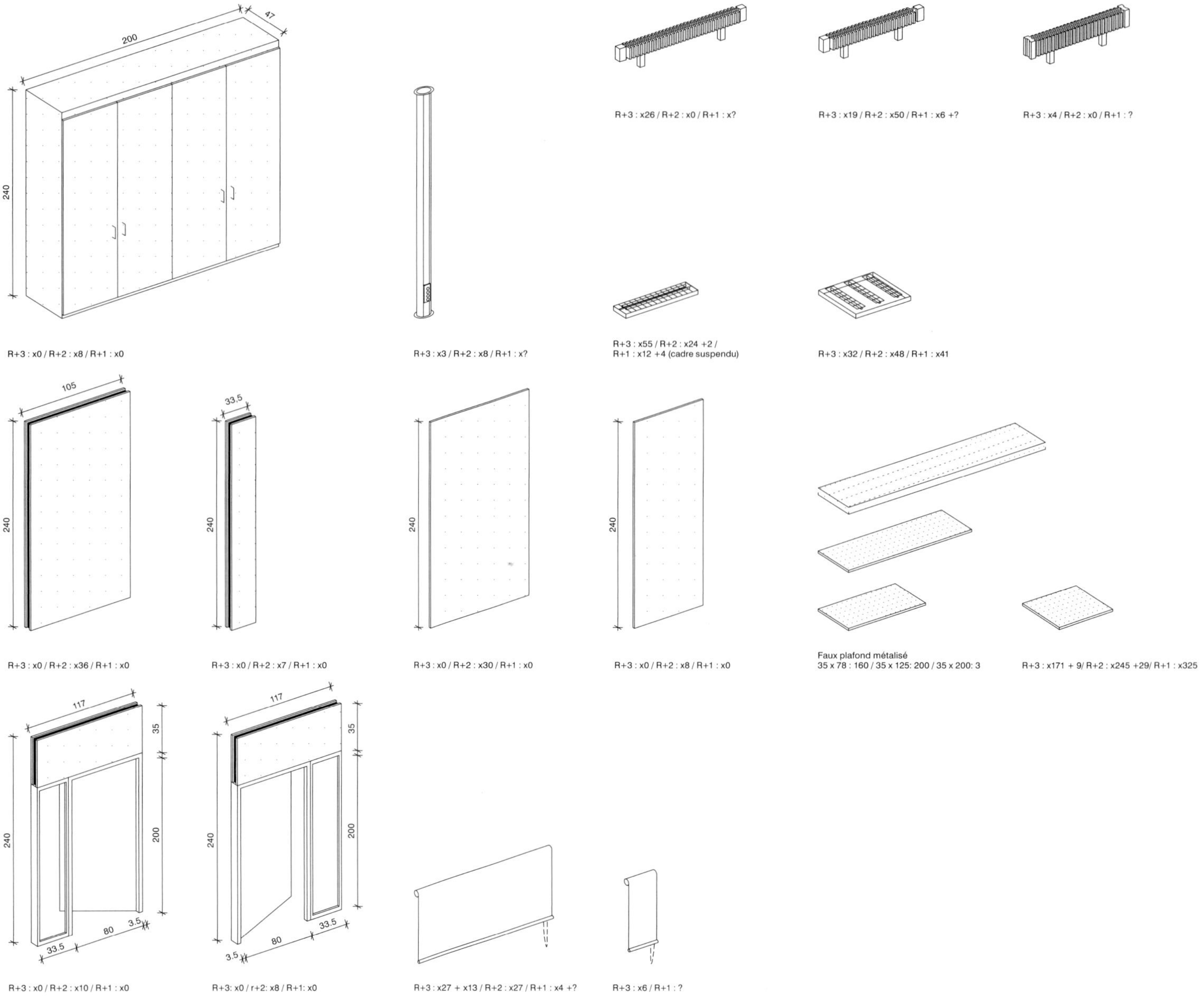

KARREVELD 1

transformation of an office building into a secondary school

2016–21

Molenbeek-Saint-Jean, Brussels

02

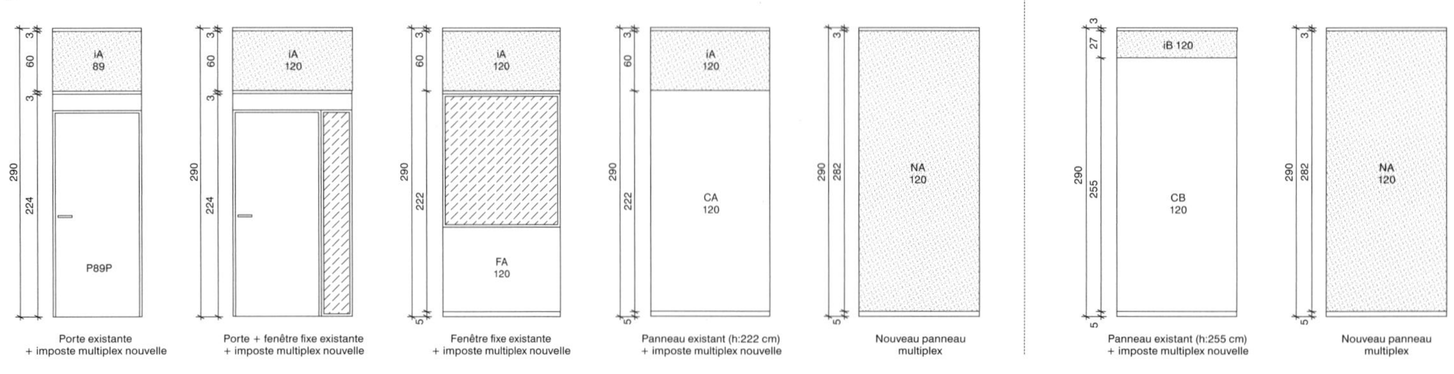

03

04

05

06

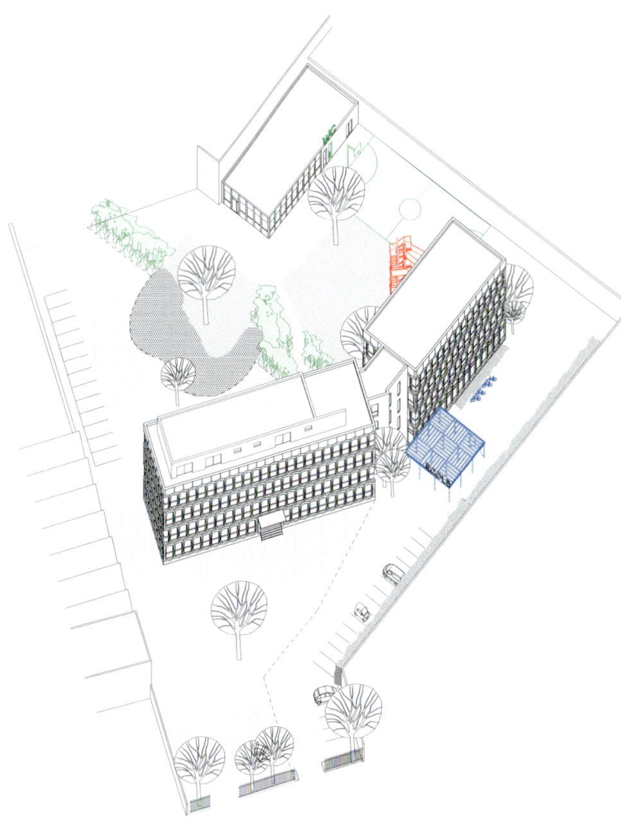

Characterized by prefabricated concrete façades typical of the 1970s, this former office building is to be converted into a secondary school. This first phase aims at housing classrooms in one wing, awaiting the future competition and project for the complete school. A canopy and emergency staircase were added, forming a dismantlable wooden construction. The classrooms were organized by reusing 90 per cent of the existing partition walls, suspended ceilings and techniques. Adaptations to the outdoor spaces were minimal. All interventions anticipate potential reuse or disassembly in the second phase.

see p. 168–171

01
inventory of reusable construction elements, execution phase (2019)

02
inventory of adapted partition walls, execution phase (2017)

03–04
storage of reusable elements, suspended ceiling and insulation, construction site (2018), © Arvi Anderson (AgwA)

05
assembly of partition walls and their adaptations, construction site (2019)

06
axonometric view, competition phase (2016)

07

08

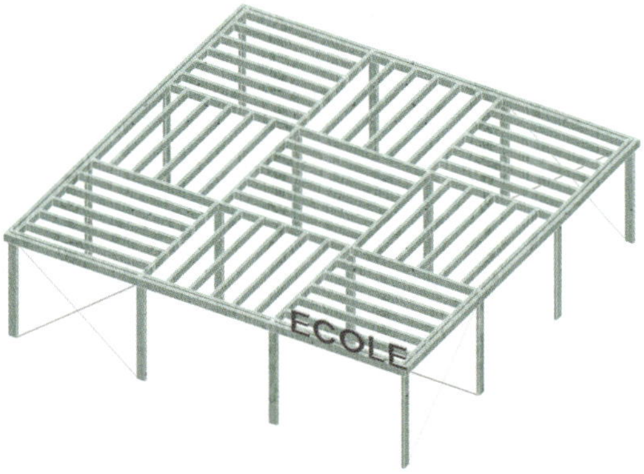

09

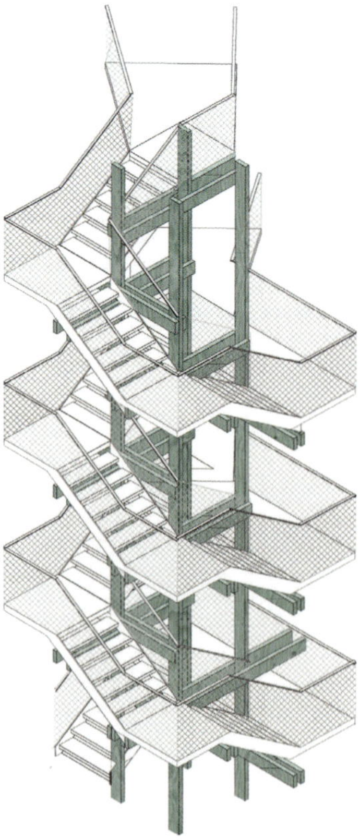

07
construction of dismountable entrance canopy, construction site (2018)

08–09
axonometric view, entrance canopy and emergency staircase, competition phase (2016)

10
construction of the emergency staircase, construction site (2018), © Arvi Anderson (AgwA)

01

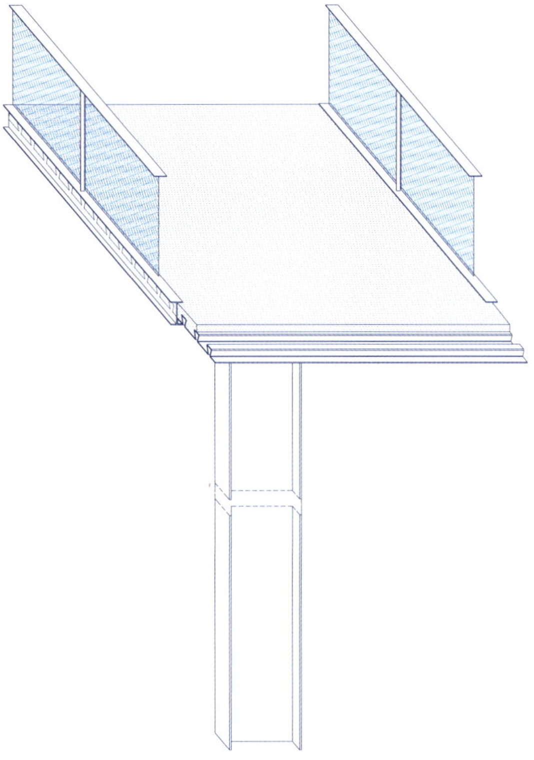

02

03

04

SERAING **construction of a pedestrian and bicycle bridge** **2017–ongoing** **Seraing**

07

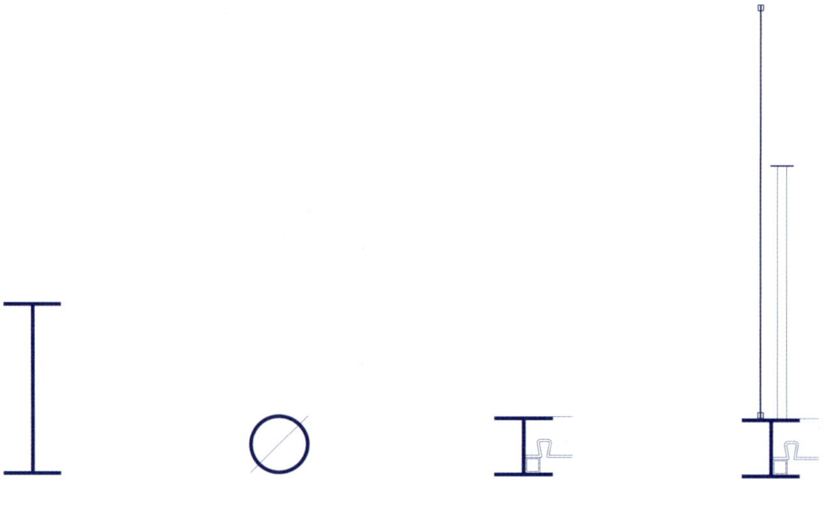

08

05

06

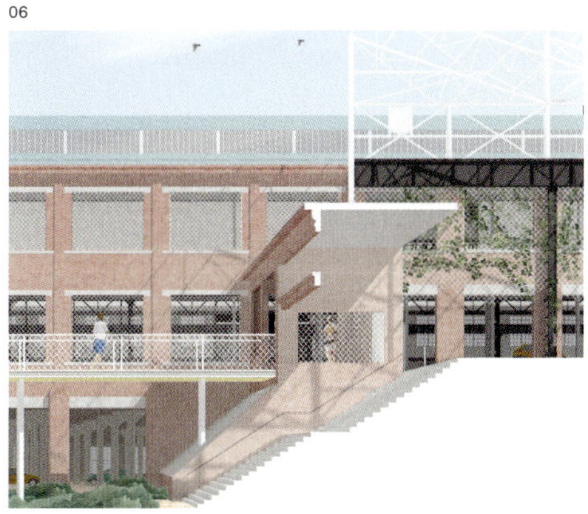

Instead of the short footbridge over the railway tracks suggested in the competition brief, the proposed infrastructure binds together the Ateliers Centraux neighbourhood, the railway station and the Trasenster park along the river Meuse. It does so by means of a simple, economical steel structure, resulting in a 250 m pedestrian and cycling bridge. The straight-forward footbridge animates the post-industrial landscape with public green pockets where the infrastructure touches ground with slopes and straight staircases giving access to the public areas and the railway platforms.

see p. 164–167

01
axonometric view of assembly of construction elements, competition phase (2017)

02–06
footbridge in a fragmented landscape, competition phase (2017)

07
principal steel construction elements, competition phase (2017)

08
situation plan

level +1, execution phase (2020)

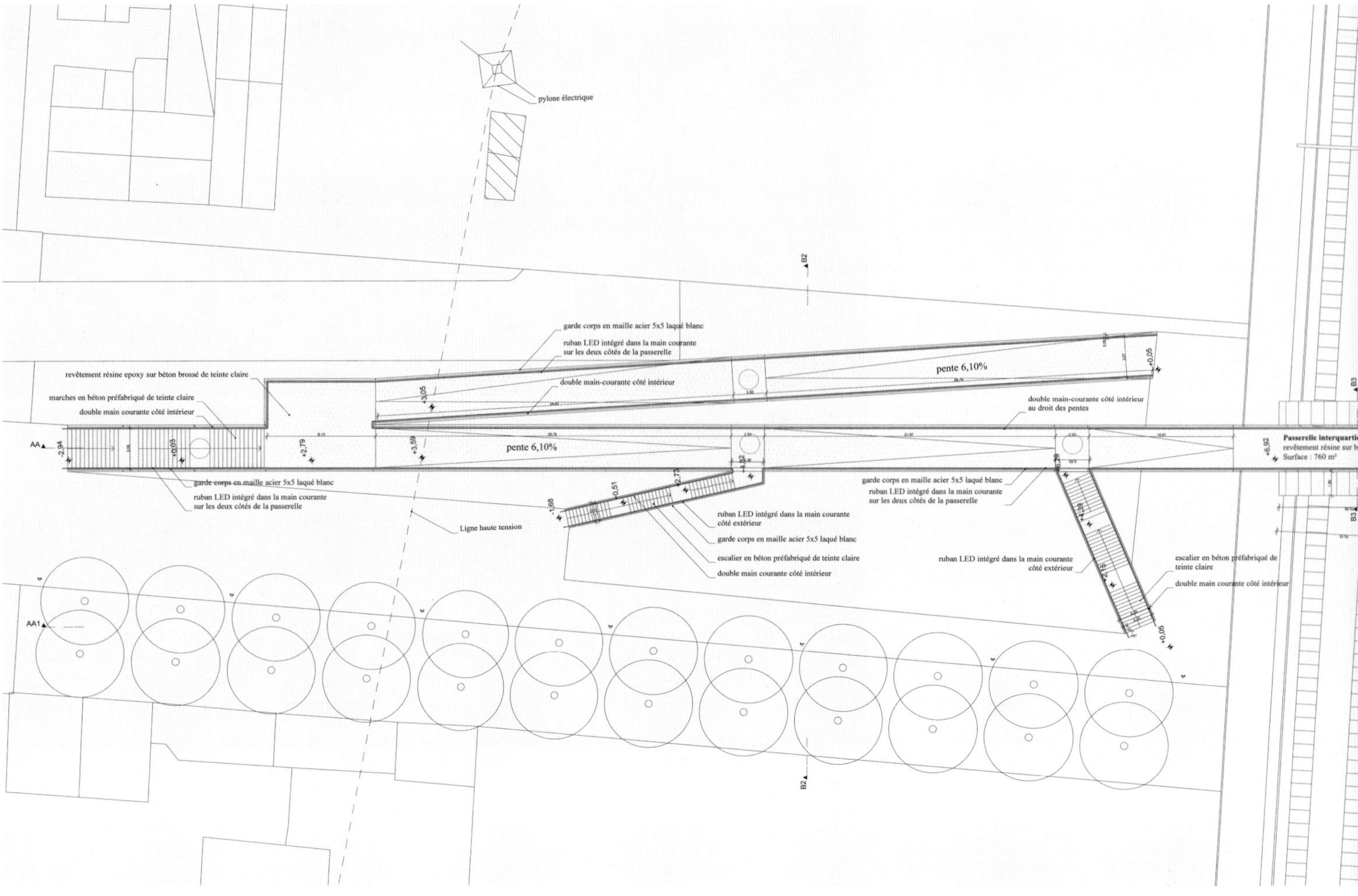

west elevation, execution phase (2020)

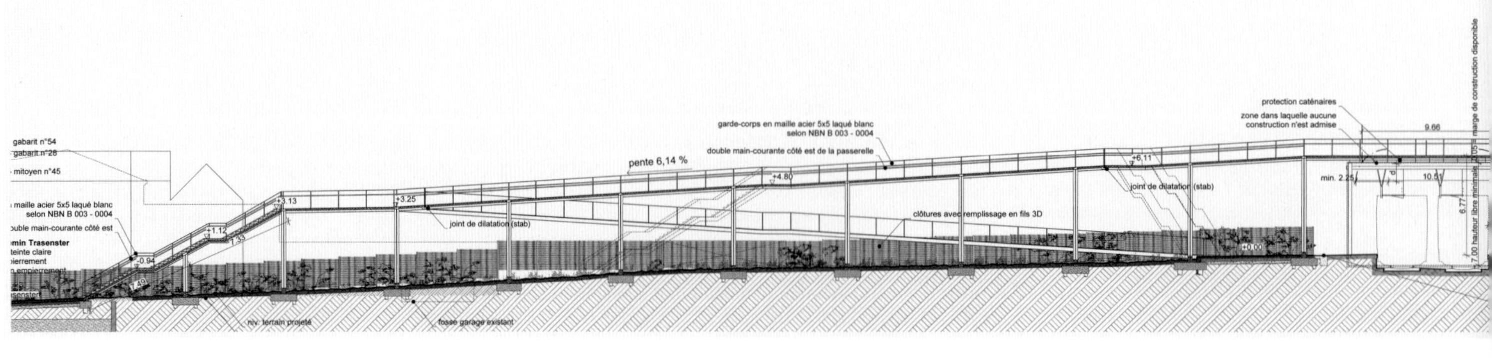

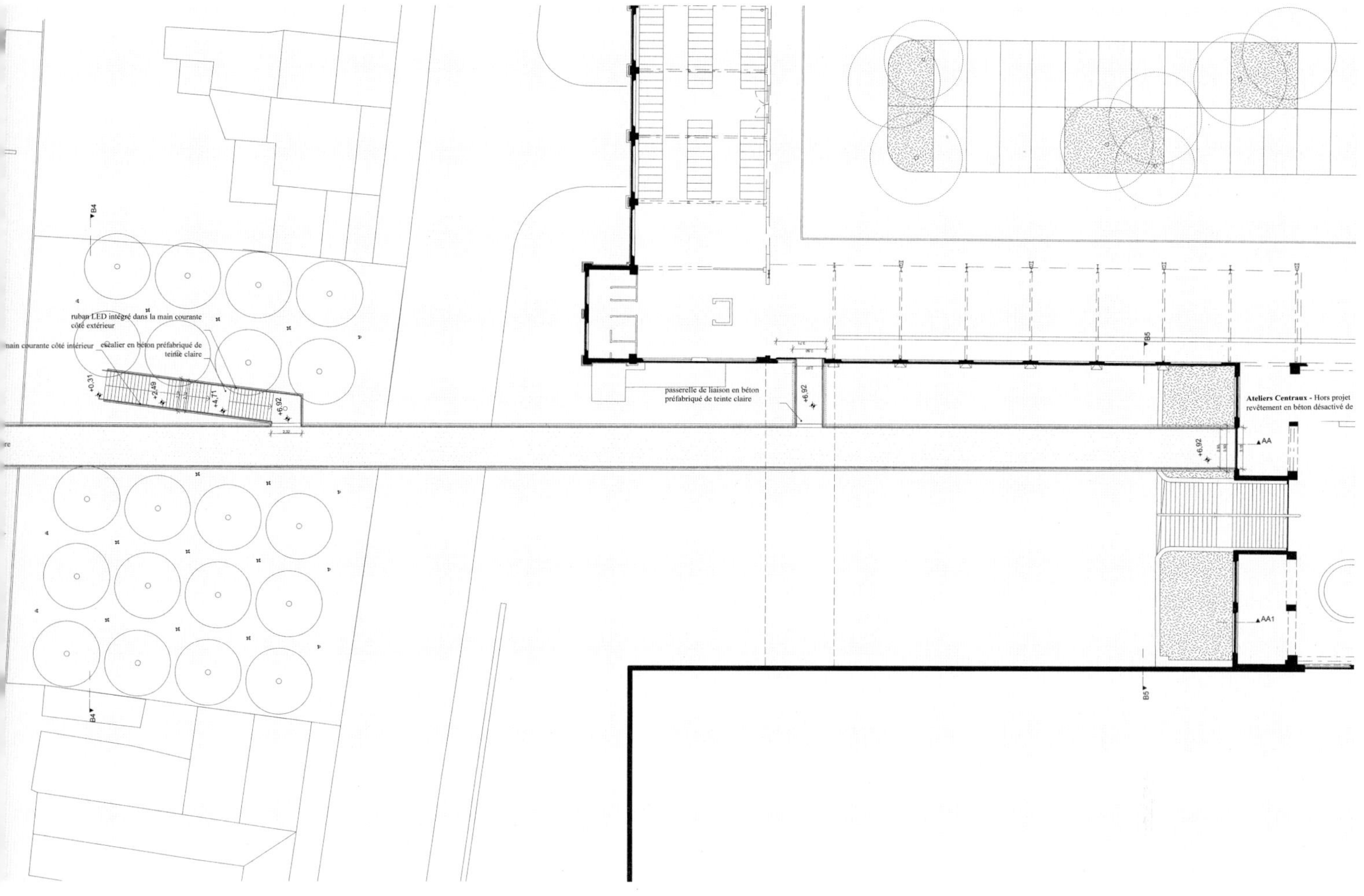
ruban LED intégré dans la main courante côté extérieur
main courante côté intérieur
escalier en béton préfabriqué de teinte claire
passerelle de liaison en béton préfabriqué de teinte claire
Ateliers Centraux - Hors projet
revêtement en béton désactivé de
+6,92
+4,71
+2,49
+0,31

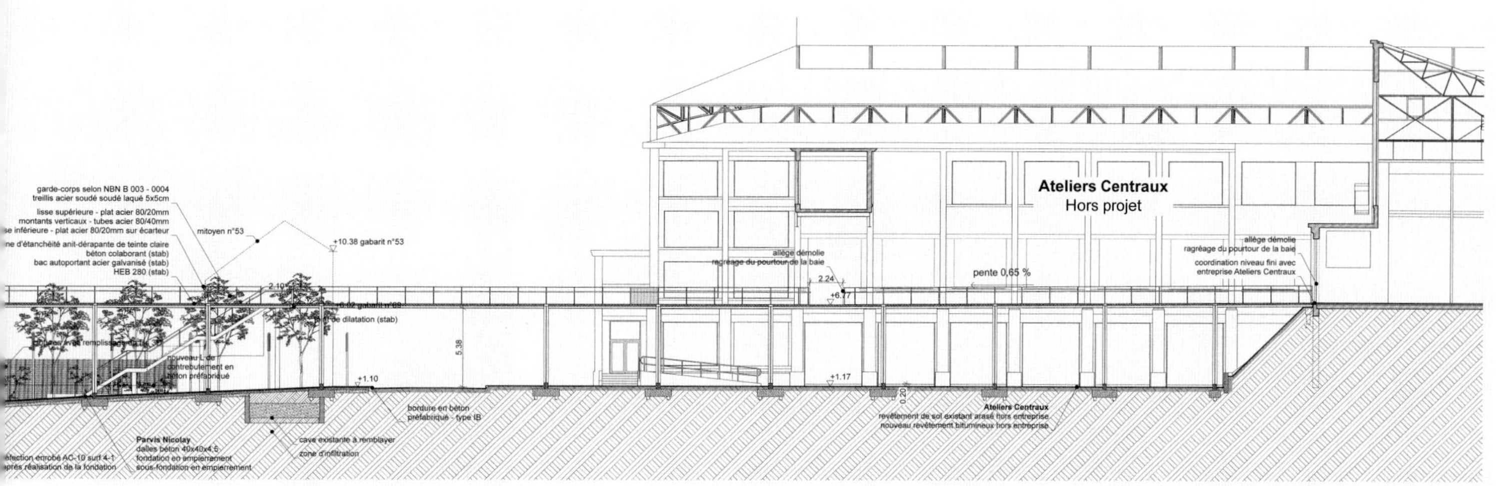
garde-corps selon NBN B 003 - 0004
treillis acier soudé soudé laqué 5x5cm
lisse supérieure - plat acier 80/20mm
montants verticaux - tubes acier 80/40mm
se inférieure - plat acier 80/20mm sur écarteur
ne d'étanchéité anit-dérapante de teinte claire
béton colaborant (stab)
bac autoportant acier galvanisé (stab)
HEB 280 (stab)
mitoyen n°53
+10.38 gabarit n°53
2.10
de dilatation (stab)
5.38
nouveau L de contrebutement en béton préfabriqué
+1.10
bordure en béton préfabriqué - type IB
Parvis Nicolay
dalles béton 40x40x4,5
fondation en empierrement
sous-fondation en empierrement
éfection enrobé AC-10 surf 4-1
après réalisation de la fondation
cave existante à remblayer
zone d'infiltration
Ateliers Centraux
Hors projet
allège démolie
ragréage du pourtour de la baie
2.24
+6.77
pente 0,65 %
coordination niveau fini avec entreprise Ateliers Centraux
+1.17
0.20
revêtement de sol existant arasé hors entreprise
nouveau revêtement bitumineux hors entreprise

0 1 5 10

09

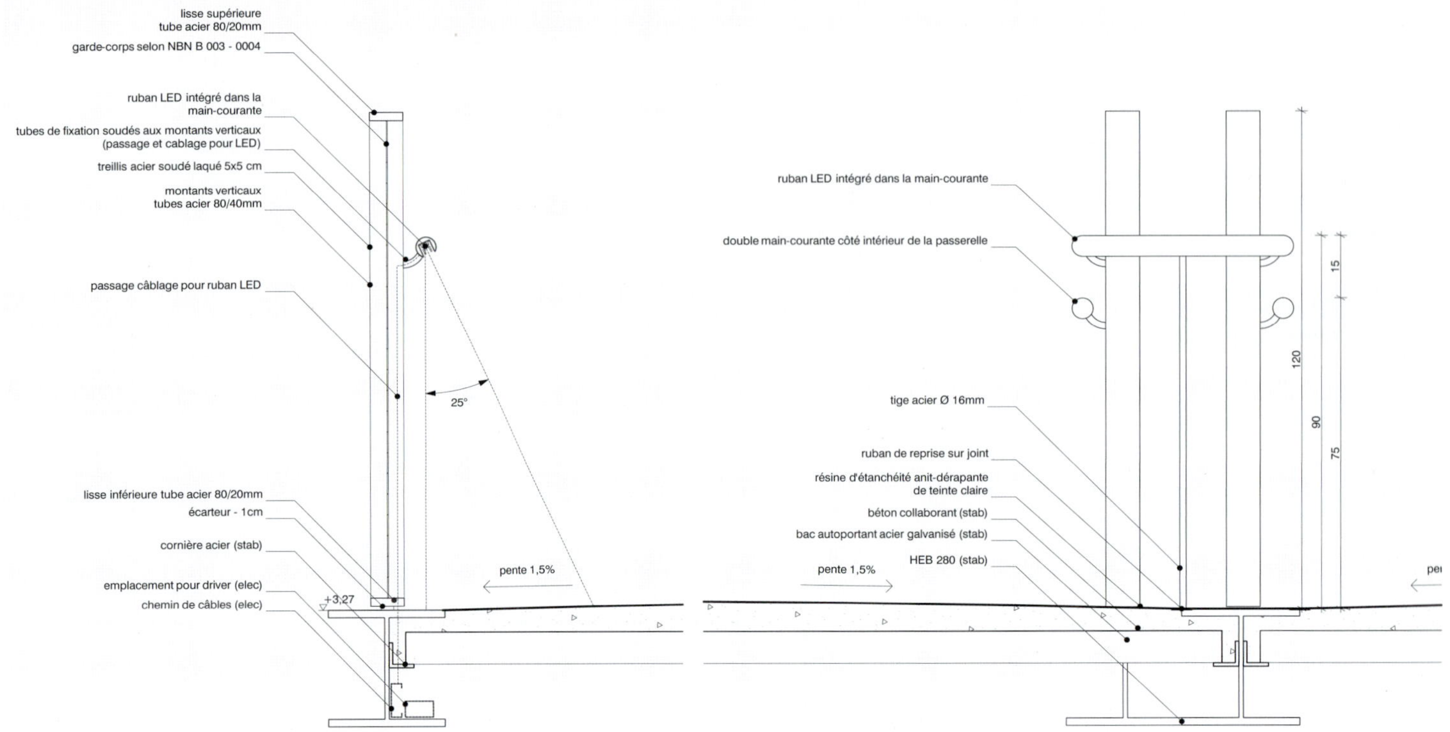

lisse supérieure
tube acier 80/20mm
garde-corps selon NBN B 003 - 0004
ruban LED intégré dans la
main-courante
tubes de fixation soudés aux montants verticaux
(passage et cablage pour LED)
treillis acier soudé laqué 5x5 cm
montants verticaux
tubes acier 80/40mm
passage câblage pour ruban LED
25°
lisse inférieure tube acier 80/20mm
écarteur - 1cm
cornière acier (stab)
emplacement pour driver (elec)
chemin de câbles (elec)
+3,27
pente 1,5%
ruban LED intégré dans la main-courante
double main-courante côté intérieur de la passerelle
tige acier Ø 16mm
ruban de reprise sur joint
résine d'étanchéité anit-dérapante
de teinte claire
béton collaborant (stab)
bac autoportant acier galvanisé (stab)
HEB 280 (stab)
pente 1,5%
120
90
15
75

10

11

12

13

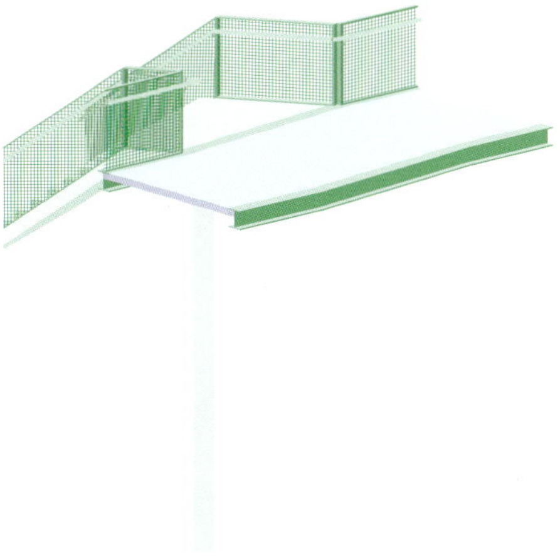

14

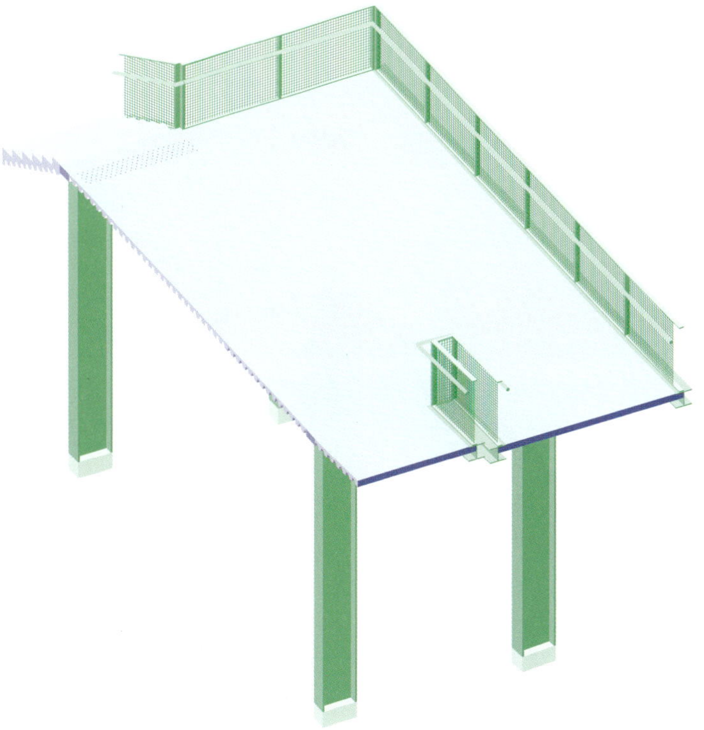

15

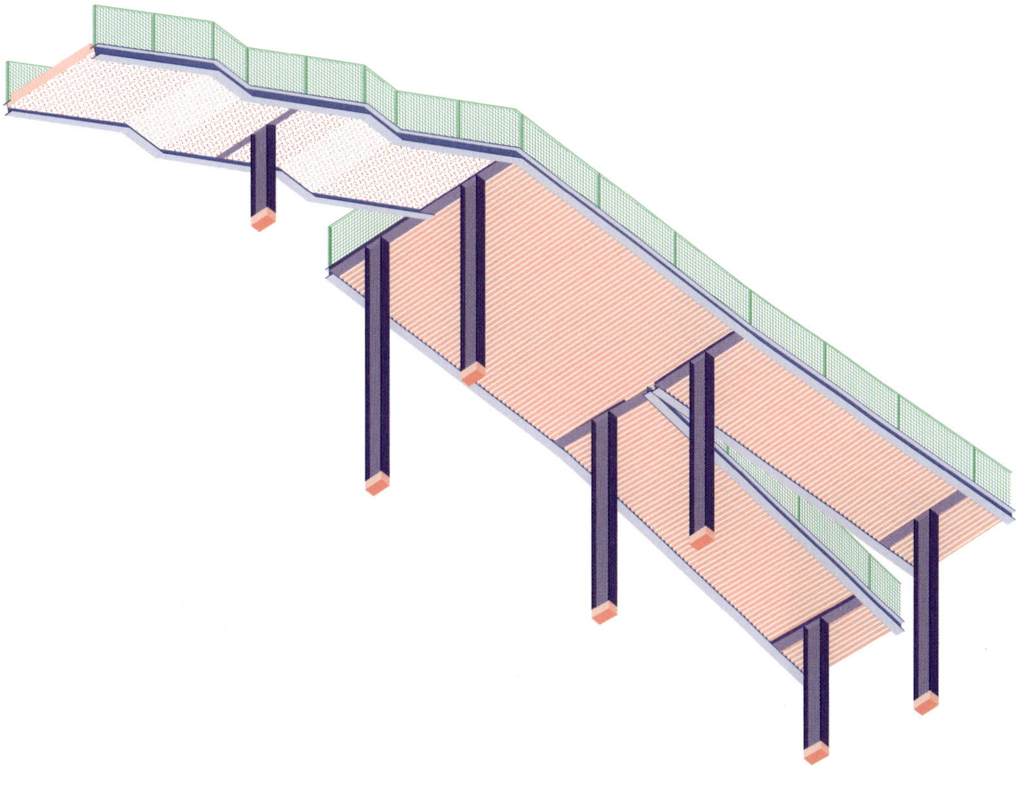

09
detail section, execution phase (2020)

10–12
axonometric views of relation between footbridge and public space, building permit (2019)

13–15
axonometric views of articulations and junctions, execution phase (2020)

01

KANAL – CITROËN

transformation of a former garage into art museum and architecture centre

2017

Brussels

in collaboration with 6a architects and architecten de vylder vinck taillieu

02

03

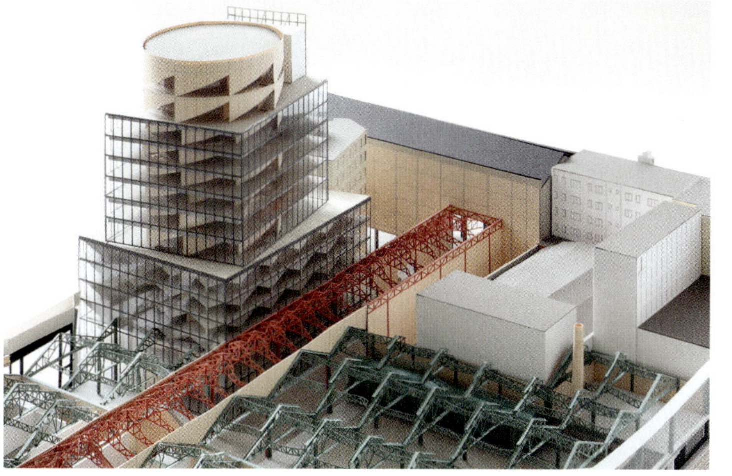

04

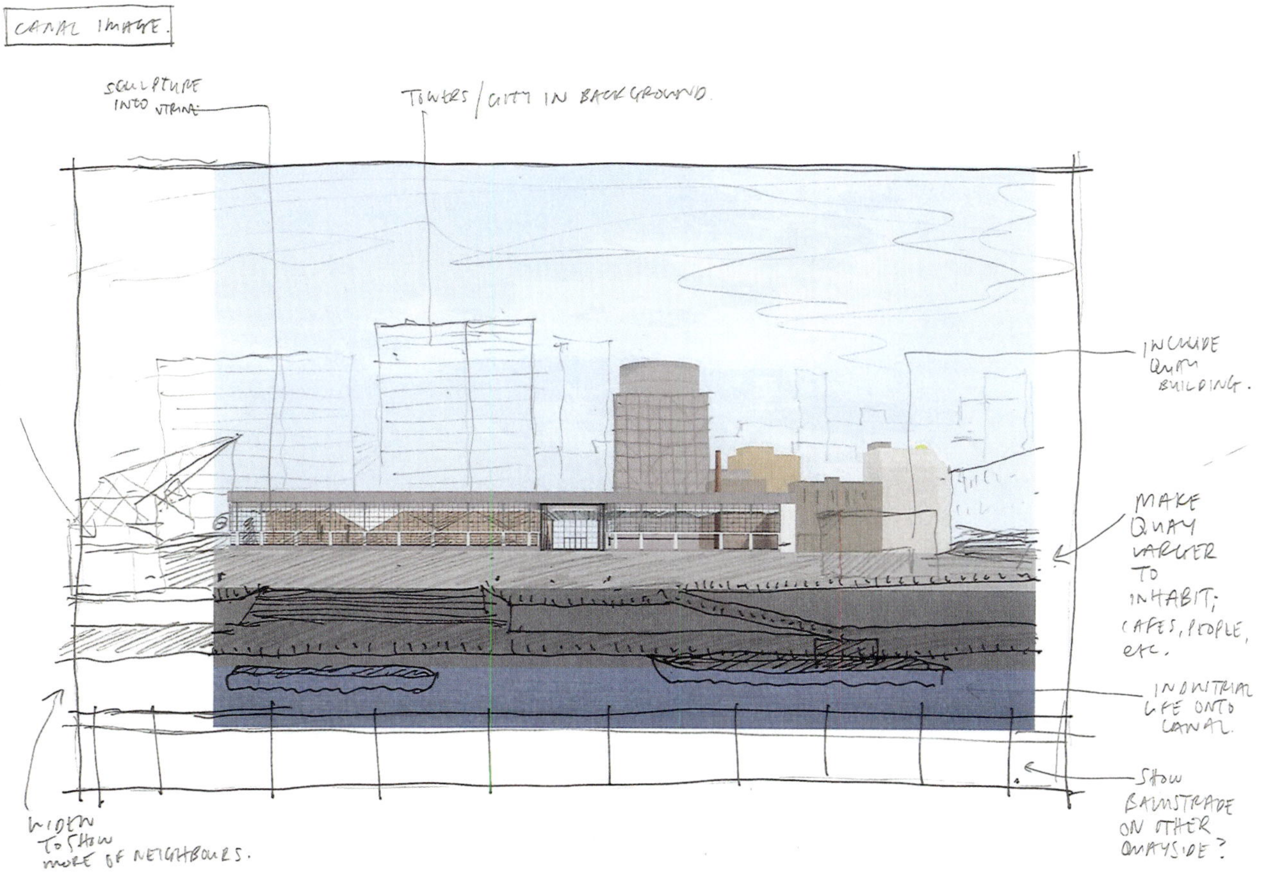

This competition entry for the transformation of a former Citroën garage into KANAL, a modern and contemporary art museum and architecture centre, starts with the complete emptying of the space under the huge shed roof. A shared square museum space is created on two levels under the sheds, with a peripheral exhibition gallery. A reference to Citroën's formal invention of a V-shaped gear, a circular tower marked by four staircases wrapped around a silo with double-height rooms fits all the building's support functions. It is the gearbox of the building, driving the mechanics of the museum: auditoriums, archives, restaurant, ticket office and more. A unitary covered public space for experimentation and large-scale events draws the city and the theatre next door into the heart of the museum.

see p. 156–163

01, 03
competition model
© Filip Dujardin

02
archive photo of the Citroën workshop (c. 1935)

04
preparation of the collage depicting the canal side

ground floor

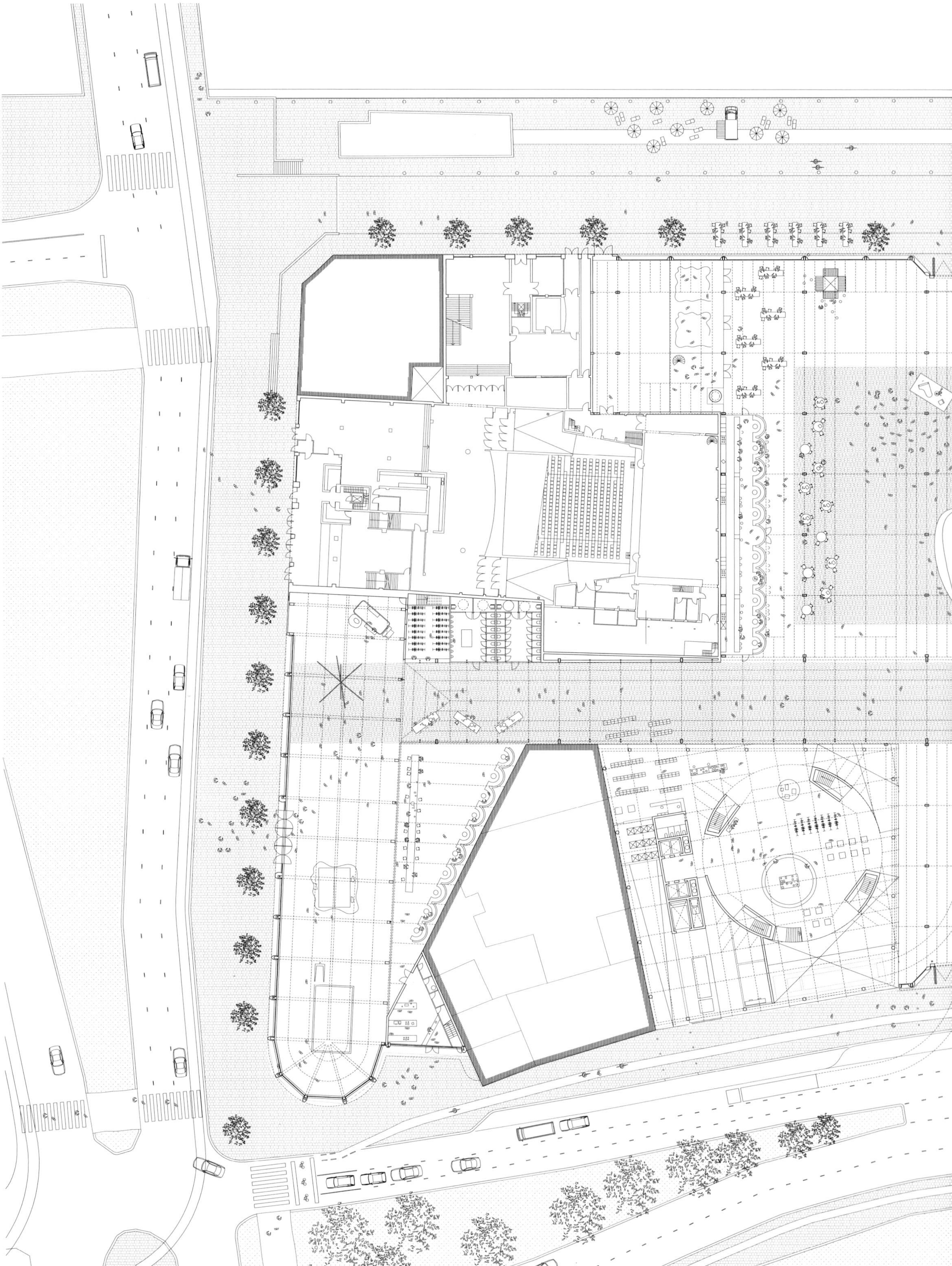

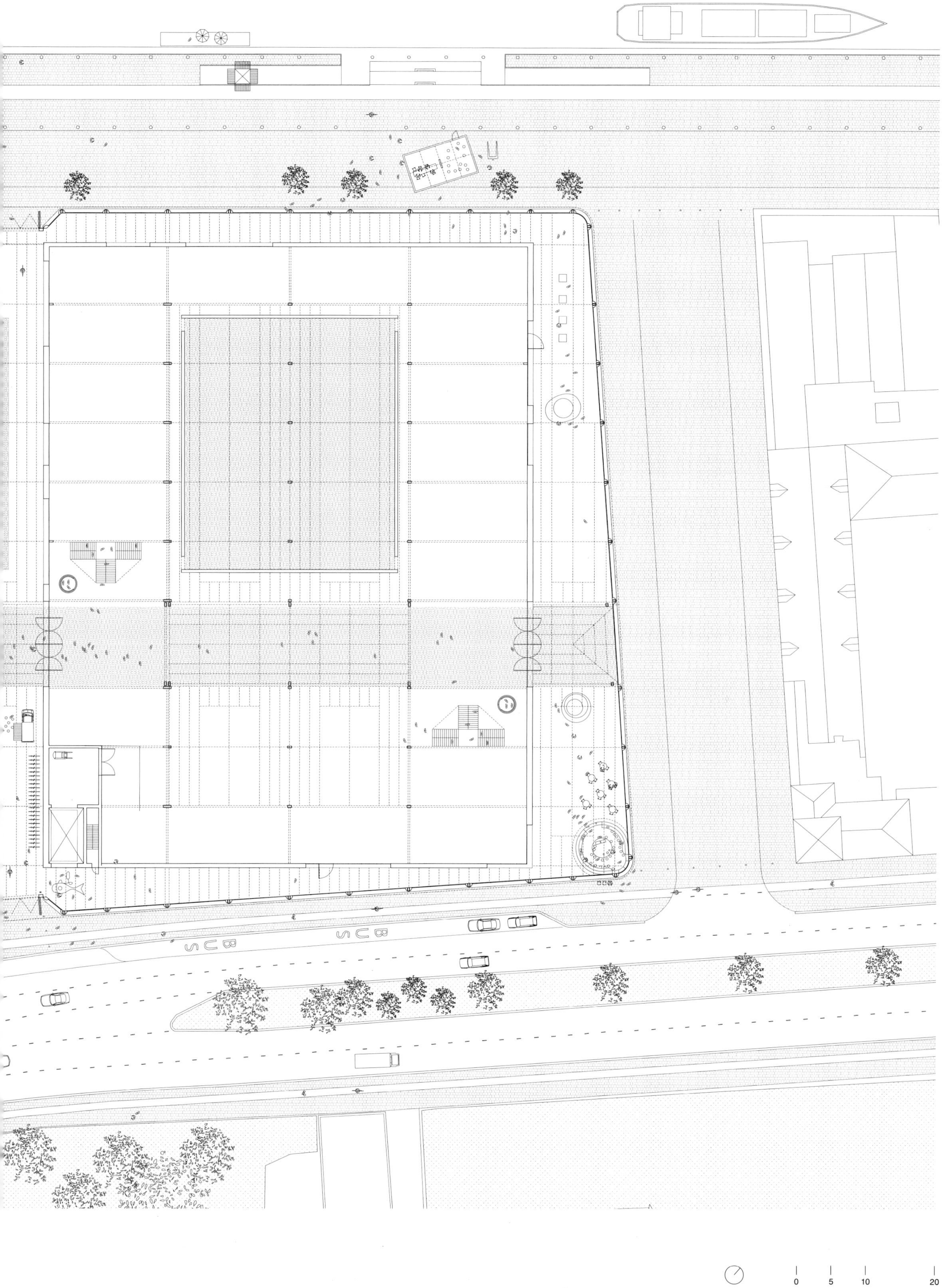
BUS
BUS
0
5
10
20

level 3, archives

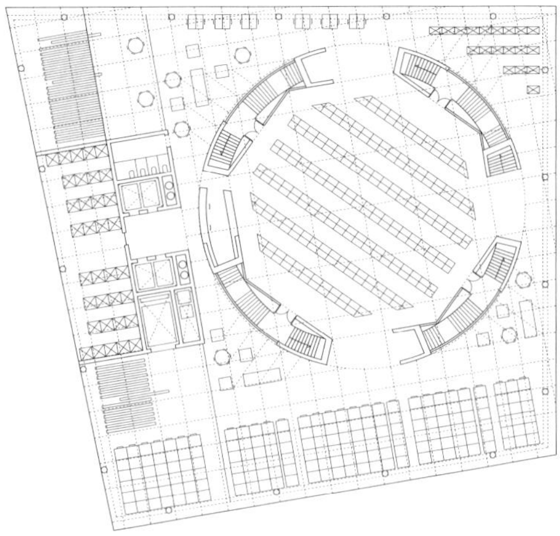

level 2, auditorium and exhibition spaces

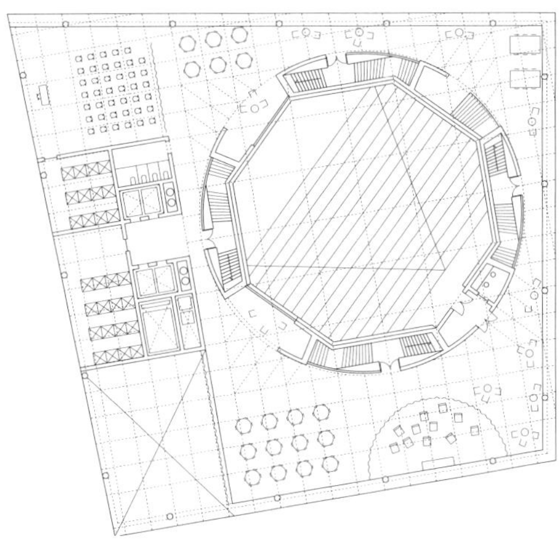

level 1, auditoriums and exhibition spaces

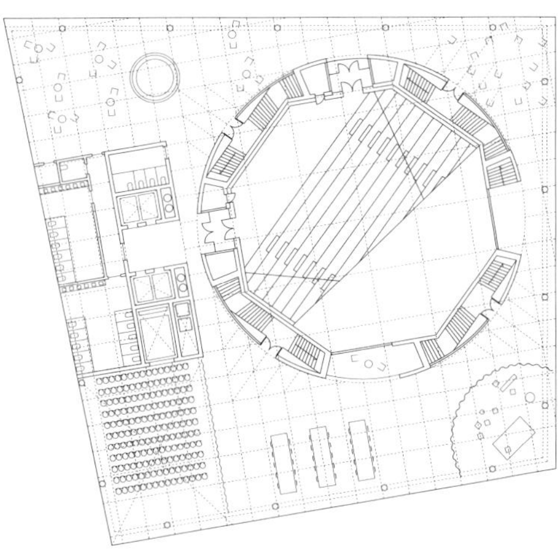

level 0, foyer

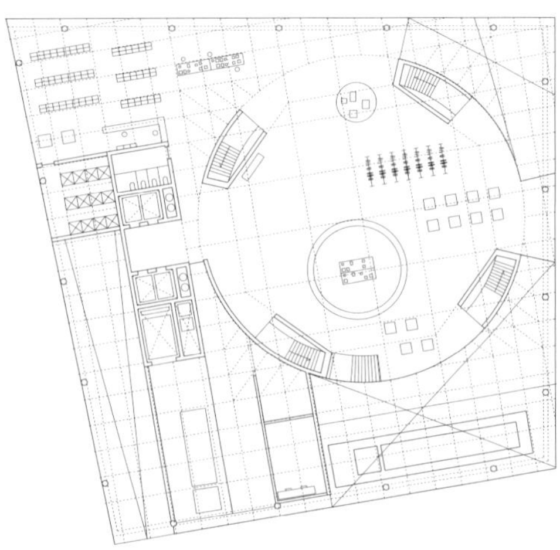

level 7, library

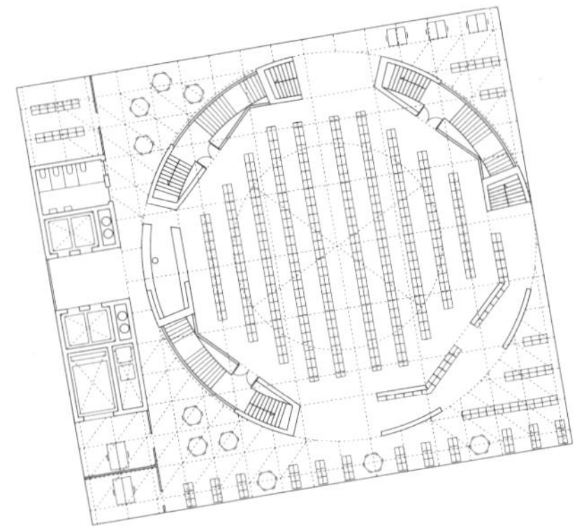

level 6, social spaces

level 5, archives and documentation centre

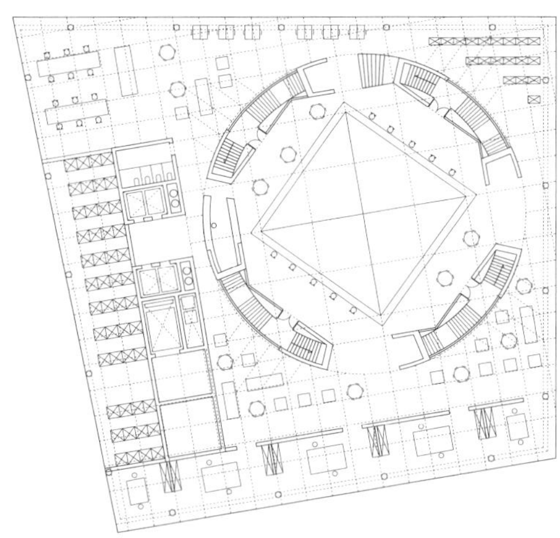

level 4, archives

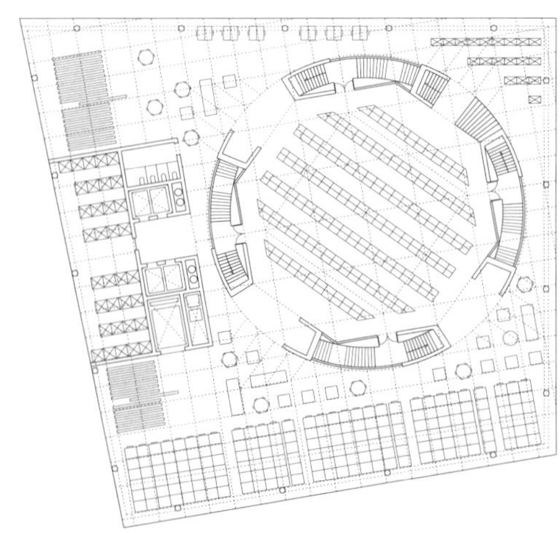

level 11, offices

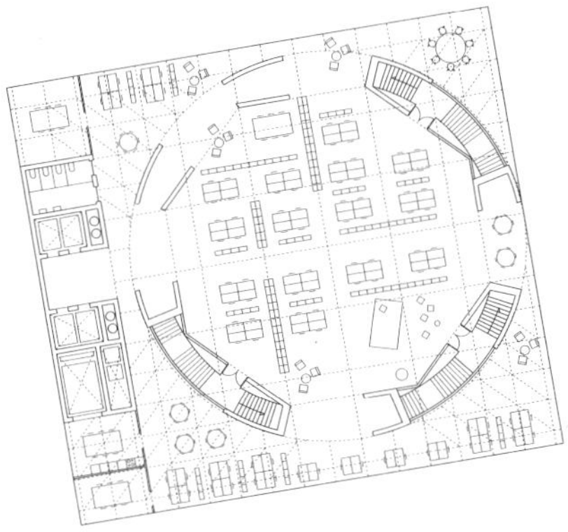

level 10, offices

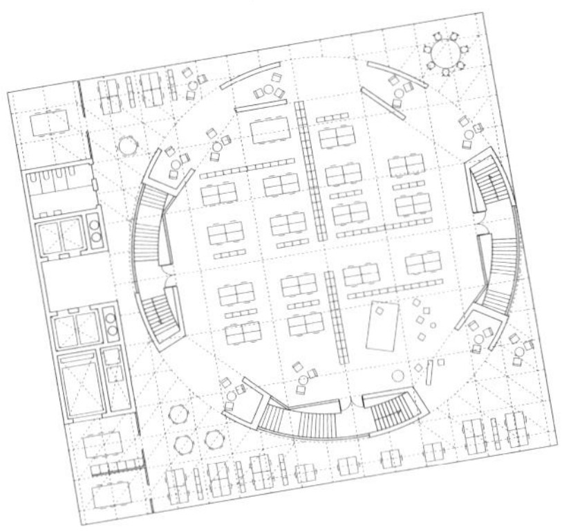

roof

level 9, offices

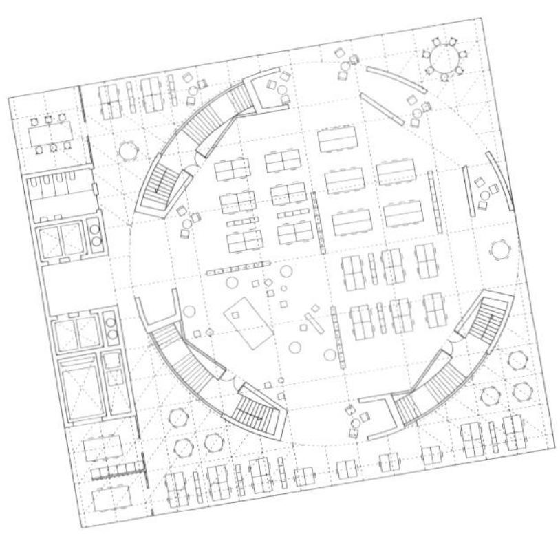

level 13, VIP spaces

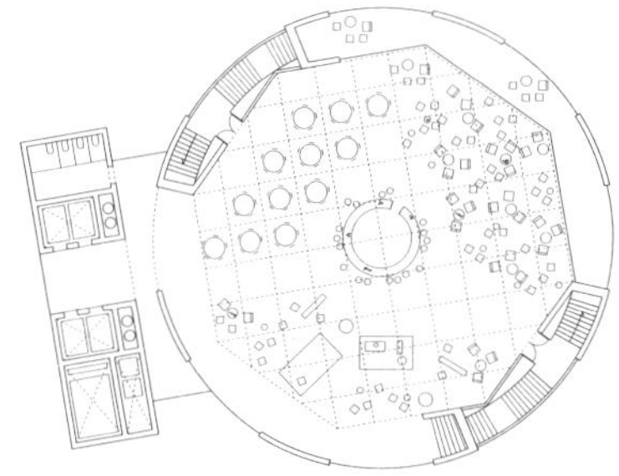

level 8, library

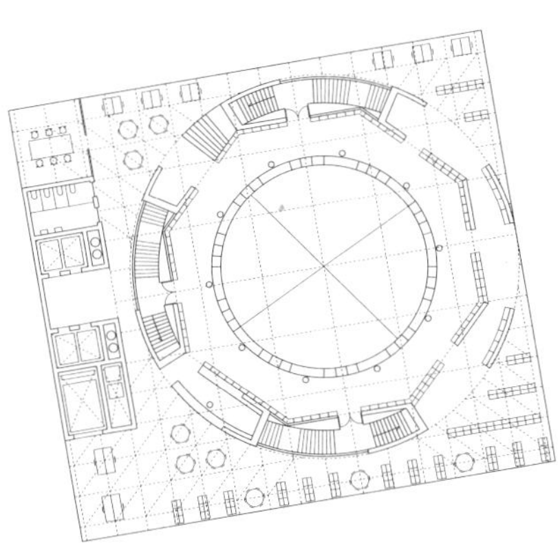

level 12, restaurant and terrace

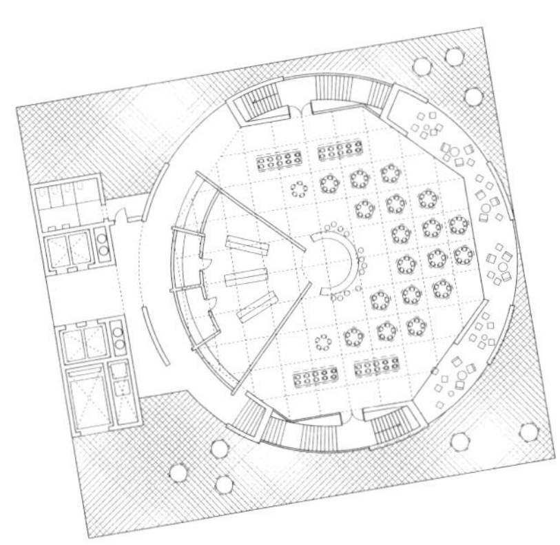

05

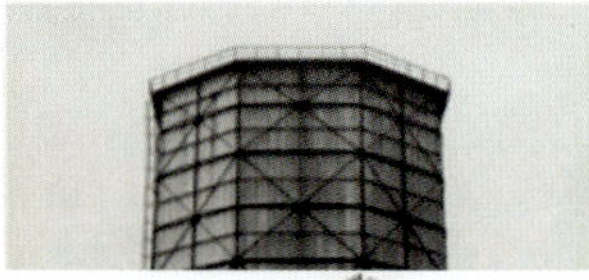

silo

cube

square

06

07

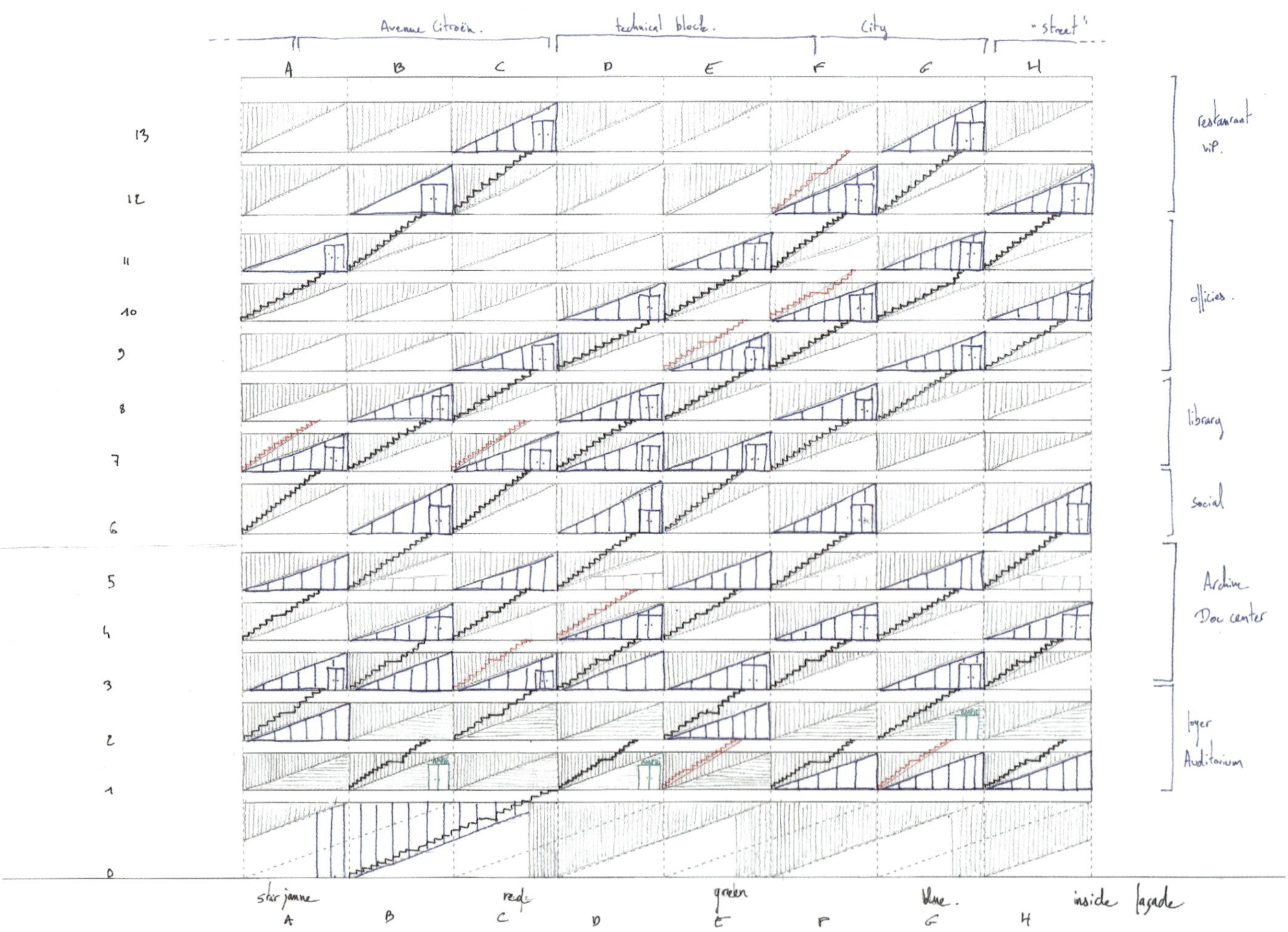

08

09

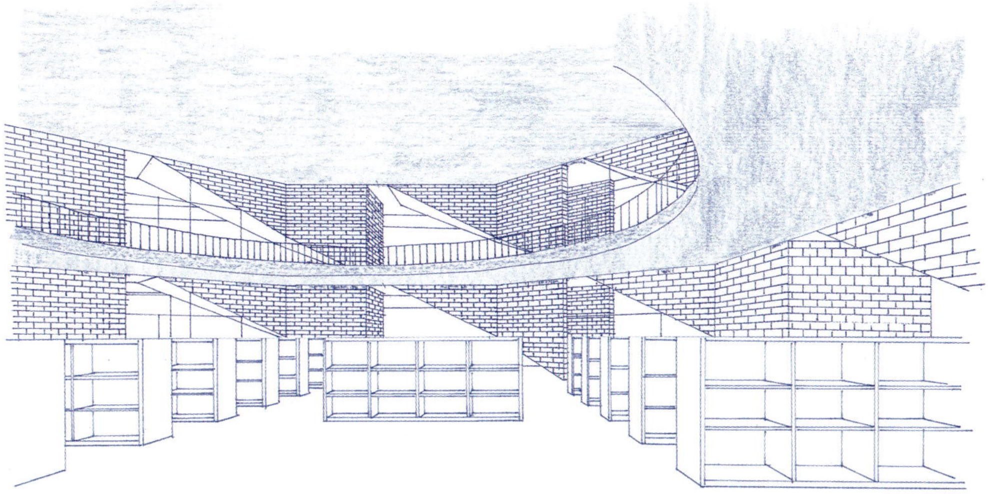

10

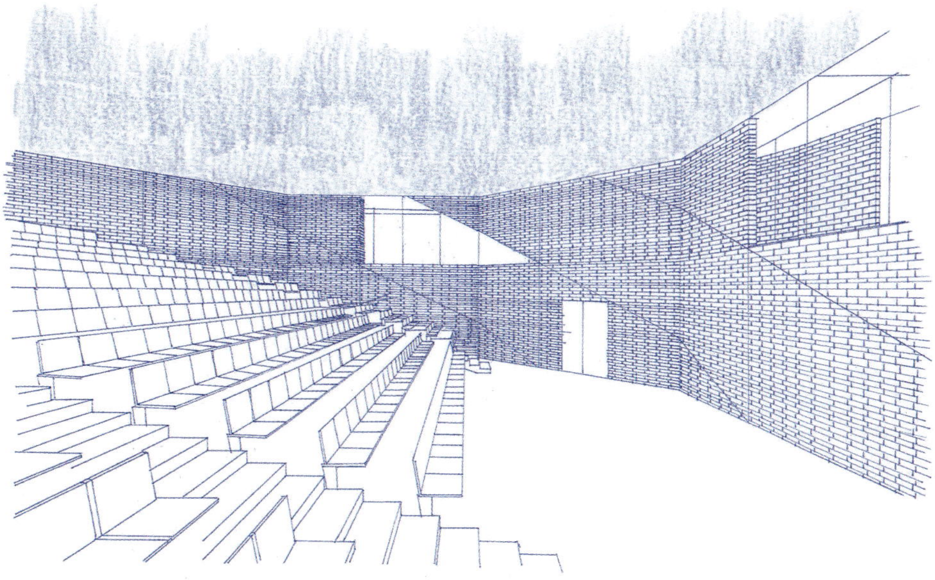

05
circular tower as an assemblage of reworked references

06
collection of working models of the circular tower

07
study of vertical circulation and inner façade

08–10
library, auditorium, foyer on ground floor

01

02

03

04

LAS ARADAS construction of a civil war massacre memorial 2017–ongoing Chalatenango, El Salvador

implantation plan

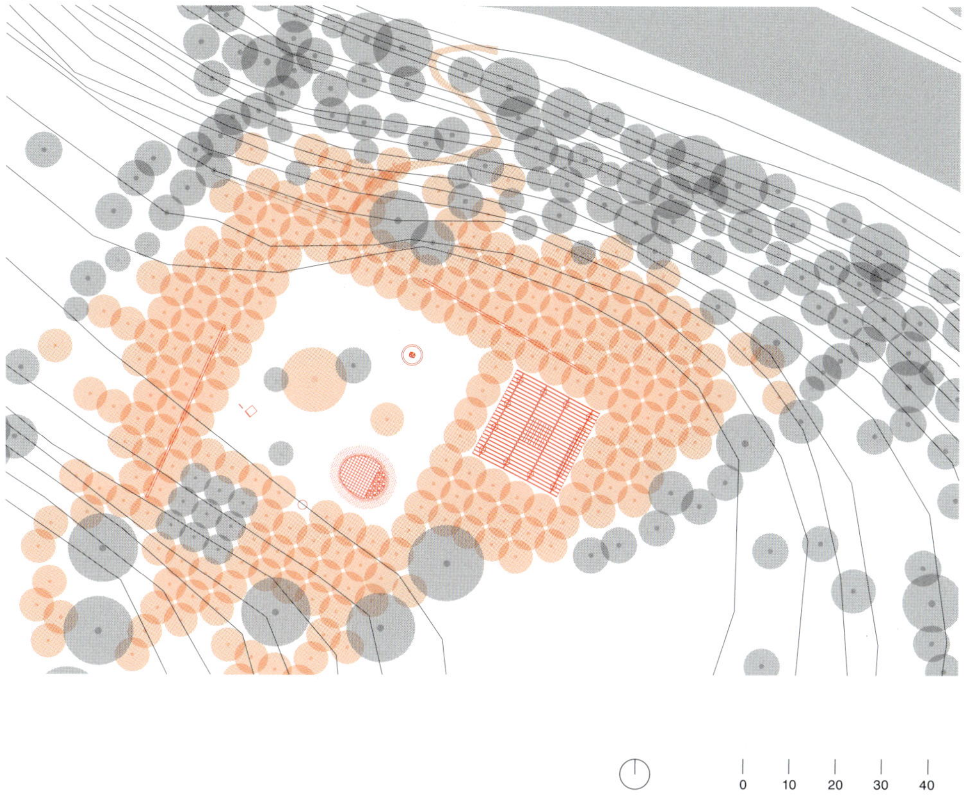

05

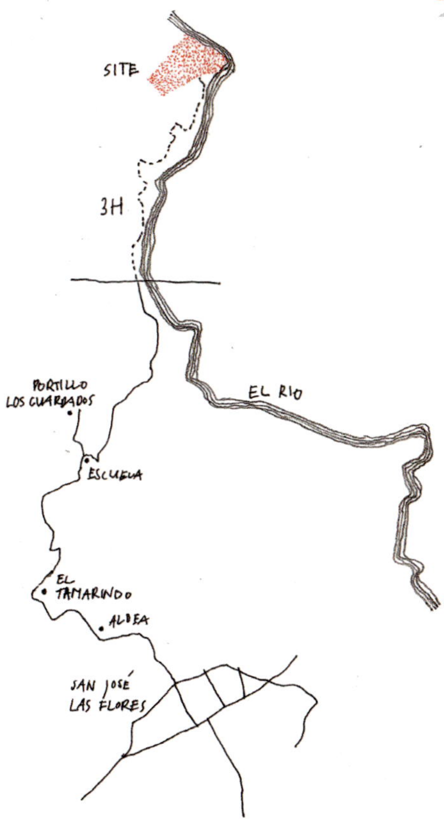

06

Two hundred red flame trees were planted to frame the memorial site of Las Aradas in El Salvador, where more than 600 civilians were killed in 1980 by the army and paramilitary groups. The flame trees blossom in May for the commemorative ceremonies. Several infrastructures were built in the clearing and between the trees. A square roof made of clay tiles burned on site covers a long adobe wall with a fresco. A circular bench frames a large fireplace. The original monument, which dates from 1993, was renovated. A ceramics memorial and life-size statue of Archbishop Romero were realized by the School of Arts of the National University. This community-based project was carried out in the context of a post-war memory research project led by Western University (Canada) and KU Leuven, funded by SSHRC (Social Sciences and Humanities Research Council of Canada).

01–03
preliminary design (2018)

04
overview of construction site (2022), © Shawn Robertson

05
plan of journey by car and by foot from one of the villages to the memorial site

06
drawing based on the recollection of the massacre by survivor Felipe Tobar, from *Memorias del Sumpul*, Equipo Maíz, august 2019

07

08

09

10

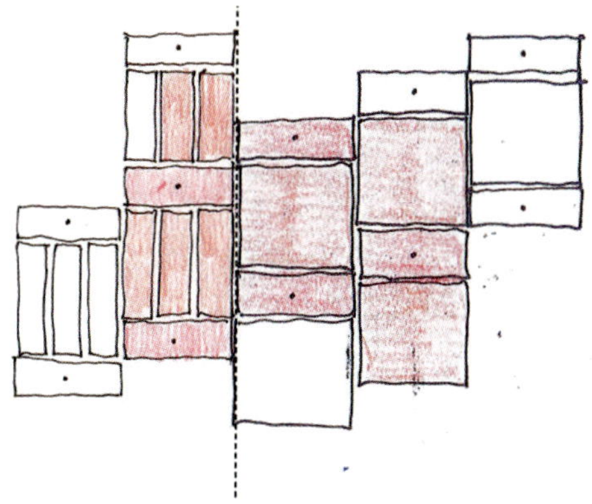

11

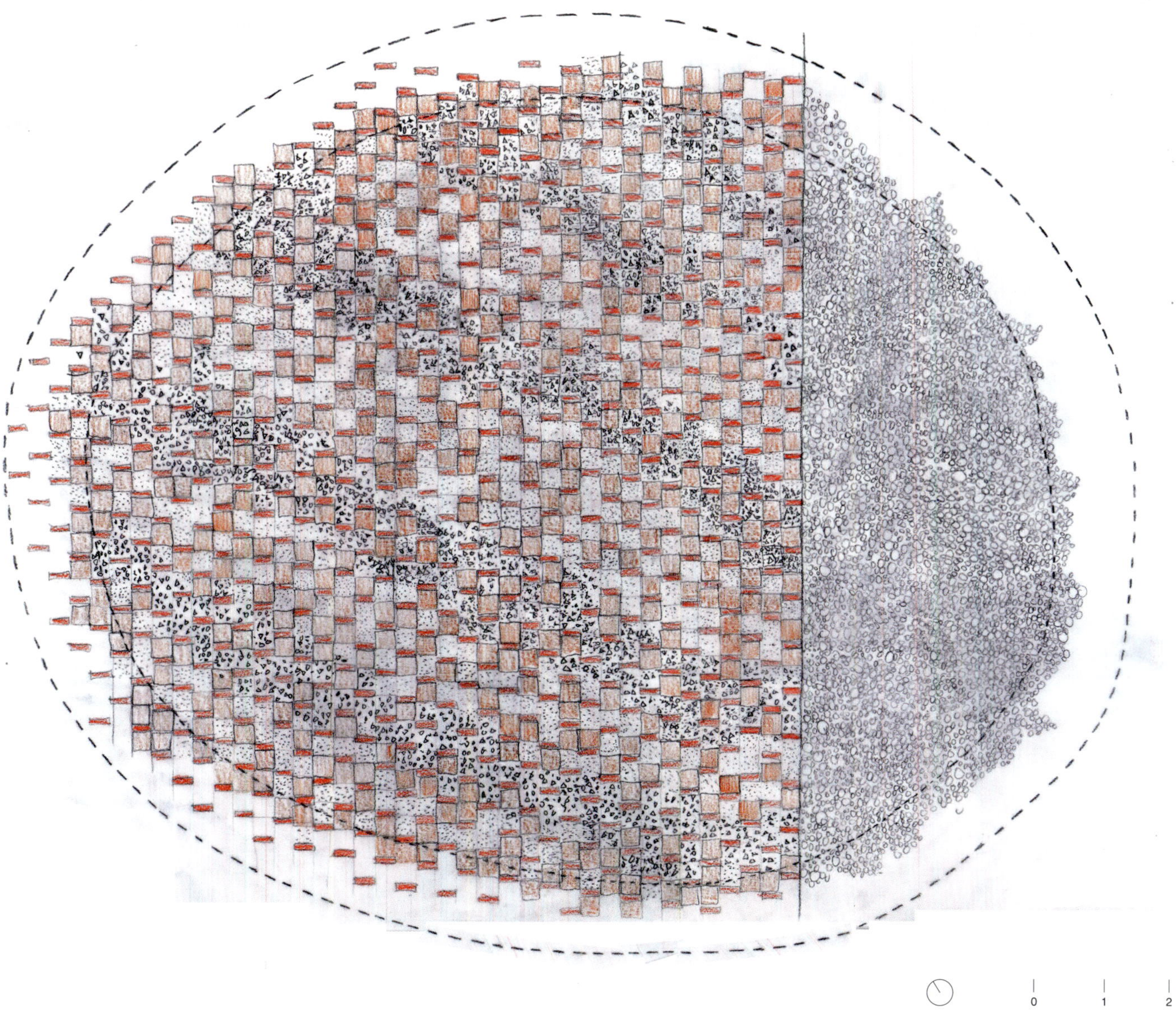

07
memorial bearing the names of the victims, construction site (2022)

08
drawing of flame trees that constitute the planted forest (2020)

09
researchers, art students and workers laying tiles and ceramics of the memorial, construction site (2022)

10
motif of tiles and ceramics, preliminary design (2019)

11
plan of the memorial, construction phase (2020)

12

13

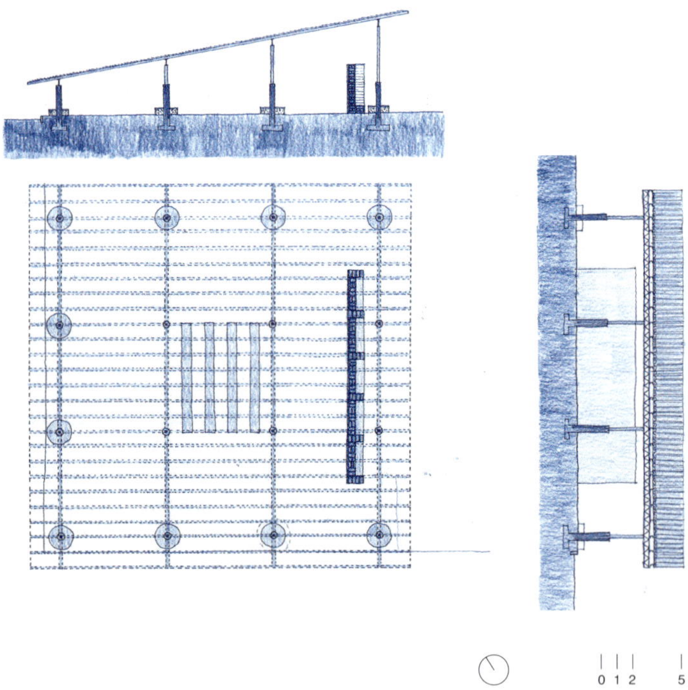

14

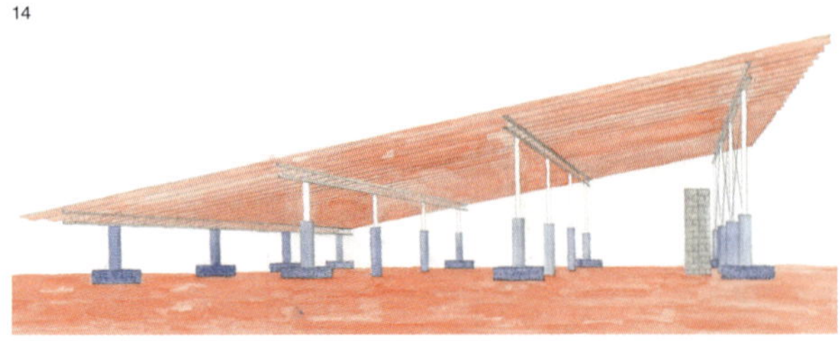

15

16

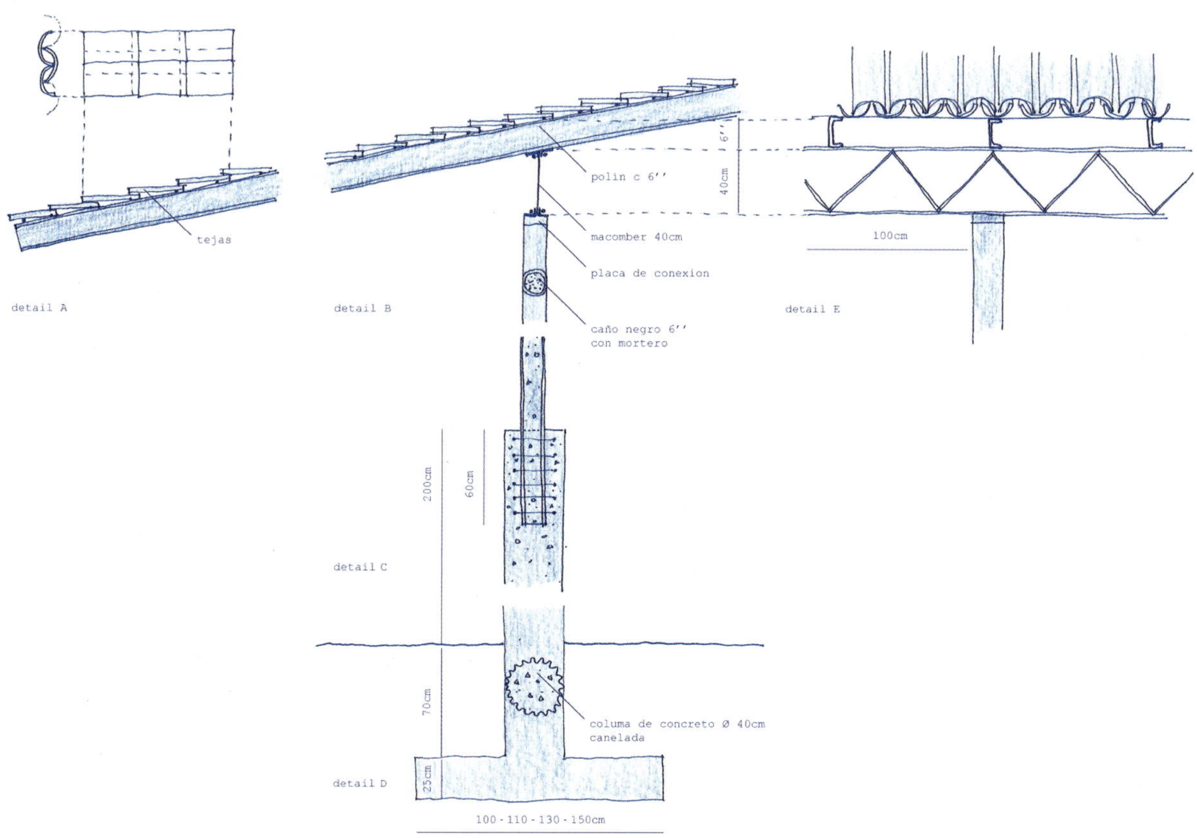

12
roof structure, construction site (2022), © Shawn Robertson

13
plan and elevations of roof structure, execution phase (2019)

14
perspective drawing of the roof structure realized for the 40th commemoration of the Sumpul Massacre (2020)

15
overview of construction site (2022), © Shawn Robertson

16
details of roof structure, execution phase (2019)

01

VERBIEST

transformation of an industrial warehouse into a single-family house and workshop

2017–20

Molenbeek-Saint-Jean, Brussels

in collaboration with Maria Evelia Macal Guerra

02

03

This former warehouse was transformed into a single-family house with a shared ceramic workshop on the ground floor. The limited demolitions aim primarily at creating a terrace and two gardens planted with productive plants and trees while maintaining the primary structures. Three small heated zones colonize the vast non-climatized spaces, depending on the seasons. Part of the roof made way for an agricultural greenhouse. Reinforced with idiosyncratic wooden crutches, the concrete structure is the backdrop for the overall use of materials recovered from the warehouse, personal stocks and other projects.

see p. 150–155

01
construction site (2019),
© Séverin Malaud

02
building permit scale model, reworked for the *Brussels Architecture Prize* (2022)

03
perspective section prepared for the *CA^{2}RE* conference, Ghent (2019)

04

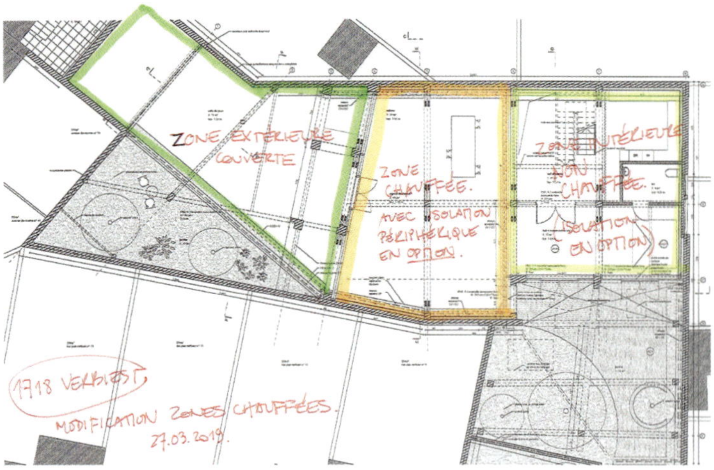

ground floor

05

07

level +1

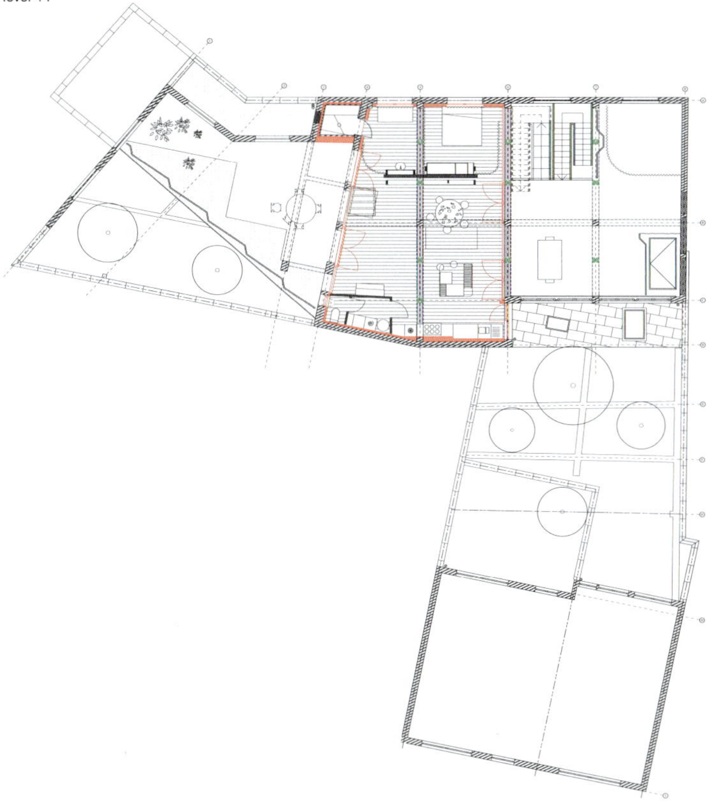

level +2

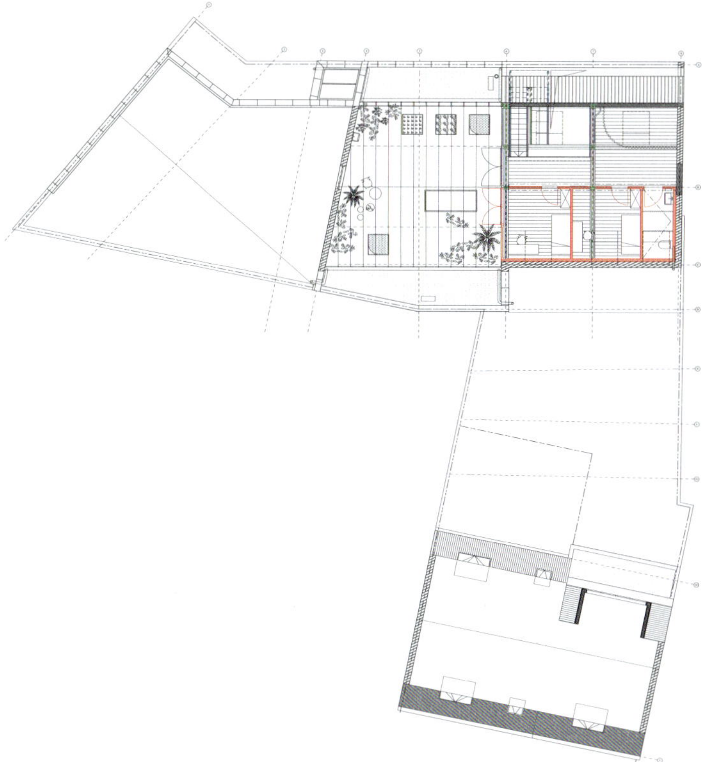

06

04
reduction of the heated areas,
construction phase (2019)

05–06
demolition phase (2019),
© Séverin Malaud

07

08

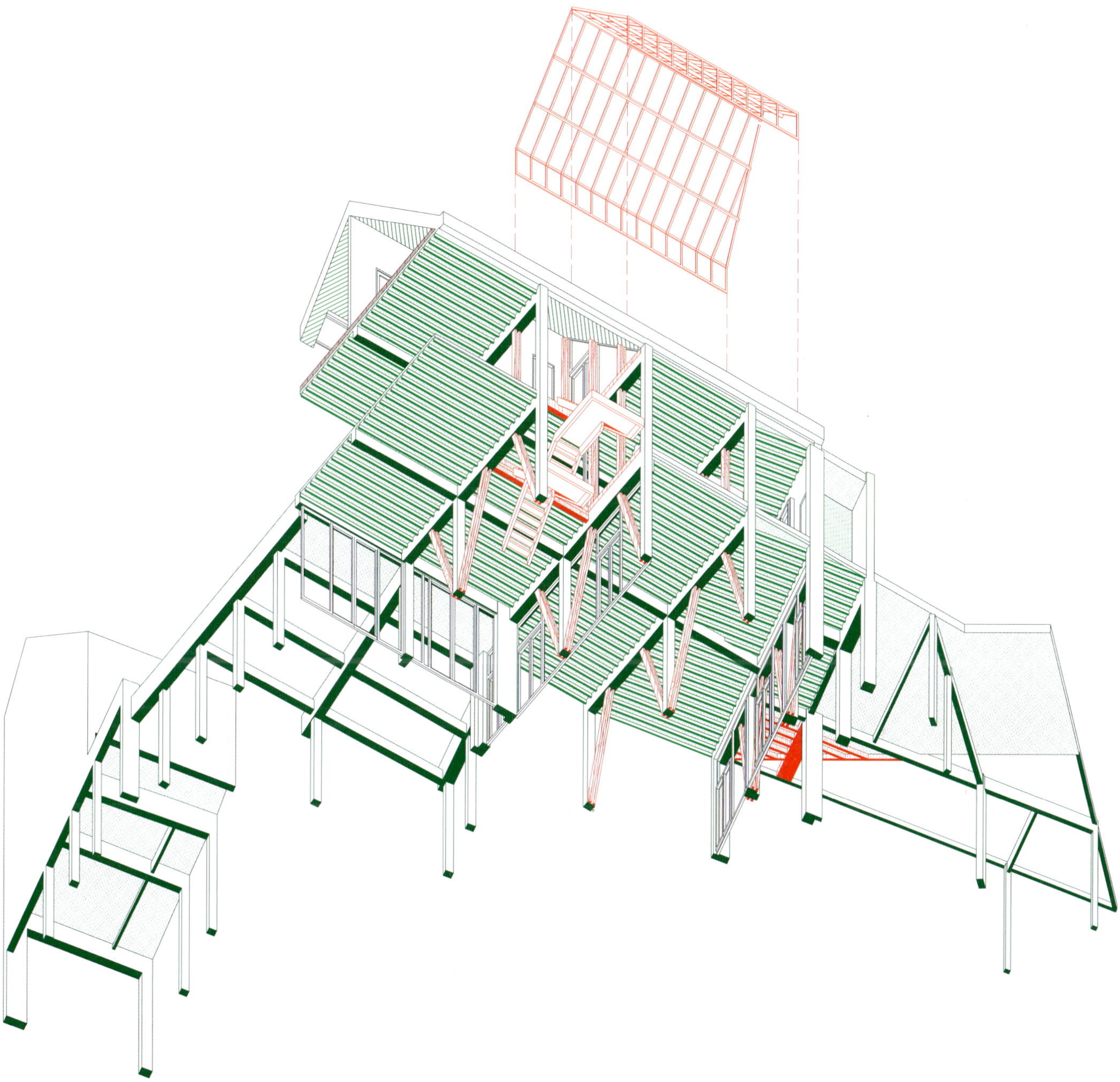

07–08
wooden reinforcements, construction site (top 2019, bottom 2020), © Séverin Malaud

09
axonometric view prepared for the *CA²RE* conference, Ghent (2019)

10

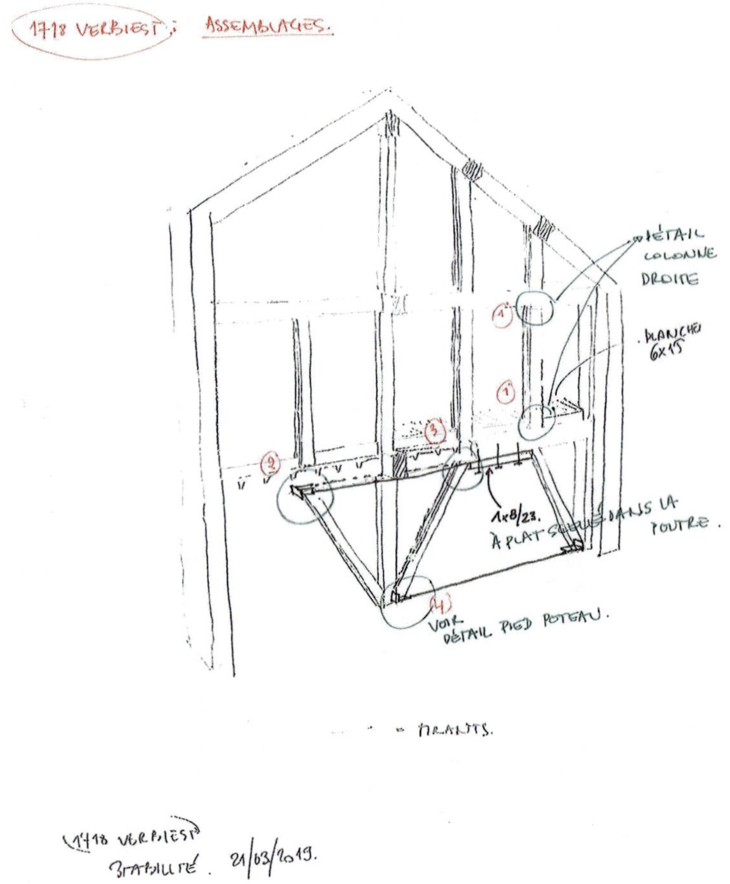
1718 VERBIEST : ASSEMBLAGES.
DÉTAIL COLONNE DROITE
PLANCHER 6x15
1x8/23. À PLAT SCELLÉE DANS LA POUTRE.
VOIR DÉTAIL PIED POTEAU.
TIRANTS.
1718 VERBIEST STABILITÉ. 21/03/2019.

11

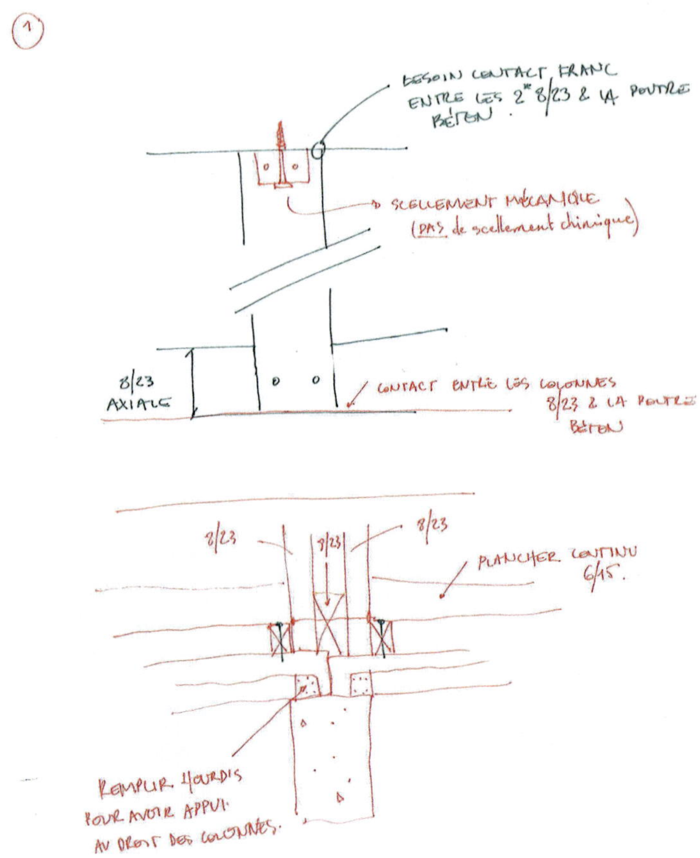
BESOIN CONTACT FRANC ENTRE LES 2* 8/23 & LA POUTRE BÉTON.
SCELLEMENT MÉCANIQUE (PAS de scellement chimique)
8/23 AXIALE
CONTACT ENTRE LES COLONNES 8/23 & LA POUTRE BÉTON
8/23
8/23
8/23
PLANCHER CONTINU 6/15.
REMPLIR HOURDIS POUR AVOIR APPUI AU DROIT DES COLONNES.

12

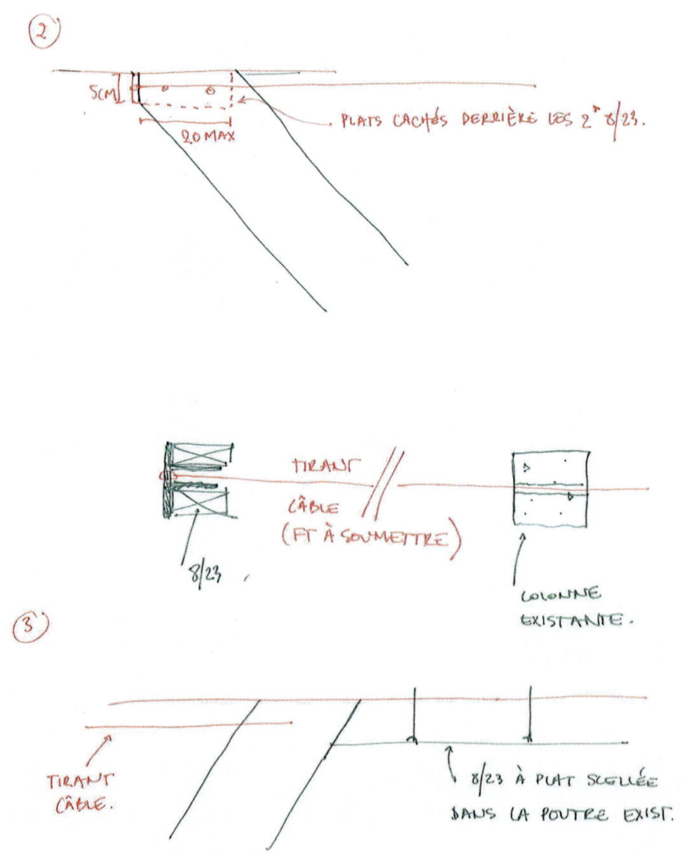
5CM
PLATS CACHÉS DERRIÈRE LES 2* 8/23.
20 MAX
TIRANT
CÂBLE
(FT À SOUMETTRE)
8/23
COLONNE EXISTANTE.
TIRANT CÂBLE.
8/23 À PLAT SCELLÉE DANS LA POUTRE EXIST.

13

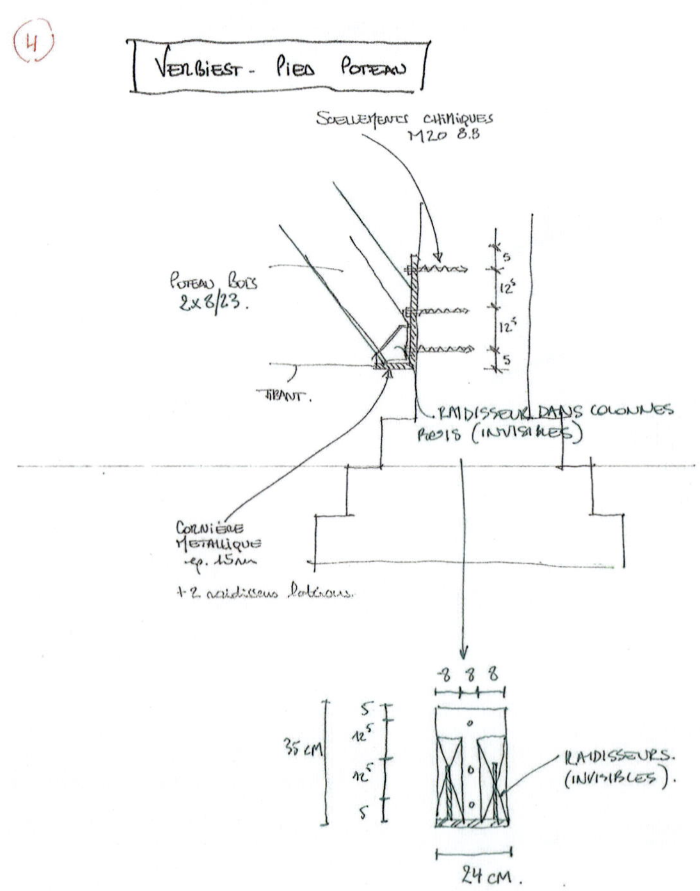
VERBIEST - PIED POTEAU
SCELLEMENTS CHIMIQUES M20 8.8
POTEAU BOIS 2x8/23.
TIRANT.
RAIDISSEUR DANS COLONNES BOIS (INVISIBLES)
CORNIÈRE MÉTALLIQUE ep. 15mm
+ 2 raidisseurs latéraux
8 8 8
35 CM
RAIDISSEURS. (INVISIBLES).
24 CM.

14

15

16

17

10–13
structural details by
Benoît Meerseman (2019)

14–17
construction site (2020),
© Séverin Malaud

01

KARREVELD 2 **extension for a secondary school and sports hall** **2018–ongoing** **Molenbeek-Saint-Jean, Brussels**

02

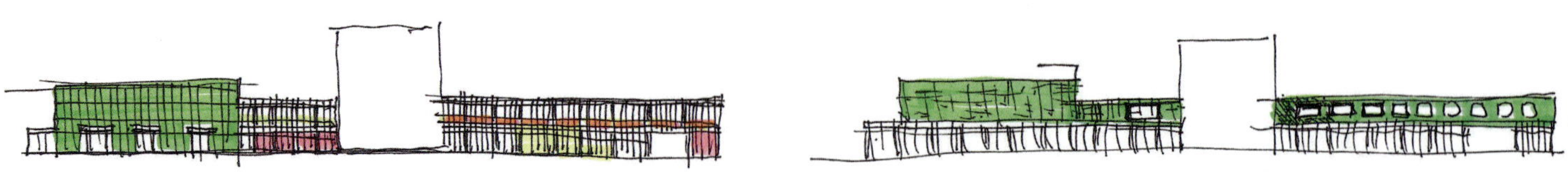

03

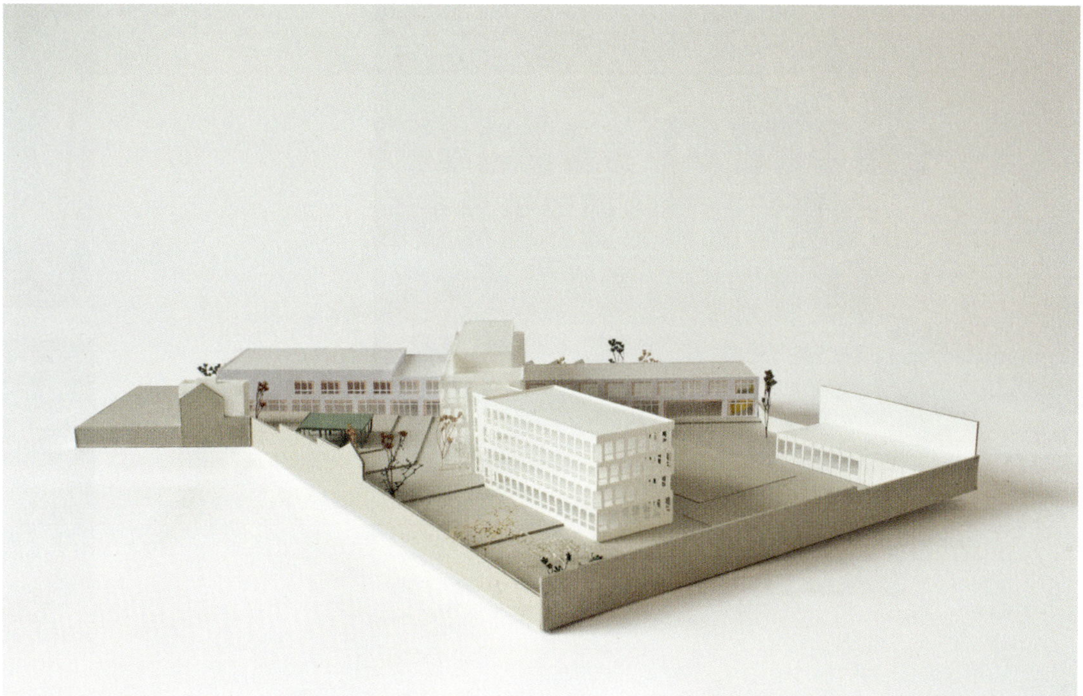

04

05

The second phase of this project involved the complete refurbishment and extension of the 1970s office building into a school with a sports hall. The first phase (see p. 70–73) **was retained in its entirety. The same approach was applied to the second wing of the existing building. A long volume was added along the border of the plot, from the street to the back of the site. Its interior spaces are free from structural elements.**

The sports hall adjoins the street and can be used when the school is closed. The cafeteria is connected to the playground at the back. A new entrance hall articulates both volumes, opening up towards generous staircases and informal meeting spaces.

see p. 146–149

01
axonometric view,
building permit (2019)

02
study of the façade,
competition phase (2018)

03
scale model, competition
phase (2018)

04
construction phase (2021)

05
execution phase (2019)

06

07

08

09

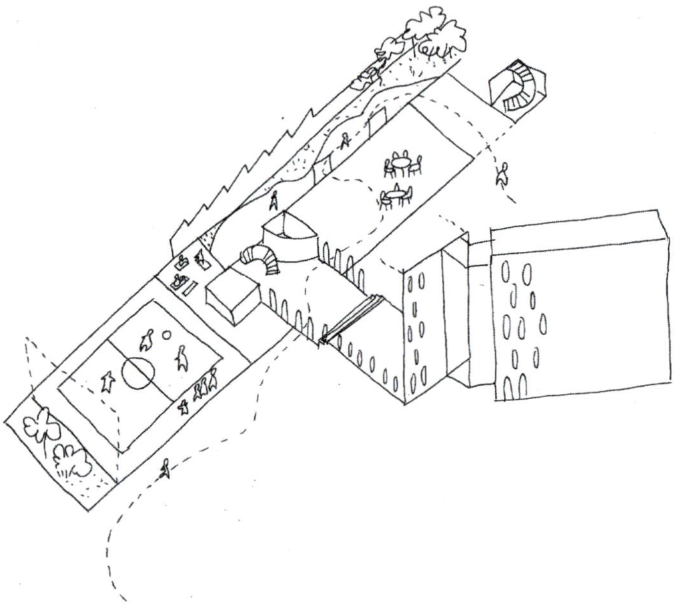

10

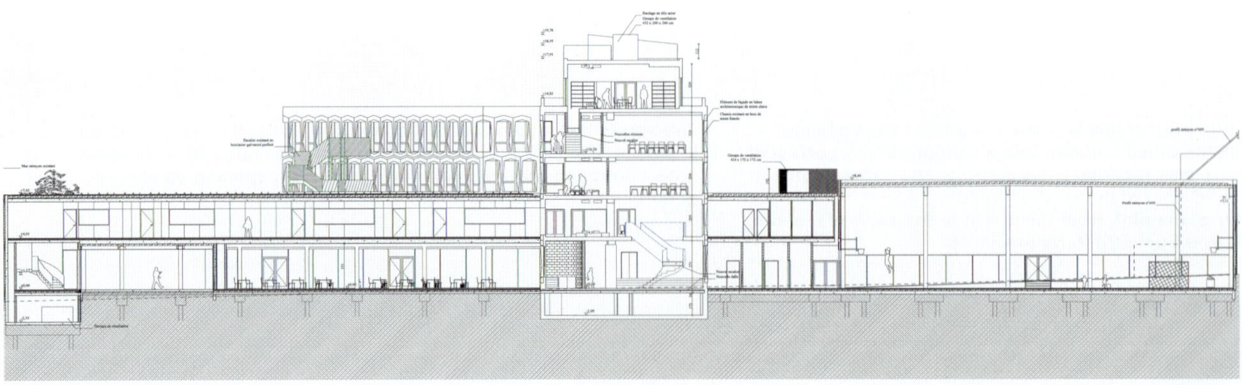

11

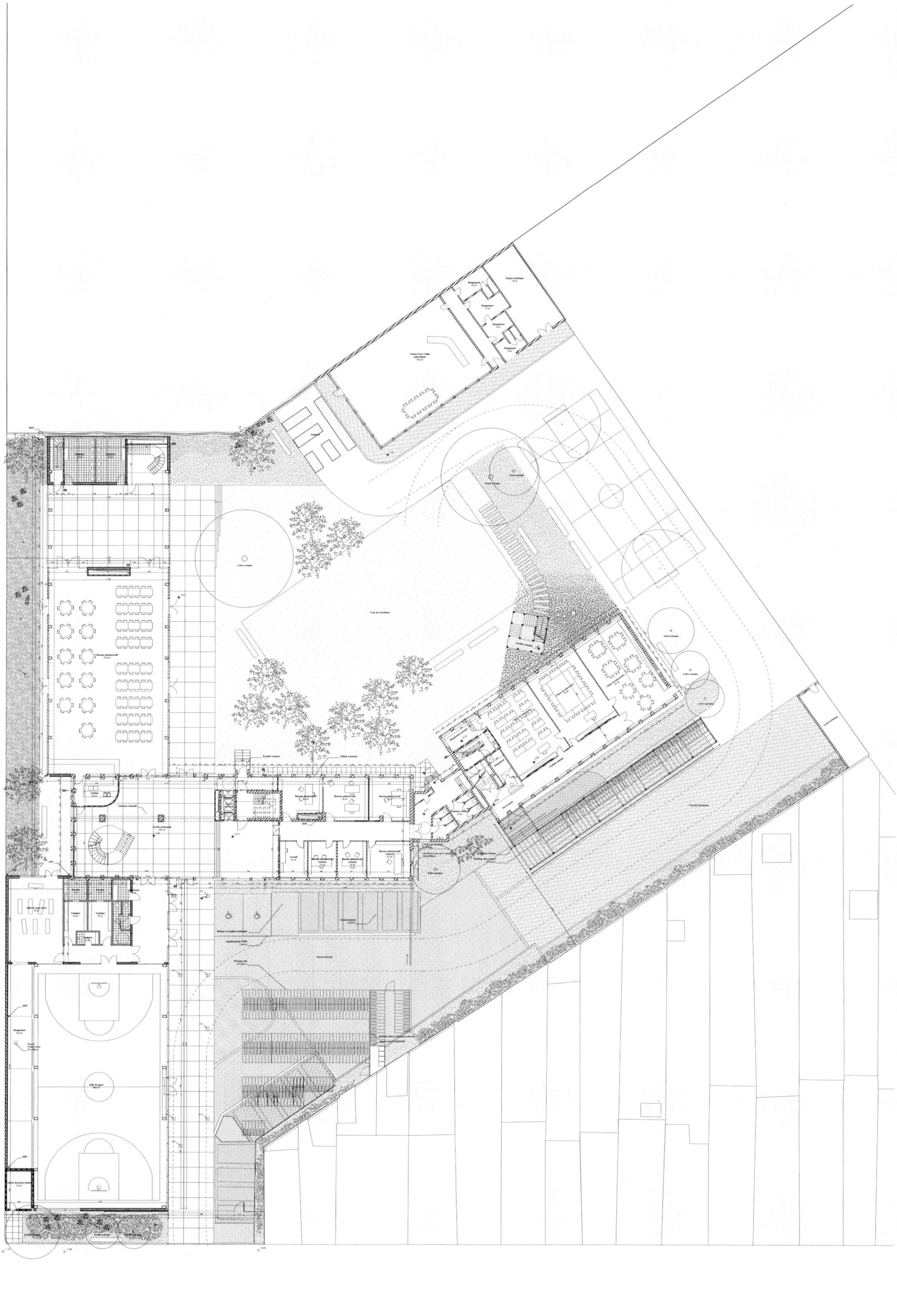

06–08
construction site (2021),
© Séverin Malaud

09
articulation of extension and existing volume, meeting of sports hall, cafeteria and entrance area, competition phase (2018)

10–11
building permit phase (2019)

0 5 10

01

JERUSALEM	**transformation and extension of farmhouses into a kindergarten, social housing and community garden**	**2019–ongoing**	**Schaerbeek, Brussels**

02

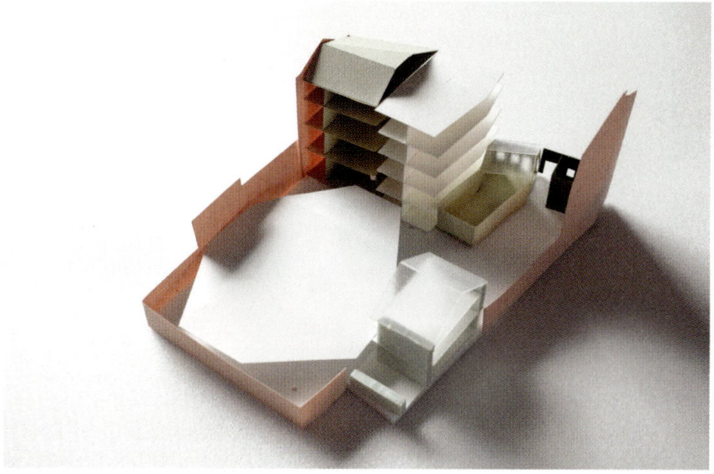

03

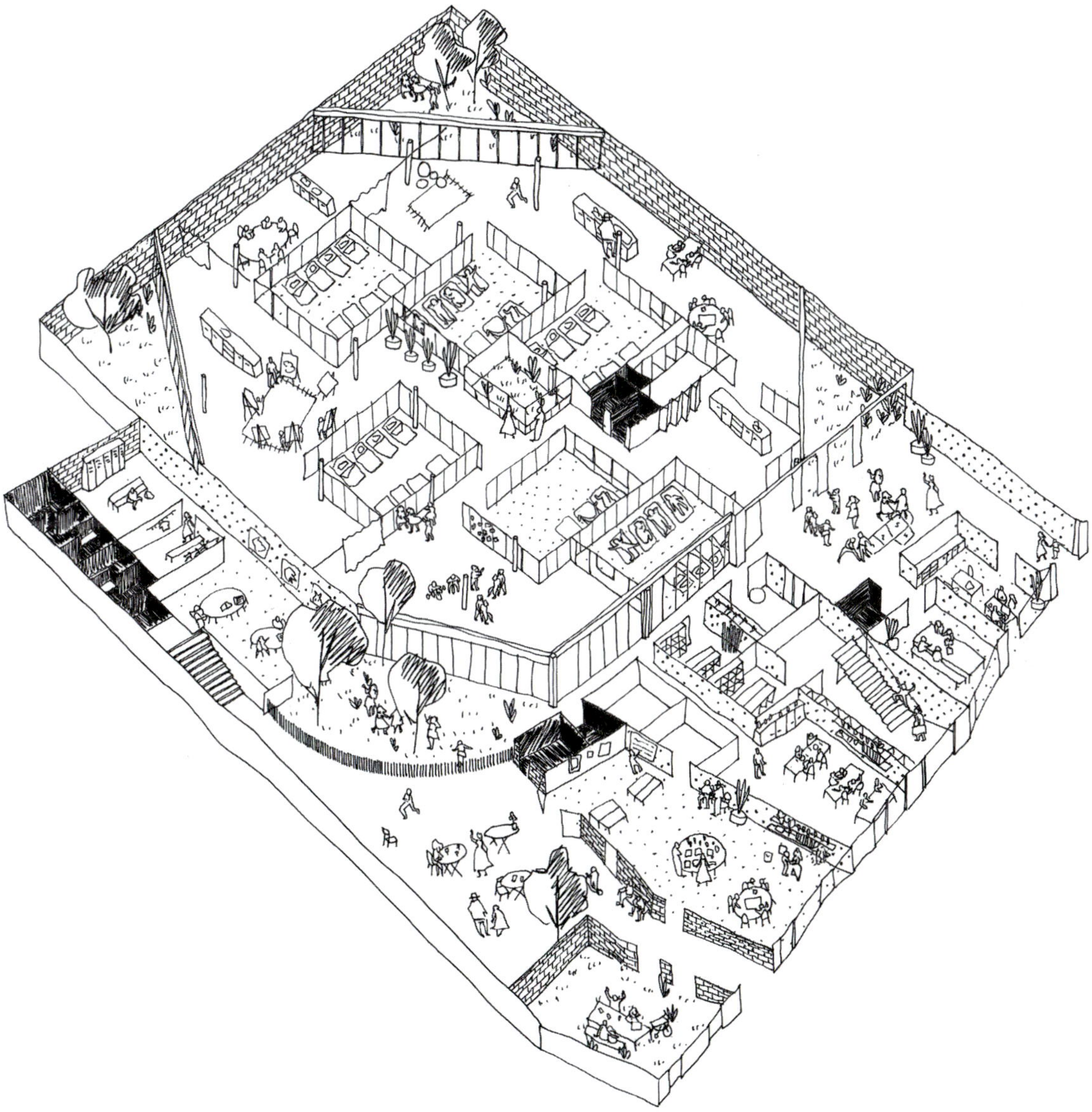

This complex programme includes housing, a kindergarten, a community centre and an urban vegetable garden on a densely occupied site. Avoiding superfluous demolitions, the existing housing, extended by a construction replacing a small town house, offers a surprising, open perpendicular façade.

At the back, the plot is filled by an octagonal kindergarten with a rooftop vegetable garden. A public walk-through gives access to the gardens and to the community centre in the two small nineteenth-century farmhouses. A pre-existing greenhouse completes the dense patchwork of constructions.

01
render of the street façade, preliminary design (2020)

02
concept model, competition phase (2019)

03
axonometric view of the ground floor and its uses, competition phase (2019)

04

0 1 2 5 10

05

06

07

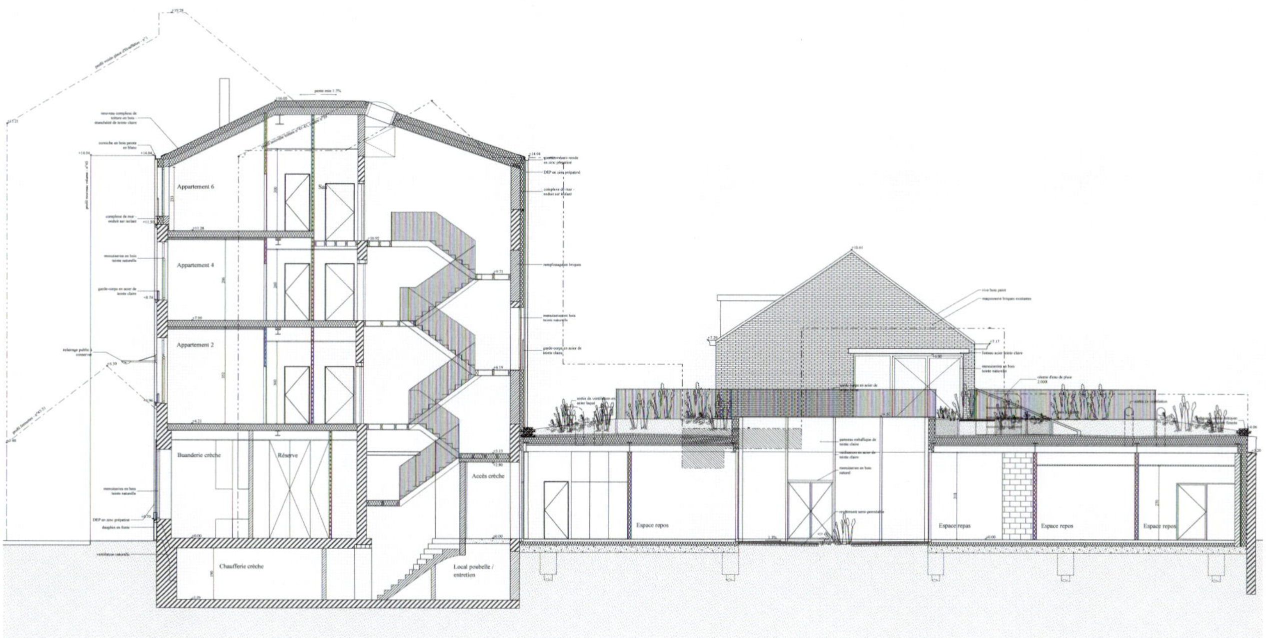

04
ground floor plan, execution phase (2021)

05
street façade, preliminary design (2020)

06
existing street façade (2022)

07
section A, execution phase (2021)

08

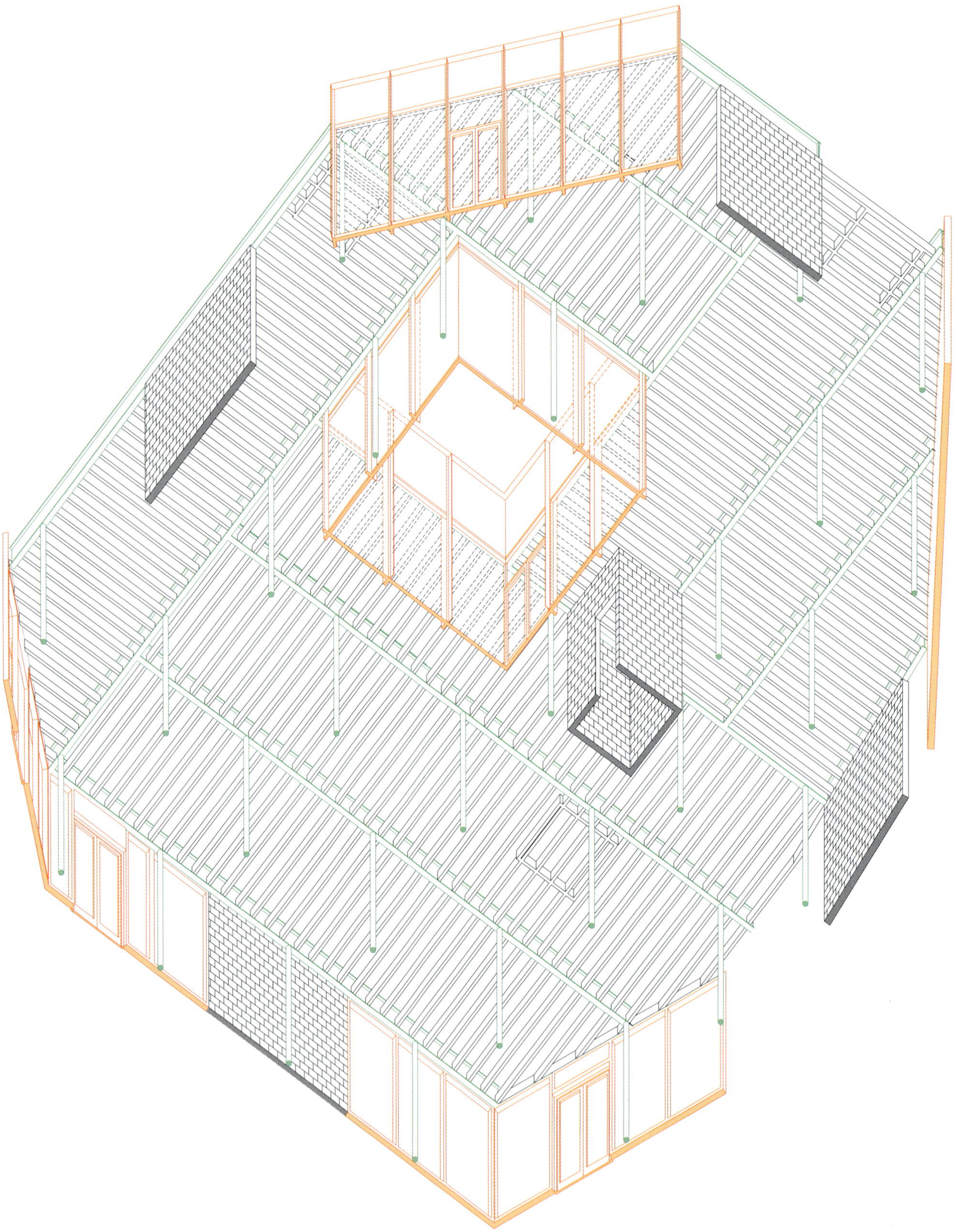

09

10

11

12

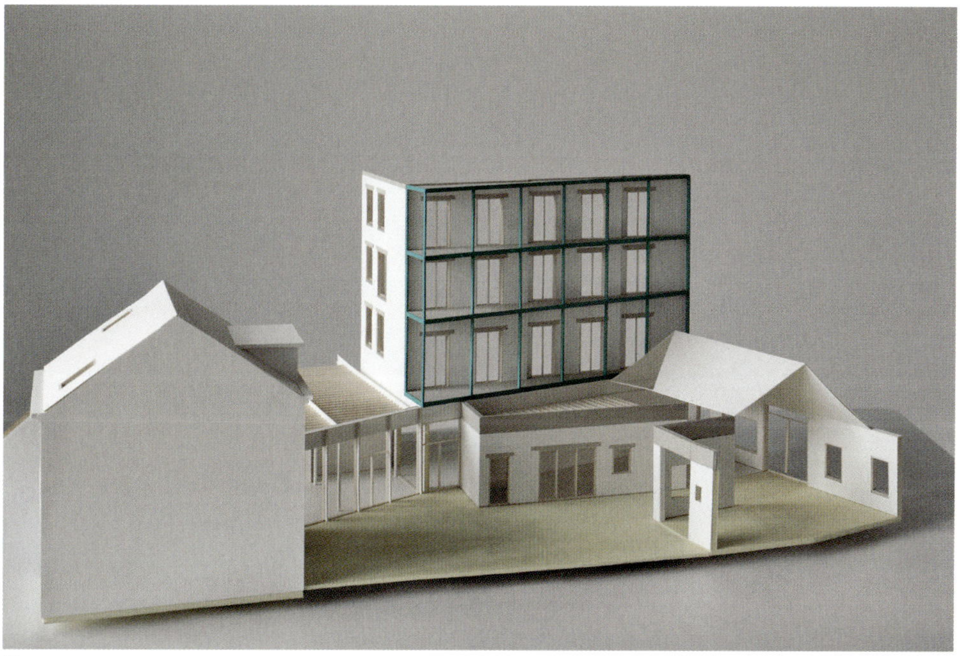

13

08
axonometric view of architectural elements of the kindergarten, execution phase (2021)

09–11
interior and exterior studies, execution phase (2021)

12–13
scale model (fragment), execution phase (2021), © Filip Dujardin

01

level +5

02

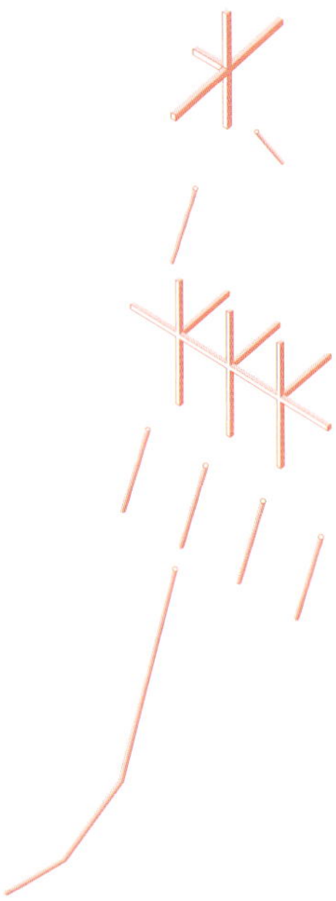

03

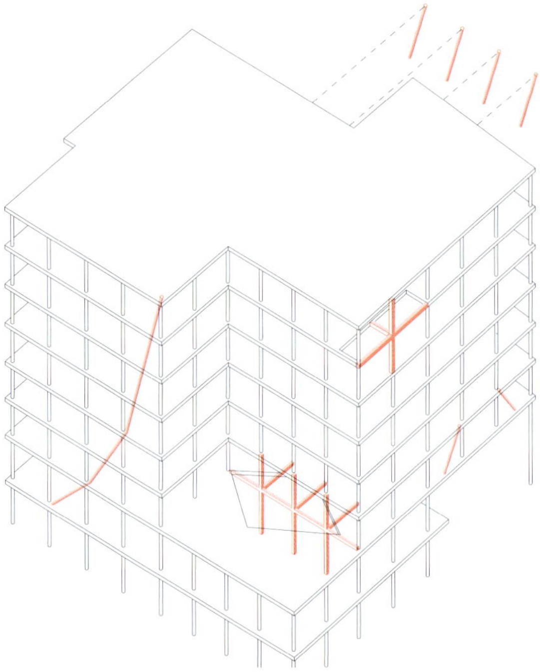

04

ABRICOTIER

construction of an office and social housing building with a kindergarten, a shop and parking spaces

2020–ongoing

Brussels

05

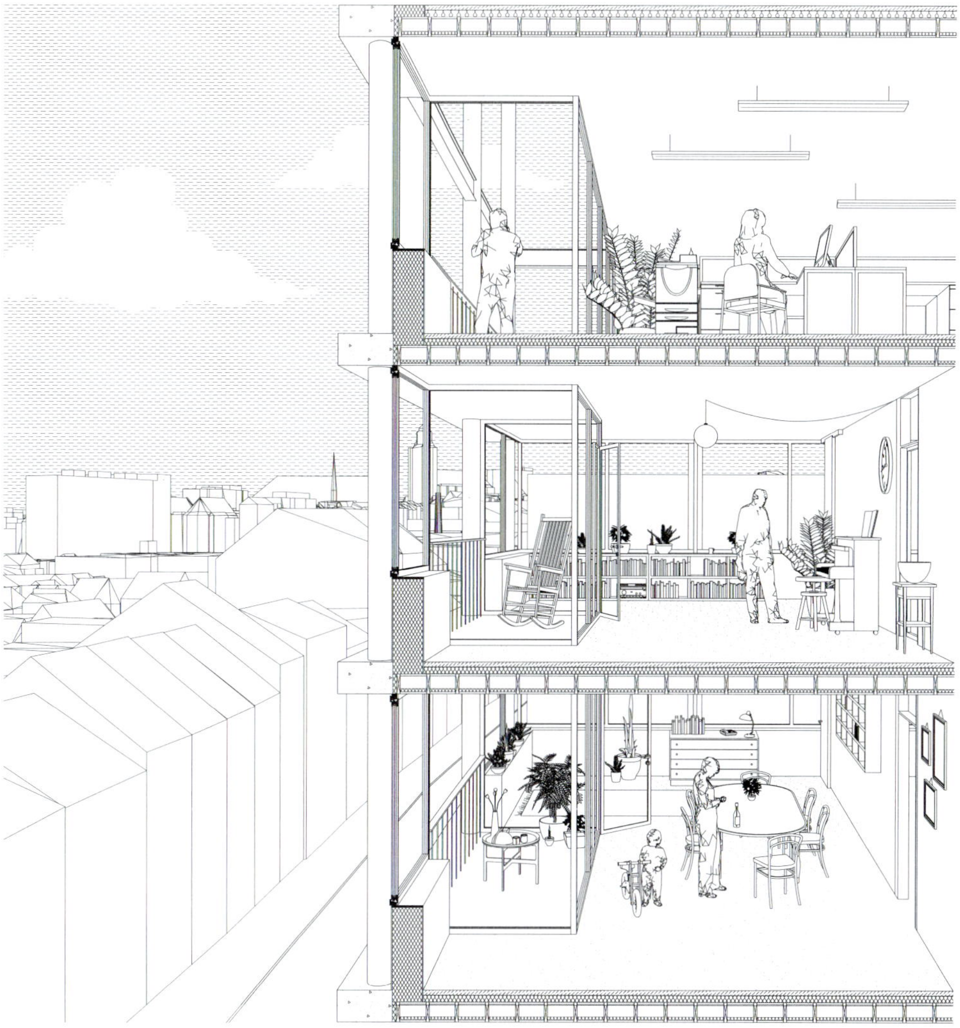

06

07

Located at the corner of a sloping street, the extension of the Brussels headquarters of the Public Centre for Social Welfare (CPAS/OCMW) – which includes housing units, a kindergarten and a shop – maintains the access to the hospital's emergency service next door. The upper levels contain a flexible office and housing programme thanks to an empty 'typical plan' with two cores and load-bearing façades.

The minimal concrete columns and beams are completed with crutches in steel (bracing, patio, ambulance passage, etc.) and combined with hemp and lime infills and timber floors. They form a geometric and structural system that makes possible the changing use of the building and its volumetric adaptation to the context.

see p. 144–145

01
north facade

02–03
axonometric views of the bracing elements and structure

04
primary concrete structure, hemp and lime infills, wooden frames

05
perspective section of the housing units

06
housing unit with bracing element

07
kindergarten around the central patio

THE VOICE OF THINGS: THE OBJECTIVE ARCHITECTURE OF AGWA

Pierre Chabard

In June 2021 the jury of the brand-new Brussels Architecture Prize 2021 met to draw up a shortlist of thirty-one projects from the 175 that had been submitted. AgwA achieved the feat of making it onto this highly selective list twice, with two projects nominated in two different categories ('small' and 'large' intervention). Although neither of the projects won a prize, this dual nomination shows the special and abiding place that AgwA has occupied for almost twenty years in the Brussels architectural scene: an active and continuous presence on all the main fronts and an abundant, varied and empirical production. It is difficult to single out a characteristic project from among their oeuvre, however, just as it is difficult to identify a clear stylistic approach or firm doctrinal stance. Harold Fallon and Benoît Vandenbulcke have been working together since 2003, first with Raphaël Cornelis until 2008 and then with Benoît Burquel from 2011 onward. They are like those writers whose new books are nothing like their previous ones, like those scholars who keep investigating new fields instead of always ploughing the same furrow. They have developed an agile, exploratory practice that responds to evolutions in the architectural debate and in the production conditions of the built environment and, more generally, to evolutions in our world and the crises it faces. Their practice is as resistant to the traditional exercise of the retrospective critical essay as the renegade researcher is to the 'accreditation thesis', but it presents that rare quality of leaving its future direction open and unpredictable.

Noticed in 2003 during the famous alternative call for ideas for Place Flagey, the Brussels office has not stopped working, researching and building since, holding itself to the same high standards in private commissions as in public competitions, in *savoir faire* as in *faire savoir*.[1] AgwA's architects, who are involved in teaching[2] and research[3] and who speak regularly at conferences and round tables, are very active on the cultural scene, as can be seen from their participation in numerous exhibitions.[4] Having won several awards, they regularly appear in the architectural press, including in special issues on Belgium by leading international magazines (like issue 1454 of *The Architectural Review*).

FLAGEY (2006)

Ubiquitous and enterprising, they elude classification. Indeed, what does the very Koolhaasian Vertigo project for the Walibi theme park (2007) – the project that put them on the map – have in common with the low-tech, thrifty conversion of the warehouse on Rue Verbiest (2020), which has just been nominated for a couple of awards? Or the extraterrestrial ETFE canopy of the school on Baron Leroystraat in Antwerp (2021) with the round-arch brick arcades of the school on Bredastraat, also in Antwerp (2016)?

VERTIGO (2006)
© Marie-Françoise Plissart
see p. 008–011 & p. 240–243

To varying degrees, AgwA's architects certainly display the main characteristics of their generation, which has driven the renewal of French-speaking Belgian architecture these past two decades: formal neutrality, economy of means, programmatic and urban intelligence, social and political commitment. But other approaches taken by the office based at Rue des Palais in Brussels, particularly regarding the autonomy of the discipline and the constructive essence of the architectural act, also link it to the Flemish scene with which it is often associated.[5] Navigating freely and pragmatically between these spheres, working and teaching alternately in Brussels, Wallonia and Flanders, AgwA is charting a course in circumstances that remain critical, marked by crises on several levels (economic, ecological, sanitary, etc.), fragile commissions, rapidly changing social demands and pressure on material resources.

VERBIEST (2021)
© Séverin Malaud
see p. 094–101 & p. 150–155

BREDA (2016)
© Delphine Mathy
see p. 028–029 & p.212–217

1 This definition of architectural practice at the intersection of *savoir faire* and *faire savoir* was the theme of the inaugural lecture that Benoît Vandenbulcke gave at the Faculty of Architecture of ULiège on 24 October 2017.

2 Harold Fallon teaches at the Faculty of Architecture of KU Leuven, Benoît Vandenbulcke at the Faculty of Architecture of ULiège, and Benoît Burquel at the Faculty of Architecture La Cambre-Horta of ULB.

3 Harold Fallon and Benoît Vandenbulcke each hold a PhD. The title of Fallon's thesis is *Metarbitrariness? AgwA, an Architecture of Practice* (RMIT University, 2012) and that of Vandenbulcke's *Abstraction, Concretion: Reading and Producing the Architectural Project through Immersion* (UCLouvain, 2015).

BARONNEKE (2021)
© Séverin Malaud
see p. 054–057 & p. 180–183

Inclusive Reparation

The long and erratic history of the redevelopment of the Adeps sports centre 'Le Grand Large', surrounded by the waters of the artificial lake of Péronnes-lez-Antoing, is indicative of these circumstances. Selected through a competition in 2009, the AgwA project has still only partially been built, due to the drastic budgetary phasing imposed by the client in the aftermath of 2008's economic crisis. This vast, almost insular water-sports centre was occupied by a collection of buildings of varying quality. Some have been slated for demolition, others will be preserved. AgwA's proposal manages to bring coherence to this heterogeneous group without confining it to a rigid and definitive order. A long, white-lacquered steel portico keeps the linear assembly of old and new buildings tightly together and allows other structures, like the new sailing centre, to sit more freely on the rest of the site. Eventually, this abstract line – by turns a gallery, footbridge, pontoon or simple path – will cross the road that still separates the old gymnasium and will act like a yardstick giving the full measure of the landscape. Pending its completion, it serves as a metaphor for the entire history of the operation. Its potential, derived from its clear geometry, seems to guarantee the continuity of the architectural intentions in the long term, despite the vagaries of time and the spatial complexity.

PÉRONNES (2019)
© Séverin Malaud
see p. 018–023 & p. 226–233

From one commission to the next, Burquel, Fallon and Vandenbulcke have learned to deal with this state of uncertainty and these erosive forces that thwart the very idea of a project. To define the current role of the architect, they have appropriated the clever metaphor used by Rem Koolhaas in the mid 1980s: the architect is no longer a 'master' builder, dominating the forces at work, but is 'a bit like a surfer on the waves: he doesn't control them, but he knows them; he knows how to make use of them and also how to go against the current'.[6]

Taking advantage of the resources of a situation, knowing when to concede a point, exhibiting smartness and turning a position of weakness into a strength, this is the agility that architects need today to make architecture happen. Not being in a dominant position, they have less to gain from rigid obstinacy than from lucidly adapting to ever-changing circumstances and drawing on 'the blows that (they) are dealt', as Henri Michaux would have said.[7]

The redevelopment of the vacant offices of Takeda Belgium in Molenbeek (2017–22) to house the pluralist Karreveld secondary school is an illustration of this constant balancing act in AgwA's practice between strategy

4 From *(Re)nouveaux plaisirs d'architecture #2* in 2007 to the Belgian Pavilion at the Venice Biennale 2020 by way of *Collection d'architectures (sans titre)* in 2007, *(Un)City* in 2013 and *Operational Aesthetics* at CIVA in 2018.

5 In 2009 already, AgwA, together with the Flemish offices 360 architecten, noAarchitecten, Jan De Vylder architecten and Dierendonckblancke architecten, was among the first to be invited to the NICHE Young Belgian Architecture programme, a series of micro exhibitions and conferences organized by Iwan Strauven at the Centre for Fine Arts in Brussels.

6 Rem Koolhaas, 'We Are Like a Surfer on the Wave: Work Methods at OMA', *Rem Koolhaas: Projectes Urbans/Urban Projects. 1985-1990* (Barcelona: Quaderns, 1990), 6.

7 Henri Michaux, 'Épervier de ta faiblesse, domine!', in *Épreuves, exorcisme, 1940-1944* (Paris: Gallimard, 1949), 21.

and tactics. Divided into two phases (with the risk that the second phase, itself subject to consultation, will never materialize), the operation will initially consist of temporarily refurbishing one of the wings of the 1970s building with its honeycomb façades made of prefabricated concrete cells. Both its qualities and defects will be systematically exploited, in particular to circumvent the absurdity of certain standards. Is the building not wide enough to accommodate two rows of classrooms? No matter, we will gain a wide corridor bathed in light, something which is generally left out in current school architecture. Is the budget for the operation too tight? This will justify the reuse of certain existing elements, in particular the ingenious modular partition system of the former offices, which is more solid and elegant as well as glazed and, above all, less ordinary than the ubiquitous plasterboard. For the same reasons, the suspended ceilings but also the ventilation and heating devices will in part be reused. Although not substantially cheaper, this strategy will at least finance labour rather than the frequently delocalized materials industry.

KARREVELD 1 (2019)
see p. 070–073 & p. 168–170

A twist on Reyner Banham's 'design by choice'[8] – where it is no longer a matter of choosing the components of a building from a catalogue but directly from reality – this method of producing 'architecture in reverse'[9] explored by AgwA (in the same way as Rotor) favours, where possible, the rearrangement of existing objects over the prescription of new ones and above all examines the combination of the two. Like 6a in the UK (with whom they competed for the KANAL project), AgwA thus revisits the 'as found' aesthetic of the Smithsons, another exponent of realism and empathy towards architecture objects that time has left behind, beyond strictly heritage or ecological concerns.

KARREVELD 2 (2021)
© Séverin Malaud
see p. 102–105 & p. 146–149

This inclusive attitude not only applies at the level of the element but also at the level of the building and city: for instance, in the Adeps sports centre in Péronnes, where the old buildings with postmodern motifs are integrated into (and accepted by) the project, but even more so in the conversion of the former site of the École Centrale des Arts et Métiers (ECAM, 2014–22) in Saint-Gilles. In this vast block interior, AgwA created a set of seven architectural objects to house community programmes. Three buildings of the former school were transformed and repurposed according to their spatial capacities: the laboratories (on the street side) into a flexible, multipurpose structure (community centre, youth house, collective kitchen, etc.); the classrooms and the workshops (at the heart of the block's interior) into a large kindergarten and a sports facility, respectively. Four new buildings were constructed, mostly replacing lower-quality structures that clogged up the interior of the block and prevented it from being crossed. Undoing, redoing, adding, subtracting, transforming, replacing, juxtaposing, adjusting, opening up certain walls, erecting others – this mix of operations combining DIY with precision work results in the arrangement in fluid, self-evident spaces of a temporary compilation of programmes that do not share the same status, the same users or the same schedules.

ECAM (2021)
© Séverin Malaud
see p. 030–037 & 198–211

This musical arrangement does not mix everything together, however. Rather than smooth out the differences, AgwA assumes on the contrary a resolutely composite and additive aesthetic. Like Guy Debord who claimed that he could 'make a film out of anything'[10] (images from archives, advertisements, other films), AgwA creates architecture with a variety of fragments, with both foreign and found objects. In this way, each part of ECAM has its own unique character, a specificity of structure and envelope, whether grey diamond-shaped cladding, white lacquered steel, a black bituminous membrane, membrane, an insulated render, a glazed, a glazed façade, corrugated fibre cement, or the original brick and stone architecture. Far from being cacophonous, this collage extends and assumes the variegated diversity of the block's interior, enhancing the ordinary landscape with its involuntary beauty.

Typical of the 'neighbourhood contracts' that the Belgian capital has been experimenting with for the past thirty years, this exercise in urban acupuncture has a long history that can be traced back to the 'conservative surgery' conducted in the 1890s by Patrick Geddes in the old Edinburgh, then a working-class slum[11]: a long-term undertaking to repair a neighbourhood from within, using an approach that was less extensive than intensive, less utopian than eu-topian *(eu-topos)* – in other words, one

8 Reyner Banham, 'Design by Choice: 1951-1961,' *The Architectural Review 130* (July 1961): 43–48.
9 See Lionel Devlieger, 'L'Architecture à l'envers', *Criticat 18* (autumn 2016).
10 Guy Debord, voice-over from his film *In girum imus nocte etconsumimur igni* (95', 1981), whose title Harold Fallon used for his lecture at TU Dresden, 18 January 2022.
11 Jim Johnson and Lou Rosenburg, *Renewing Old Edinburgh* (Edinburgh: Argyll Publishing, 2010), 134-41.

that sought not so much to create an ideal place as to bring out the best in a place. By challenging the modern, hylomorphic[12] notion of 'project', this 'repairing' mission that AgwA is on redefines the role of the architect. As Francis Ponge said of the artist, perhaps the architect too should 'open up a workshop and take the world in for repairs, the world in pieces, as it comes to them. From then on, any other plan is wiped out: it is no more a question of transforming the world than explaining it, but merely putting it back into running order, piece by piece, in their workshop'.[13]

Structural Resistance

As Harold Fallon acknowledges, '(e)ven if local influences can be traced, architecture today is not predictable, it escapes causality and necessity. Architecture happens in response to a multitude of unspoken reasons, operated influences, uttered wishes, contingent constraints and implicit urges'.[14] But most of all, it has to deal with fragile and fragmented public commissions and the ensuing programmatic instability that makes it difficult to envisage a built object in the long term. At ECAM, the uncertainties surrounding the nature of the occupants of the wing facing the street or the size of the crèche inside the block (first thirty places, then 150) illustrate this common yet uncomfortable situation that triggers a clear response from AgwA: to produce spaces that derive their character not so much from their function as their structure and that are not so much volatile contents as robust containers. In their view, there is no fundamental difference between the workshop of the former ECAM and the gymnasium that replaced it: it is above all a vast parallelepiped with windows along its length, almost as wide as it is high, and which only exists thanks to the repetition of four porticoes with a span of ten metres.

The project as a whole consists at bottom in identifying key sites within this complex block where the few construction efforts that the budget allows should be concentrated in order to make human activities possible and to guarantee the necessary conditions for architecture to happen. Here, the architects use the necessary support structure between the exposed adjoining walls to prop up two floors and a roof, thus creating an impromptu space for workshops or festivities. There, they underpin the street-facing building to open up a wide passage. Elsewhere still, where the flows meet, they install a vast foyer without intermediate load-bearing points. These structural acts are rare yet strategic and clearly expressed: respectively, huge oblique jambs; a girdle-beam raised by four posts; and two porticoes crossed at right angles, a centrifugal figure that is perfectly suited to this crossroads-like site. Diagonals, a square, a cross – these structural figures arise from situations that are always very specific and tied to particular circumstances, but they achieve a formal autonomy that ultimately frees them.

CARRÉ (2014)
© Marie-Françoise Plissart
see p. 016–017 & p. 234–239

AgwA's architects love to build and know how to. Unlike some of their fellow architects who leave this field to specialized engineering offices, they have never shunned the building site, which they treat on the contrary as an operating theatre, a lever for action, a transitional moment of potential architecture. Vertigo, their first project, taught them how to create architecture out of

12 For a critique of the hylomorphic theory of the modern project, where the idea of a form is always imposed vertically on inert matter that is 'waiting to receive the projects that will be imposed on it from the outside', see Tim Ingold's preface to *Making: Anthropology, Archaeology, Art and Architecture* (London: Routledge, 2013).

13 Francis Ponge, The Voice of Things (New York: McGraw-Hill, 1974), 163.

14 Harold Fallon, 'Evidence', in *Raamwerk In Practice, Lichtervelde Youth Centre*, eds. Harold Fallon, Benoît Vandenbulcke and Benoît Burquel (Ghent: MER. Borgerhoff & Lamberigts, 2020), 167.

technical infrastructure, even for mass entertainment. In 2014 their project for the removable canopy of the courtyard in the Carré des Arts in Mons was reduced to a very obvious structural act, a large, white translucent membrane strung across an empty space, forming two series of parallel and inverted arches: the convex ribs are attached to plates under the cornices and seem to extend the asymptotic slope of the roofs; the concave arches channel the rainwater towards the draining holes. In 2017 AgwA even won a competition for a bridge, a structural act par excellence: a bridge for cyclists and pedestrians intended to connect the former Ateliers Centraux to the train station in Seraing and that AgwA proposed to extend to the future Trasenster Park on the banks of the river Meuse. Between these two zones in a state of slow and uncertain transition, the architects drew a bold structure that will extend in a straight line from the ground floor of Boulevard des Ateliers (ten metres above the embankments), span the railway tracks, dip down towards the park before bouncing back to reach the station platforms in a gentle slope. Like the gallery in Péronnes, this stripped-down, distinctly linear and deceptively simple object that will reconnect the grounds of a chaotic, post-industrial geography, affirms AgwA's belief in the powerful agentivity of the art of building.

SERAING (2017)
see p. 074–079 & p. 164–167

It is on the ground and in the secret time of the building site, in a world closed to the uninitiated that has been invaded by new experts, that they find room for manoeuvre and, if not power over reality, at least joy in its metamorphosis. What a conundrum, building an auditorium to modern acoustic standards, nested in an existing warehouse, itself set in the heart of a city block with low soil-bearing capacity! And yet it is thanks to its taste for building sites that AgwA achieved this feat of constructive choreography for the community centre De Kriekelaar in Schaerbeek (2015). Left visible (apart from the system of double acoustic curtains), masonry work is the beginning and end of the project – a cyclopean act that creates a box within a box but is embodied in subtle details that express the architecture: the slight folding of the load-bearing walls to provide bracing and break up the reverberation; the contrast between the smooth surface of the concrete and the rough surface of the solid blocks; the stacked arrangement of the latter to convey their filling function; and the concrete cornice that encircles the room at a third of its height, adding scale and emphasizing the height of the doors and the bottom of the curtains at the same time.

KRIEKELAAR (2015)
see p. 024–026, p. 220–225

As you leaf through the *AgwA: Chantier / Construction Site publication* [15], you move from one project to the next almost without noticing it, as if you were walking through the same raw heterotopia, the same indecipherable and moving landscape made up of cranes and scaffolding, freshly raised earth and unfinished walls, suspended cables and spiky props, formwork boards and rusty irons, chalky dust and shimmering wet surfaces. Together with Jan De Vylder (who wrote the book's preface), Burquel, Fallon and Vandenbulcke share the conviction that a key moment, which is infraformal but profoundly architectural, is being enacted here, that a crucial 'game' is being played out, revealing latent opportunities, inscribed in the circumstances of the very evolution of the building site. 'Opportunities that, prior to the design, defy estimations and predictions. Opportunities that are only found in the ultimate moment of the building site itself. Not a moment sooner. And often only available from one moment to the next. In other words, for as long as the moment lasts.' [16] More than a space, the building site is therefore a time in which architecture is embodied in a specific mode of existence whose powerful qualities are usually erased once the building has been handed over.

The search for this moment is perhaps one of the keys to the formidable project that AgwA is currently undertaking with architecten Jan de Vylder Inge Vinck in Charleroi: the renovation of the huge Palais des Expositions (66,000 m^2) that was built in 1953 to the plans of Joseph André and that has been in a state of virtual neglect for years. Rather than spend the inadequate budget on replacing the 'hall of honour' – the oversized legacy of the economic euphoria of post-war Wallonia – with a zero-energy building, they proposed to transform it into a kind of vertical, open architectural garden and to redistribute the resources to rehabilitate the adjacent exhibition halls (removal of asbestos, renewal of sheds, recalibration of heated spaces, development of a conference centre, greening of the surroundings, etc.). With the same disenchanted and empathetic vision that architecten jdviv displayed in their project for Caritas in Melle, here the architects are not seeking to compete with a glorious, bygone past, but rather to make the most of what remains of it in our architecturally impoverished age. Stripped of its façades, marble facings and bluestone slabs, and equipped with a few additional vertical circulations, the hall of honour thus becomes a huge, open, covered public space on three levels, connecting the different parts of the Palais and of the city, the perched historic centre and the former industrial valley. Reduced to its rough and robust concrete framework, to its Piranesian tangle of columns and entablatures – like a superposition of Greek temples – this architecture tells us something about itself and

15 *AgwA: Chantier / Construction Site* (Ghent: MER. Borgerhoff & Lamberigts, 2019), 167.
16 Jan De Vylder, 'Work in Progress: A Verb/Living in Progress: A Context', in *AgwA: Chantier / Construction Site*, 6.
17 The first session resulted in a publication: *Real Estate Architecture #1: The Apartment Building*, eds. Benoît Burquel, Thaïs de Roquemaurel, Martin Dumont and Guillaume Joachim (Brussels: Real Estate Architecture, 2018).
18 2A+P/A, Fala, Architectenbureau Bart Dehaene, OMMX, Piovenefabi, Gafpa, Something Fantastic, Dyvik Kahlen, Buero Kofink Schels, Plan Común, Conen Sigl Architekt:innen and Jean-Benoît Vétillard architecture

the moments that define it. Rather than musing on its own ruin, it invites us to delve into the impure moment of its actual execution. Could this architectural garden be seen as a metaphor for the lost paradise of the construction site?

CHAPEX + CHAPCO (2022)
© Filip Dujardin
see p. 038–049 & p. 184–197

Geometrical Inscription

Conducted with architecten jdviv, the operation of the Charleroi Palais des Expositions demonstrates an approach to architecture that is less about the expression of a creative ego or an identifiable signature and more about shared and constantly renewed experimentation, where the process is at least as important as the result. At a time when new problems and issues are emerging, Burquel, Fallon and Vandenbulcke, who already form a richly diverse collective, see architectural practice as a privileged framework for tackling these problems and extending the process of reflection to a wider community.

Since 2016, for example, Benoît Burquel has co-organized three summer schools called 'Real Estate Architecture' that explore private real-estate production in Belgium in the 1960s and 1970s. In each session, the transformation potential of architectural types such as the apartment building in Liège (2016)[17], the office tower in Brussels (2018) and the shopping centre in Ghent (2019) is the subject of a design-based investigation led by a series of emerging architectural firms.[18] Among this wide network of European counterparts and interlocutors, Burquel, Fallon and Vandenbulcke also find participants for another cross-cutting project, 'In Practice', launched in 2018. Here, they invite an office to give a lecture on the process of one of its projects, before producing a book.[19]

Alongside these collective, project-based research initiatives, AgwA also likes to collaborate on competitions with architects they esteem and with whom they want to enter into dialogue, a circle that extends far beyond linguistic and even Belgian borders. Besides Jan De Vylder and Inge Vinck (architecten jdviv) on five occasions[20], they have collaborated on competitions with, among others, Kersten Geers and David van Severen (OFFICE)[21], Sophie Laenen, Christine Fontaine, Ariane Van Craen and Veerle Nys (ZED)[22], Muck Petzet[23], Tom Emerson and Stephanie Macdonald (6a architects)[24], Louis Leger, Laurent Didier and Mathieu Le Ny (BAST)[25], and Martino Tattara and Pier Vittorio Aureli (Dogma).[26] Although most of these projects did not come to fruition, they served as opportunities to interpolate an informal cluster of ideas, themes and forms and to collectively rethink the position of the contemporary architect in relation to temporal and material, social and political, conceptual and disciplinary issues. As an echo to these exchanges, which make it one of the most Flemish of the French-speaking offices, AgwA is developing an architecture that is more strategic than stylistic, more process-oriented than formal, more rhetorical than syntactic; an architecture that has accepted the drastic reduction of its means without renouncing its pioneering role; an architecture that is faced with the instability of social demand and seeks within itself its own raison d'être; an architecture that becomes at bottom its own subject and that sleepwalks a tightrope between two temptations – disciplinary fundamentalism and 'new mannerism'[27], with, as a safeguard, a lucid and anxious empathy for the things of the world.

This 'play of order and compromise'[28], of autonomy and heteronomy, runs throughout AgwA's work. It is acutely reflected in a project like the extension of the

19 To date, three titles have been published by MER. Borgerhoff & Lamberigts: *Philippe Vander Maren & Richard Venlet* (2019), *Raamwerk* (2020) and *Buero Kofink Schels* (2021). The next publication is on a project by Dyvik Kahlen.
20 Besides several unsuccessful bids, the competitions for the Charleroi Palais des Expositions, 2015; the Waasmunster Sports and Leisure Centre, 2016; the KANAL museum (with 6a and Muck Petzet) in Brussels, 2018; the Welcome Centre for the NGO Transit, 2020; and the renovation of the former CGER/ASLK headquarters for BNP Paribas Fortis, 2022.
21 Competitions for the new exhibition centre, Liège, 2018; and the headquarters of the Walloon Social Credit Company (SWCS), Charleroi, 2019.
22 Competitions for a crèche and after-school daycare centre in Molenbeek, 2012; the conversion of a school in Vilvoorde, 2014; a mixed building in Waterloo, 2016; and a social housing building, Brussels, 2022.
23 Competitions for the KANAL museum (with 6a and jdviv) in Brussels, 2018; the conversion of the former USquare barracks in Ixelles, 2018; and the conversion of the Royale Belge building in Watermael-Boitsfort, 2019.
24 Competition for the KANAL museum (with jdviv and Muck Petzet), 2018.
25 Competition for the ENSAPC, Cergy-Pontoise, 2021.
26 Competitions for the San Giovanni di Dio market, Rome, 2019; the master plan of the tip of Buda Island in Kortrijk, 2020; and a social housing building, Brussels, 2022.
27 Cf. Bart Verschaffel, 'Add a Little More: A New Mannerism in Recent Flemish Architecture', *Flanders Architectural Review 12* (2016): 126-33.
28 Robert Venturi, *Complexity and Contradiction in Architecture* (New York: MoMA, 1977), 42.

DURLET (2019)
© Séverin Malaud
see p. 058–065 & p. 172–179

secondary school on Durletstraat in Antwerp (2016–19). From a distance, the immaculate cubic volume may resemble a 'machine célibataire', a minimalist UFO that landed by accident in the middle of this Flemish neo-Renaissance architecture. Up close, however, the project is nothing more than breathing, listening, relating. Confirming the fact that this fourth wing could not, for reasons of urban prospect, budget and production conditions, resemble the three other wings symmetrically flanking the courtyard building, the architects emphasized its exceptional character in order to dialectically introduce into this architectural system qualities that it lacked: extraversion, oblique axes, suspension and cantilevering, and large openings. At the same time, specific details testify to a subtle reading of the site, such as the projecting elevator shaft that engages in dialogue with the chimneys of the old building, or the nine-centimetre offset of the joints of the concrete blocks, which organizes the whole façade and recalls the old Flemish art of brickwork. Even the prow formed by the cube, rotated 53 degrees in relation to the axis of the courtyard, seems like the horizontal rabatment of the Flemish gables that already give the landscape a triangular appearance.

PRINS DRIES (2014)
© Marie-Françoise Plissart
see p. 026–027 & p. 218–219

AgwA's architecture is often seen as the paradoxical inscription of an abstract, autonomous geometry in ever-changing and impure urban and human circumstances. The triangular covered playground of the Prins Dries school (2013–15) and the circular one of the Baron Leroy school in Antwerp (2015–21), the polygonal plan of the crèche in the Jerusalem block in Schaerbeek and the square one of the Durlet school, all introduce forms into the turbulent ocean of reality which are intended to be as obvious and immutable as their structure. However, they are rarely regular in the geometric sense – like the curved line that circumscribes the almost circular plan of the Waasmunster leisure centre (competition with architecten jan de vylder inge vinck, 2016) – but are rather the result of a slow process of approximation and adjustment. More perfect than pure because carefully negotiated, these objective figures transcend the mere stylistic register and above all tell us something about the way they are perceived and were constructed.

JERUSALEM (2019)
see p. 106–111

AgwA's architects produce architecture by addition, not subtraction. They put things together rather than extract them from a single material by hollowing-out or sculpting. Their architecture is not a plastic act but an assembly. They usually compose their façades by constructively adding elements that serve to frame horizontal openings rather façades by abstractively piercing through the neutral substance of a wall.

Preserving their integrity or at least their legibility, engaging in dialogue beyond their differences, building an open and inclusive order, these things are added to one another in a process, not of infinite expansion, but of intensive inscription; a deepening of the real within itself.

In these conditions, architecture does not derive its expression from an overarching, all-embracing aesthetic statement but, on the contrary, from listening to the dialogue that takes place within the ever-open family of things that are there, a dialogue that establishes a meaning that is always circumstantial. This objective aformalism of AgwA is in line with the approach of Francis Ponge. It echoes the attention that the writer paid not only to the most insignificant things but also to the process of putting them down in writing: 'May my work be one of continual rectification of expression on behalf of the raw object (with no *a priori* concern about the form of that expression).'[29]

29 Francis Ponge, *Mute Objects of Expression* (Brooklyn, NY: Archipelago Books, 2006), n.p.

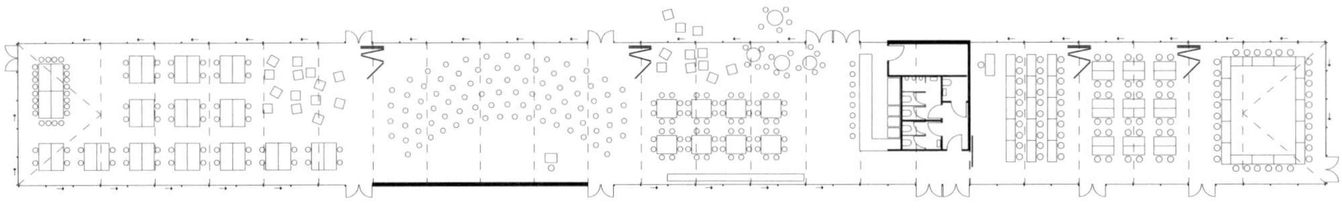

0 2 5 10

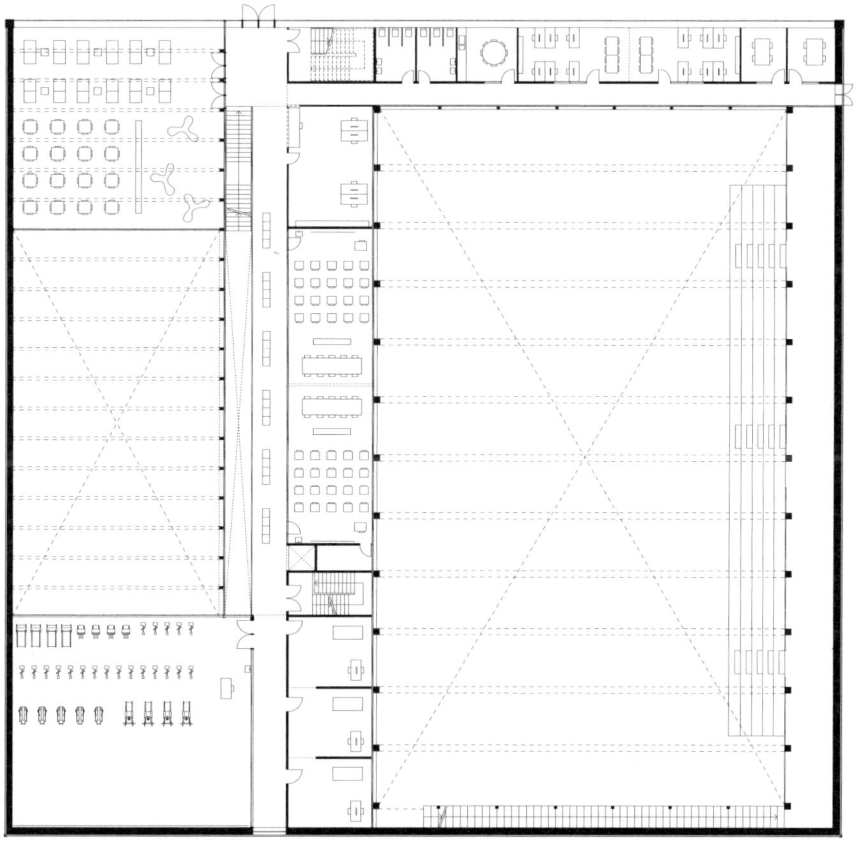

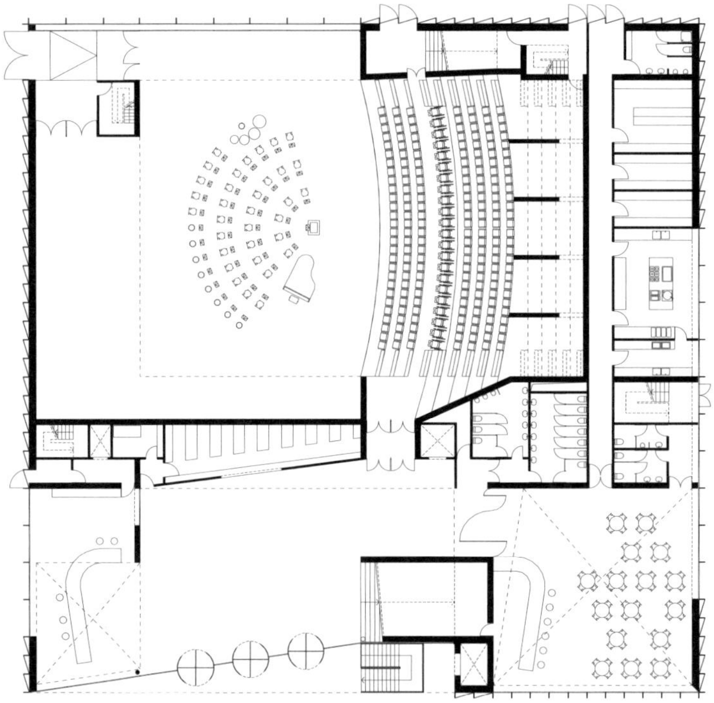

0
2
5
10

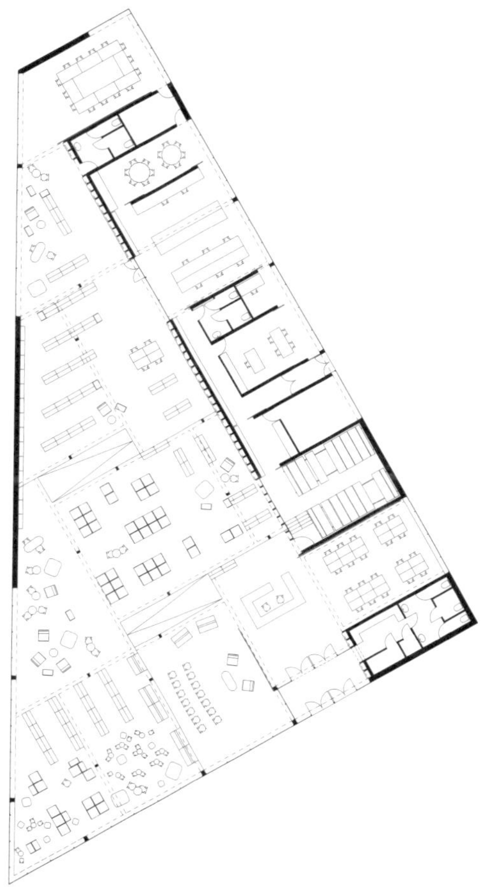

0 2 5 10

PRACTICE OF ARCHITECTURE

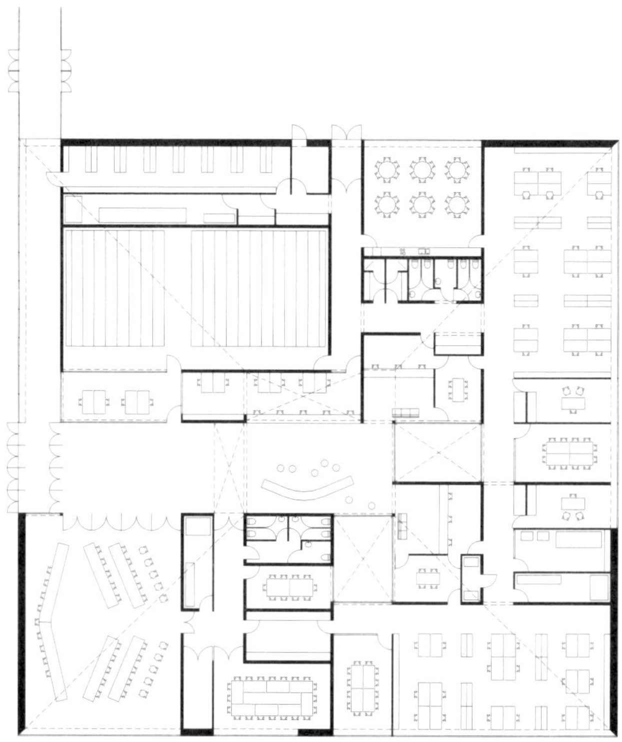

0 2 5 10

0 2 5 10

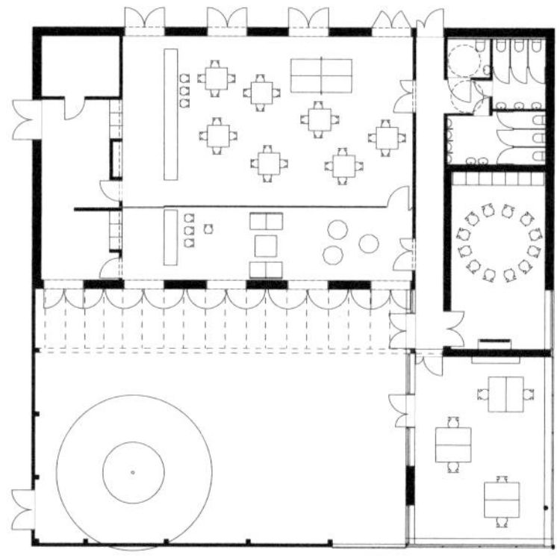

0 2 5 10

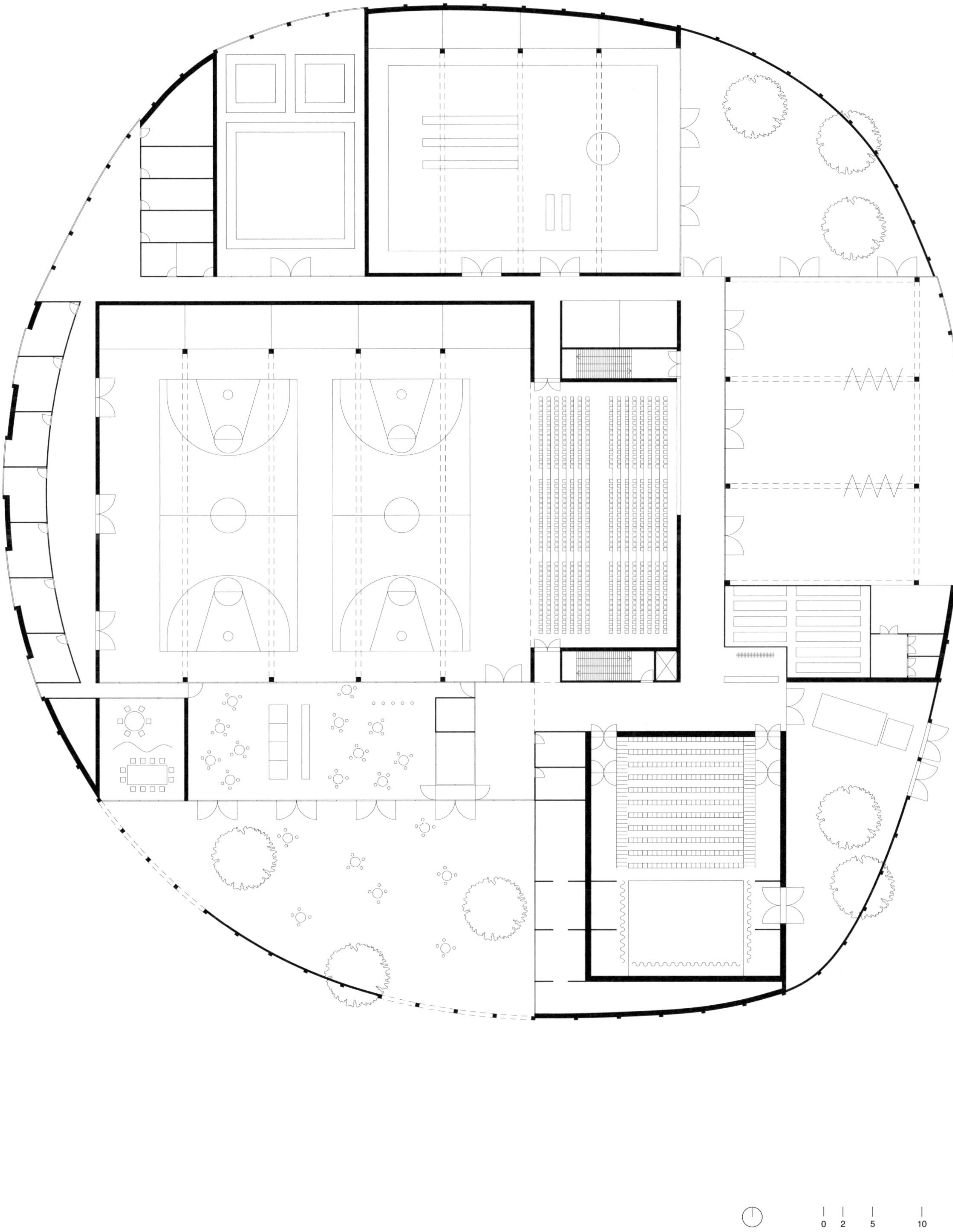
0
2
5
10

A CONVERSATION WITH BENOÎT BURQUEL, HAROLD FALLON AND BENOÎT VANDENBULCKE

Lisa De Visscher
Iwan Strauven

AgwA has been around for more than fifteen years. What is the most important evolution that your office has gone through?

AgwA gradually came into existence between 2003 and 2006. There were three of us at the time: Benoît Vandenbulcke, Harold Fallon and Raphaël Cornelis. We had studied together – architectural engineering at UCLouvain in Louvain-la-Neuve – and worked on projects in different constellations. Raphaël soon changed direction and left the firm in 2008. Meanwhile, we continued to grow. Benoît Burquel, who also studied architectural engineering but at ULiège, joined us in 2011. By then, there were six of us. Today we are eighteen, but we still see the office as a family environment, even though it is getting a little cramped.

We do not work in a strictly hierarchical system. Everyone takes on different tasks and there is a constant exchange of knowledge. Of course, everyone has their own specific competences, but it is nice to have someone who is very good at following up construction sites do a competition now and then, and vice versa. That keeps things interesting, for both the office and the collaborators.

We see the office as a space where a lot of freedom is possible within the projects. All three of us teach at the university and many of our collaborators also have an academic job alongside AgwA. The architects at the office get a lot of autonomy early on. It often happens that young members of staff, who have only just joined us, are immediately put in charge of a large project or are sent off to a major construction site. That is how we started and it is the best way to learn rapidly to deal with responsibility.

The biggest difference with ten years ago is probably that we used to work together much more intensively on each project. We would spend hours together around the table. Today that is impossible. We work in different constellations. Consultation between the three of us and within the office in general has become more diverse and flexible.

We still make the most important decisions together, the three of us. Since we mainly work on public buildings, we always choose together what projects to apply for. Not that we have strict criteria for these choices. We are a large team, and we select broadly, perhaps a little too broadly. It may sound like an exaggeration, but we are actually interested in almost all the projects that come onto the market. We are curious, want to discover new things and therefore say 'yes' to everything. (*laughs*) We ourselves are sometimes surprised which projects we get chosen for in the end. Once we have them, the projects are distributed among the partners and collaborators according to their availability at the time. So it is not the case that someone only deals with Brussels or Flanders or Wallonia, or someone only with pre-schools and someone else only with large-scale projects. Saying 'yes' to every project can be both an advantage and a disadvantage, but it has ensured a rich and diverse production.

Do you have a particular 'signature', or do you aspire to one?

That is rather for you to tell us. (*laughs*) We do not have a specific image of what AgwA is or what its buildings should look like. We do not have references which we constantly refer to in our architecture. Nor do we have that ambition. We probably even try to avoid this signature effect.

That is also due to our background. At UCLouvain (where Benoît Vandenbulcke and Harold studied), we were hardly given any references. One of our lecturers, Yves Lepère, had previously worked for Louis Kahn and our training was largely based on his work, as if nothing else existed, as if the entire history of architecture was essentially irrelevant. What we did get out of it, however, was a rooted understanding of the intrinsic mechanisms of the architectural discipline: How do you design a plan? What is a wall, a window, a niche, a volume, etc.? At ULiège (where Benoît Burquel studied), hardly any sense of architectural movement existed at the time. You had to build up your own architectural culture, contingently.

We were just talking about how our curiosity keeps making us enter all kinds of competitions. Well, that curiosity was really born in that period for the three of us, together with the belief that we do not have to create a specific image with our architecture in order to give shape to a certain office identity. The result is that we explore the discipline of architecture through structure, the autonomy of the form or the use of materials.

What do you mean by that?

We are all three architectural engineers and the question of how buildings are made, both from a technical design point of view and a purely structural one, is very important to us. In the end, the structure of a building is what remains. We devote a lot of time to collaborating with engineering firms and designing the structure in order to identify it with the architecture. A building becomes so much more interesting when the structure also contributes to the spatial quality and to the flexibility of use. The way the users claim the space does not much matter to us. We see our architecture more as an invitation to interact with the buildings, which in turn requires a strong identity of what is permanent. In that sense, we work with colour and furniture as a first occupation of space rather than an essential condition of our architecture.

The use of materials also defines our design process. In recent years, we have increasingly asked ourselves which material is the right one for each project. This is not only a matter of aesthetic consideration, but also of the social, ecological or energy impact of the material. The choice of material can also be a real driving force for a project. This was the case with the sports centre in Péronnes. The sketch design for the competition

the office of AgwA (2022), © Filip Dujardin

was ready, but the material for the façade had not yet been decided. Then we had the idea of working with concrete blocks. This decision had a major impact on the project. Not only did the volumetry of the building change, but the architectural idiom also had to be defined differently. The concrete blocks raised new construction questions in terms of joints, lintels and so on. Concrete blocks often feature in public projects in Belgium as they are cheap and there is usually little budget available. But they are often used as a kind of 'wallpaper', without taking into account their intrinsic structural properties. We enjoy fully exploring the possibilities and limitations of a particular material and getting to work with it. And we are not just talking about concrete blocks, of course. For a while, we used a lot of wood in our work, or polycarbonate. Currently, we are interested in hemp and materials sourced on the construction site itself. We look at how we can use the material constructively or architecturally and how we can possibly reverse its use to bring about unexpected twists in the project.

Several projects are based on autonomous geometric forms. Is that a thread in your oeuvre that is part of a specific modus operandi?

We have indeed made a whole series of designs with a square footprint and internal geometric rules of composition. Like the competition for a restaurant in Philippeville (which we lost, for that matter) or the Jokot youth centre in Niel or the Belgian embassy in Beijing we are currently working on. There was a period when we were very interested in this, almost as a research project.

Similarly, the Prins Dries school in Antwerp is a triangle and the competition for a leisure centre in Waasmunster is an almost perfect circle.

The form of these projects confers a certain autonomy from the context. It is not about using autonomous forms to create a certain image or identity for the office. It is not a play of forms. There are two things at work here. First, it is a way to avoid a servile relationship to a context. These projects stand in a context, they are carefully positioned. But their form, their identity, is not servile. In that way, they can continue even when the context changes around them. Second, it enables an internal thought process in which we try to define the mechanisms of geometry. This is about the composition of the plan and about the role of the construction. We carry the fruits of this process into future projects. Maybe this use of form is indeed a common thread. In any case, it is a way of working that is also picked up by our collaborators and that they pass on and therefore it forms part of the DNA of our office.

Although you do not present yourselves as 'adaptive reuse architects', a large number of the projects you realize are transformations of existing buildings. How come?

As we said before, we never set out to look for a certain collective identity or, economically speaking, for a certain market segment. The fact that we carry out many conversion projects is mainly due to opportunities. In a city like Brussels, few new buildings are being built anyway. There is little space and you have to learn to work with what already exists. We also ask ourselves many questions in relation to the energy and ecological impact of new buildings. Ten years ago, in 2012, we took part in a competition for a small public programme called 'Bonnevie' in Molenbeek. There was a building on the site that had to be demolished and replaced by a passive new construction. It turned out that the existing building perfectly met part of the requested programme in terms of surface area and layout. To us it seemed absurd to demolish it.

Moreover, we had certain reservations regarding the uniformity of the architectural expression of passive standard projects, those compact volumes made up of plastered insulation fitted with small windows. Does the city really have to look like that? We proposed to keep the building. We calculated that it would also be far more interesting energetically if you took the grey energy into account and that the new passive building would take about 300 years to recover the investment through the low heating costs. We did not win the competition, but it was an eye-opener both for the critical questioning of competition briefings and for the insight into the strength and potential of the existing built environment, regardless of its aesthetic or historic quality.

Does the growing demand for repurposing influence the way you look at architecture?

The way we relate to what exists already can form the basis for an architectural discourse. That in itself is not new. During modernism and later among postmodernists, the way in which one dealt with the heritage also played a major role. The fact that existing buildings can accommodate a new programme is also not new. Buildings have been reused since ancient times. What is perhaps new is the theoretical framework that has been developed in recent years around reuse in which context plays a major role. We find it interesting to confront an existing context, which is far richer than an unbuilt plot. The question is rather how we relate to that context and whether we should intervene at all. Whether it is not simply a question of putting a few chairs and tables in an existing space, so to speak? But even then, our office is convinced that we can still create an autonomous oeuvre, even if it is within an existing and binding context.

Repurposing is certainly one of the motors of our practice and therefore it has a certain theoretical potential within that practice. Actually, we are also active in theory, writing and editing, but it is really grounded in practice. We want to engage with the reality of architecture, to experiment with construction methods and materials and we want to let the way we work evolve. Our discourse is embedded in our work, not in the words we use to describe that work.

How does your vision of repurposing manifest itself in the two major repurposing projects that are currently under way, Chapex in Charleroi and Karreveld in Brussels?

Chapex, the former Palais des Expositions in Charleroi, is a gigantic building of 60,000 m². The idea, at the time of the competition, was to maintain it as a venue for fairs and shows, with a large part devoted to parking. We are developing the project with Jan De Vylder and Inge Vinck.[1] Together we decided to be very restrictive in the demolitions. We already had experience with this type of question, like in Bonnevie, which we were just talking about, or in the Jerusalem project, where we were asked to demolish all the buildings on site even though some existing ones were perfectly suited for the requested programme. There were also other projects in that vein, like Métal, which was exhibited at the Centre for Fine Arts as part of the NICHE series in 2009. Jan De Vylder and Inge Vinck shared this approach, which built on the Caritas project in Melle that they made with Jo Taillieu and Bavo.

Given the limited budget of €25 M – which comes down to about €400 per m², a sum you can actually do very little with – we decided to set to work very pragmatically. We drew up a list of all the valuable elements in the building, parts that intrigued us and that we definitely wanted or had to keep, such as the old chimneys (too expensive to demolish), the monumental entrance colonnade (too characteristic to disappear) or a tower of emergency staircases (too useful to be removed). There was also a huge entrance hall with incredible staircases and glass brick domes. We decided to keep the central

the office of AgwA (2022), © Filip Dujardin

1 Chapex was initiated with architecten de vylder vinck taillieu and is now being continued with architecten jan de vylder inge vinck.

part, about 15,000 m², which was set to be demolished, but to remove its façades and toilets. We turned two thirds of the construction into a zero-energy building by just leaving it open and using it as a vertical distribution garden or stacked car park and by leaving one exhibition hall totally unequipped, with no heating and no mechanical ventilation. That way, we did not have to insulate or heat and we could invest the budget in the remaining third of the building.

This allowed us to retain most of the building. The clients believed in the project and we won the competition. You can no longer erect a building of this scale – some rooms are ten metres high – with these spatial qualities today, or at least not with the budget available, and that existing building opens up a whole range of possibilities.

In this sense, the Karreveld project presents a certain analogy with Chapex. These former offices of a pharmaceutical company date back to the 1970s and were in perfect condition: a beautiful façade made of prefabricated concrete elements and office spaces inside where everything was still in perfect order. The assignment, in an initial phase, was to use a temporary intervention to convert the offices into a secondary school. The timing was extremely short, as the school wanted to open the same year. When we visited the building, it was immediately clear to us that we not only wanted to keep the building as it was, but also wanted to recover all the modular partition walls and suspended ceilings, among others, not as an a priori stylistic attitude, but first of all as a good management reflex. As in Chapex, we again drew up a list of the parts to be preserved. Only now it was not about spectacular skylights or colonnades, but about doors and partition walls. Strangely, as in many other projects, we were practically the only participants who limited demolition and engaged in reuse with materials sourced on site. In terms of timing and budget, this is not always the most profitable solution for the client, so you do need their commitment. But today, you simply cannot keep promoting a culture of automatically discarding things.

This is not a standard attitude, however, a kind of recipe that we apply again and again. We are not gurus of the circular economy. Of course, ecological and economic issues are important to us, but we always start from the logic of the project itself. And the decision to refrain from demolition and to reuse as much as possible in the above projects was a matter of common sense.

Does your non-dogmatic design attitude also result in a specific aesthetic in conversion projects? It can sometimes seem as if you are looking for a 'clever trick' or an 'intelligent intervention' that initially solves a localized problem, but then later also characterizes the whole project.

We are very interested in that gesture that solves everything. But it is difficult to choose between 'clever trick' and 'intelligent intervention' as a characterization of this pursuit. Intelligence is perhaps more correct because it refers to the proper understanding of all the parameters of a project, but it sounds a bit wishy-washy, while 'clever trick' sounds livelier: it is more dynamic and on the ball.

Our project for the pedestrian bridge in Seraing already shows how we can in part let go of the aesthetic issue. Because we did not make a 50 m footbridge but a 250 m one for the given budget, we managed to involve another public space in the project, which allows cyclists to circulate differently. But in order to reach that 250 m, we had to build in a super-efficient and cheap way. The technical solution here provides a specific aesthetic, which we appreciate very much. The limitation of means, the constructive aspects, structure and detailing, the spatial ambitions and the aesthetics form one whole. It is impossible to say which derives from which. It is a bit like when we used wood to reinforce the structures of the Verbiest house. Here we mainly wanted to avoid working with concrete. The precise placement of the support points allows for an efficient load redistribution and this creates a certain image that begins to characterize the whole project. Although the design process in itself is not a quest for that particular aesthetic, it is of course a research and therefore really requires work to understand how to find the 'clever solution'. This also implies a lot of iterations with other project partners, such as the stability engineers in this case.

The same applies to Karreveld, where we recovered partition walls, but differently. In order to obtain more ceiling height, we removed part of the existing suspended ceilings and reused them elsewhere. As a consequence, we complemented the modular wall system with plywood panels. This resulted in an overall aesthetic of hybridity that benefited from what was already there. The result was a bonus, so to speak.

Is this always expressed in your architecture through the use or reuse of specific materials or building elements?

No, another example of a clever trick or intelligent intervention was the competition design we made in Ixelles for the Marni theatre of the Wallonia-Brussels Federation. The former cinema, which the theatre is renting (with all the issues of commissioning that go with that), does not meet the requirements for stage performances: the slopes are not very good, it has a huge balcony and above all there is no foyer, which is what the organization really wanted. We proposed to build a floor at the level of the balcony, so that suddenly there were not one but two halls, with rather low ceilings. To be honest, the scenographer had told us that it was not really a 'good' theatre hall according to norms and customs. But it was an intervention that could be built in a fortnight and the principle also solved all kinds of other problems, such as acoustics and fire safety. The winning project proposed to demolish the existing hall and build a whole new hall 'from scratch' inside the existing building for a budget much higher than the initial one. Someone involved in the competition told us afterwards that our proposal was the winner of the lateral thinking project.

It also resulted in the denormalization of spaces. In our Marni project, the foyer was exceptionally low and large and the theatre was unusually flat. At Chapex, there are suddenly parking spaces that are ten metres high. This creates a provocative friction between programme and space, making you suddenly aware of the spatiality, instead of the usual soft cocoon that you do not even notice anymore because it is predictable and normalized.

You collaborate a lot with other offices from Belgium and abroad that have very different profiles. What are you looking for in those collaborations?

In the first place, it is just about being able to participate, because public tenders are structured in such a way that you have to provide references and often the agencies alone do not have them, so we enter into partnerships.

When the calls for tenders are published, the phone just keeps ringing. You have to be quick because everyone is taken immediately. Conversely, we also often receive phone calls but can already be engaged with another team. So it is not only a matter of curiosity or affinity, but also of pure necessity and opportunity. All the same, we have entered into collaborations with a whole range of agencies and what really counts is getting along with the people and being able to work together in mutual understanding. Of course, we look for designers who make work that we find interesting, that we have an affinity with and that we would like to get to know better. That explains why we have set up collaborations with BAST, OFFICE Kersten Geers David Van Severen and Bruther, for example. We once also worked with OMA, which was very special for us who studied at the turn of the century, but also with offices such as Studio Tuin en Wereld and ZED, with whom we collaborate regularly because of our genuine and mutual appreciation.

We have also established a very good modus operandi with the office of Inge Vinck and Jan De Vylder, with whom we have so far collaborated on five projects. What unites us is that we look critically at the assignment and that, even during the development of the project, there is always room to question things fundamentally through architecture.

What is the biggest difference in approach between your two offices?

Their aesthetic approach translates into great attention to detail. We also spend a lot of time drawing details, but in a kind of quest to make the detail disappear, to give the impression that there are no details. Just look at the ECAM project: it looks as if it has been knocked together and that it is some kind of big hut, when in fact it is all very finely tuned. It is the product of an iterative design process thanks to which things gradually start to fit together in a straightforward way.

You are involved in research at the university. In addition to teaching, Harold Fallon and Benoît Vandenbulcke have each obtained a PhD and you organize conferences and publish books. Can you tell us how this academic research is structured and how it relates to your work in the office?

To get the full picture, you should know that we are attached to a research group called *In Practice* that develops three activities: there are the *Practices in Research* conferences linked to the publication of a journal with selected contributions; there are also doctoral seminars in which PhD students are guided in developing academic research strategies; lastly, there is the *In Practice* book series.

When the architecture schools integrated the university and we were able to do research, we asked ourselves how we could run an office while simultaneously carrying out training and research at an academic level without losing ourselves in worlds that are completely sealed off from each other. Focusing on the process brings the three together in pragmatic terms. Harold's PhD at RMIT really concentrated on the understanding of the design mechanisms at the office. It was about situating the work and about the exploration of its inner workings. Benoît Vandenbulcke's PhD at UCLouvain focused on the understanding of design processes though the question of materiality and construction: construction is a common ground to situate many contemporary practices and so it is very important in education to make this explicit. We will never know what went through the minds of the architects of Sanaa when they designed and built their dematerialized buildings, but we can retrace lines of force and design mechanisms underlying their approach. There is a possibility to talk about architecture through the design process, a kind of theory grounded in practice.

To explore this further, we launched the *In Practice* book series. Each book basically tells the story of a single architecture project from the first sketches until its completion. It reconstructs this process by showing, both in words and images, what happened. Each time, we first invite architects to a lecture in which they are asked to take a fresh look at what they do. We ask them to look over their own work documents without any preconceived ideas and to question what we can discover in them. In the book, we then invite them to do the same with an external author, so that an outside view is integrated. Perhaps the books somehow echo our own interest in the work of their authors.

How do you make the selection?

For the *Practices in Research* conferences and journal, it is quite simple since it is a call. A scientific committee we are part of makes the first selection based on a fairly simple criterion, namely, whether there is really a design practice to which the research relates. We want to propose something related to ongoing practices, because with the integration into the universities, a lot of theoretical work is produced at the architecture schools that is separate from an active architectural practice. We hope that over time an interesting network of researching and reflexive practitioners can emerge from these conferences.

Do you also use a call for the *In Practice* book series?

For the book series, things are different. Initially, we organized lectures, each time inviting an architect to talk about the process of a project. We also invited a panel

the office of AgwA (2022),© Filip Dujardin

for a discussion about the project process after the presentation. Philippe Vander Maren and Richard Venlet, whom we invited to Liège, responded in a very interesting and playful way and we decided afterwards that we had to do something with this. And so the idea of the book series grew. Later, Raamwerk from Ghent and the Munich-based office Buero Kofink Schels followed. We are currently finalizing a book on a project by Dyvik Kahlen, an office whose geographic origin is not very clear (they are at once Norwegian, German, English, Portuguese and Spanish). Benoît Burquel invited these last two agencies in the context of a series of summer schools he co-organized in Liège, Brussels and Ghent. The occasion aroused our curiosity for these offices, which did not hesitate to open the black box of their design practice. It is not all that obvious. It was really Philippe and Richard who were the first to engage with this way of explaining a project exhaustively. They agreed to open up their archives, review them and tell us what they saw in them, and so not only was the project explained through selected documents, but they also showed what they tried but failed to do for one reason or another. What helped was that they were not working in the same place and everything was scanned so that the traces of their exchanges were available. So there was quite an extensive archive from the start.

Does this position you as a cultural actor?

Well, we do this mainly from the academic world. But it is clear that the books themselves occupy different fields simultaneously. They occupy both the academic and cultural fields since they are also available in bookshops and they are related to lectures. For us it was very important to have a publisher and distributor, otherwise they would remain objects only to be found in university laboratories. At the same time, each book is peer-reviewed, so they remain hybrid objects.

The *Practices in Research* seminars are open to researchers, but also to practising architects who want to make use of an exchange platform to feed the reflection on their own practice. This broadens the research field somewhat. It places the seminars also in a cultural field. In any case, it is not exclusively an academic approach for and by academics.

In general, with *In Practice* we try to establish a relation between the professional world and the academic world, something we also strive for in our other activities. As a result, we have a very diversified professional life. In one day we can face ten totally different things. There can be something on at the university, a problem on a construction site, a competition entry at the office, not to mention administrative paperwork. At the same time, we might be writing a book, organizing a lecture or working on an exhibition. It is challenging and demands a lot of energy, but at the same time it is exciting and allows us to create an environment that is very enriching. We were talking about the pleasure of working together, good relations and the family-like character of the office, but also about the fact that this allows us to develop. For example, at the office, a collaborator organizes *Approaches*, an in-house lecture series where staff members are invited to present something they are working on inside or outside the office. This allows us to rediscover the people we work with. Returning to the start of this conversation about the organization of the office, in fact, our academic activities are strongly related to our office activities. Of course there is a personal development, but it is also something that we share in the office. It is not as if everyone's own academic activity starts when they leave the office. This is also part of our modus operandi. We feel that the combination of an intense practice at the office and in the university can contribute something fundamental to both of them: it feeds the reflection, provides oxygen and makes it possible to see things in a different light.

AN ECOLOGY OF SPATIAL PRACTICES: ON SHARING KNOWLEDGE AT AGWA

Rolf Hughes

When invited to write about AgwA in relation to research, I was interested in learning how *practical knowledge* is articulated and disseminated in an architectural office that is active across practice, academic teaching and research. So I emailed the company, asking a question both simple and complex: *How is knowledge shared at AgwA?*[1] The range of responses illuminates the realities of a contemporary architectural practice. One respondent speculated that it was 'something that leads us to a point where we can (somehow) conclude that something is right, just, measured, or something that offers clarity, like the moment a connection between different points (meaningless in themselves) creates a drawing (a shape with a sense, a direction). But how do we *know* a design for a project (the shape of it; the plan; the façade; the detail; etc.) is right? Is it possible to claim to know that it's right?' Is knowledge then this 'moving towards a point of clarity'? But what does a point of clarity mean in an office that one member characterizes as 'a bit like a chameleon… a very diverse production, probably connected to all these different ways of seeing (and allowing things to be seen in different ways)'?

Others wrote of 'the experiences of failure and second chances'[2], 'a kind of disappointment' provoking further discussion about how to refine the metallic structure of a roof that remained stubbornly difficult to implement on a house extension but was resolved satisfactorily on a second, larger project. Learning from disappointment was a recurring theme. One example involved returning to a detail that had not turned out to plan and collectively working to raise a second iteration to a higher degree of aesthetic and functional resolution, almost as a shared badge of honour between architect and contractor. Another respondent emphasized the importance of developing a shared language as a means of putting words to attitudes, strategies, theories by means of common references. 'At AgwA, when we want to say that an idea (about a structure, a detail, a material, etc.) is quite nice, we say that it's rather fun (in French, *"C'est encore marrant"*). I would never have said that before arriving at the office. The use of these words is meaningful, it says something about what we are looking for – not having a beautiful, a coherent, a rational project, but finding something unexpected but that in the end sounds good, like a good joke that has to have a good punchline.' Aesthetic judgement is thereby encoded in an informal, colloquial expression – an instance, perhaps, of what Wittgenstein implies when he describes a proposition as 'a picture of reality' (and a picture, in turn, as 'a model of reality').[3]

Images are pinned in shared spaces to trigger short and informal conversations about them and to relate them to other ongoing processes. A WhatsApp group is used both for small talk and to share comments on ongoing issues of general interest – pictures from construction sites, work in progress, pictures of scale models, details of interest, newspaper articles. No reactions are expected ('it is not really a conversation'). Booklets and publications appear and disappear. Spoken words are favoured over any 'template' expert system. Questions and answers are shouted out in the office, so that everyone hears the exchange, irrespective of whether they are involved in the particular project. Starting anew is another recurring theme, not only in competitions, but as an attitude – 'new strategies, new ways of thinking and much improvisation'.

As this outline illustrates, an architectural office may be described as an *ecology of practices*. When Christopher Frayling's seminal paper 'Research in Art and Design' was published in 1993, he famously distinguished between different kinds of research that supposedly grow out of 'what we actually do'. Frayling distinguished research *into* art and design, research *through* art and design, and research *for* art and design. Research *into* art and design, he argues, includes historical research, aesthetic or perceptual research and research into a variety of theoretical perspectives on art and design: social, economic, political, ethical, cultural, iconographic, technical, material, structural, etc.

Research *through* art and design, Frayling continues, includes materials research, development work and action research 'where a research diary tells, in a step-by-step way, of a practical experiment in the studios, and the resulting report aims to contextualise it. Both the diary and the report are there to communicate the results, which is what separates research from the gathering of reference materials'.[4]

The published output of AgwA as part of their academic activities may be said to represent an example of the latter. The 'In Practice' book series, for example, invites architects 'to unravel the design and construction process of one single project by bringing the work documents to light. The architects in turn invite an external observer and writer to develop a narrative of the process'.[5] This approach nudges practice and theorization of practice into separate roles. 'The extensive and rigorous investigation of the process of a project, the perspective from within the practice combined with an external outlook, as well as the integration of complementary observations, form a layered setting which relates to the modalities of academic research involving a creative practice. The role of the architecture practice itself in this case encompasses the subject, the procedure and the motivation of the research project.'[6]

Frayling's final category – research *for* art and design – consists of research 'where the end product is an artefact – where the thinking is, so to speak, embodied in the artefact, where the goal is not primarily communicable knowledge in the sense of verbal communication, but in the sense of visual or iconic or imagistic communication'. More recently, theorists exploring the notion of the artistic or designed artefact as *research* have adapted the term identified by Hans-Jörg Rheinberger when analysing the history and epistemology of experimentation in the life sciences. Rheinberger foregrounded what he called 'epistemic things' within the dynamics of experimental scientific practice.[7]

1 *How is knowledge shared at AgwA?* By this, I'm especially interested in practical knowledge exchange: conversation, feedback, demonstration, use of examples, experimentation, use of teaching, etc. I'm interested in the realities of practice rather than an idealized/corporate statement, so reflecting on how knowledge (in other words, *value*) passes through the company and is enhanced en route is, I hope, an interesting and productive question for you.' Email from the author, 16 March 2022.

2 'What I like about AgwA is that you are allowed to make mistakes and learn from it. So when you are struggling, you do not need to hide it but can talk about it openly and without shame with one of the partners. They will find a way to help you and the project. Before AgwA, I worked at another office where I tried to manage everything on my own because I was scared to ask for help …' Anonymized response to author's question.

the office of AgwA (2022),© Filip Dujardin

AgwA: Chantier / Construction Site – AgwA's compilation of photos of construction sites – may be an example of one of Rheinberger's 'epistemic things'[8] and equally an example of Frayling's third category, 'where the thinking is, so to speak, embodied in the artefact, where the goal is not primarily communicable knowledge in the sense of verbal communication, but in the sense of visual or iconic or imagistic communication'. It is a bold move for an architectural firm to present not (only) carefully curated images of perfectly executed projects, but the raw realities of sites before *architecting* has supposedly bestowed its grace. As Tom Emerson comments, 'spaces are there but the places have not yet been stitched together'.[9]

Between AgwA's academic output, publications and the less formal exchanges on site and within the office, something important would seem to be suggested about expert knowledge. It is not about enforcing conformity to a preset template (an approach that might assign special status to virtuosity) but rather about *strengthening and extending a given practice in relation to a specific environment.* This draws on all the methods that architects evolve to solve the practical problems they confront daily, supplemented by their formal training, their historical, cultural and theoretical curiosity and contexts, their personal experience, their willingness to extend the conceptual borders of their practice to incorporate methods, patterns, materials and, not least, perspectives that might undermine architecture's otherwise uncritical pursuit of control and mastery in favour of understanding the complex (and sometimes unfathomable) dance between intention, context and actualization.

Knowledge is all around us – practical, embodied, evolving and essentially performative. Too often we restrict it to the propositional logic of institutional or disciplinary definitions, thereby losing the experiential complexity of what it is to be alive, in touch with our senses – turning around, in wonder, in space.

3 Ludwig Wittgenstein, *Tractatus Logico-Philosophicus* (London: Routledge Classics, 2001).
4 Christopher Frayling, 'Research in Art and Design', *Royal College of Art Research Papers 1*, no. 1 (1993/4): 5.
5 Harold Fallon, Benoît Vandenbulcke and Benoît Burquel, 'Curating Completeness', in *Buero Kofink Schels. In Practice: T.I.A. House 1 + 2* (Ghent: MER. Borgerhoff & Lamberigts, 2021), 9.
6 Fallon, Vandenbulcke and Burquel, 'Curating Completeness', 9.
7 See, e.g., Henk Borgdorff, 'Artistic Practices and Epistemic Things', in *Experimental Systems: Future Knowledge in Artistic Research*, ed. Michael Schwab (Leuven: Leuven University Press, 2013).
8 Borgdorff comments: 'Rheinberger has deliberately chosen the term "thing" rather than "object" in order to signify the indeterminate, not yet crystallised status of the knowledge object. Epistemic things are "chronically underdetermined".' Borgdorff, 'Artistic Practices', 14.
9 *AgwA: Chantier / Construction Site* (Ghent: MER. Borgerhoff & Lamberigts, 2019), 91.

VERBIEST

VERBIEST

chez andré

DUBLET

2.35JR+N
00

Cegelec
BEMAT
DUCHENE

CHAPEX+CHAPCO

CHAPEX+CHAPCO

APCO

ECAM

ECAM

panimatic

Grote zaal

MUSIQUE
THÉÂTRE

PLEYEL
GYMNOVA

DIMA

Vandaag:
*super*mega*fantastisch*

ABRICOTIER
2020
Brussels
4985 m²
client
CPAS Bruxelles
procedure
Public tender (two-phase competition)
structure, techniques, energy
JZH & Partners
acoustics
ASM Acoustics
security
Gbar
photography
cover, p. 144–145
Jeroen Verrecht

JERUSALEM
2019–ongoing
Schaerbeek, Brussels
1802 m²
client
Municipality of Schaerbeek
procedure
Public tender (two-phase competition)
structure, techniques, energy
JZH & Partners
acoustics
Scala Consultants
security
Codives
landscape
Plant en Houtgoed
photography
p. 111 (12–13)
Filip Dujardin

KARREVELD 2
2018–ongoing
Molenbeek- Saint-Jean, Brussels
6129 m²
client
Pouvoir Organisateur Pluriel asbl
procedure
Public tender (two-phase competition)
structure, techniques, energy
JZH & Partners
acoustics
Khale Acoustics
security
Securisan
landscape
Denis Dujardin
contractor
ACH Construct
photography
p. 104 (06–08), 146–149
Séverin Malaud

VERBIEST
2017–20
Molenbeek- Saint-Jean, Brussels
611.4 m²
in collaboration with
Maria Evelia Macal Guerra
clients
Maria Evelia Macal Guerra, Harold Fallon
procedure
Private commission
structure, energy
JZH & Partners
security
Gbar
contractor
RevGroup
photography
p. 094 (01), 096 (05), 097 (06), 098 (07–08), 101 (14–17), 150–153
Sévérin Malaud
p. 154–155
Family Fallon Macal Guerra

LAS ARADAS
2017–ongoing
Chalatenango, El Salvador
30000 m²
client
Asociación Sumpul
procedure
Interuniversity research project
structure
Civing
artistic interventions
Escuela de Arte UES
more information
elsalvadormemory.org
photography
p. 088 (04), 090 (07), 092 (12), 093 (15)
Shawn Robertson

KANAL – CITROËN
2017
Brussels
35000 m²
in collaboration with
6a architects, architecten de vylder vinck taillieu
client
Société d'Aménagement Urbain
procedure
Public tender (two-phase competition)
structure
Bollinger+Grohmann
techniques
HP Engineers
circularity
Muck Petzet
museality
Mathieu Wellner
photography
p. 162–163
Filip Dujardin
rendering
p. 156–161
AgwA, 6a architects, architecten de vylder vinck taillieu

SERAING
2017–ongoing
Seraing
191.75 m²
client
City of Seraing
procedure
Public tender (two-phase competition)
structure
Bollinger+Grohmann
techniques
A+ Concept
security
Bureau PS2
landscape
Denis Dujardin
impact studies
DREA²M
contractor
Batitec
photography
p. 164–167
Filip Dujardin

KARREVELD 1
2016–21
Molenbeek-Saint-Jean, Brussels
1170 m²
client
Pouvoir Organisateur Pluriel asbl
procedure
Public tender (two-phase competition)
structure, techniques, energy
JZH & Partners
acoustics
Daidalos Peutz
security
Sixco
contractor
Thiran
photography
p. 071 (03–04), 073 (10), 168, 169, 171
Arvi Anderson
p. 170
Séverin Malaud

WANDRE
2016–ongoing
Liège
1540 m²
in collaboration with
S2JD
client
City of Liège
procedure
Public tender (two-phase competition)
structure
Delta GC
techniques, energy
A+ Concept
security
Volon
contractor
Gustave et Yves Liégeois

DURLET
2016–19
Antwerp
1344 m²
client
City of Antwerp
procedure
Public tender (direct selection via a pool for small projects)
structure
Bollinger+Grohmann
techniques
Ingenium
energy, security
Eveka
contractor
Sogiaf
Photography
p. 059 (04), 061 (08), 065 (13–14), 171–178
Séverin Malaud
p. 063 (12)
Arvi Anderson (AgwA)

BARONNEKE
2015–20
Antwerp
154 m²
client
City of Antwerp
procedure
Public tender (direct selection via a pool for small projects)
structure
JZH & Partners
energy
2B-Safe
security
Eveka
landscape
Forest
contractor
WeGroSan
photography
p. 180–183
Séverin Malaud

EMBASSY
2015–ongoing
Beijing, China
2160 m²
in collaboration with
GeJianZhu, ZhongZhu
client
Belgian Ministry of Foreign Affairs
procedure
Public tender (two-phase competition)
structure
Greisch, ZhongZhu
techniques
AgwA, GeJianZhu, ZhongZhu
energy
Enesta
contractor
BUCG
photography
p. 051 (08)
Delphine Mathy

CHAPEX+CHAPCO
2015–ongoing
Charleroi
47000 m²
in collaboration with
architecten jan de vylder inge vinck
client
City of Charleroi
procedure
Public tender (open competition)
structure, techniques, energy
Greisch
acoustics
Progrs
security
Bureau PS2
landscape
Denis Dujardin
interior design
Doorzon
contractors
Eiffage, bemat, koeckelberg
photography
p. 039 (06), 048 (07–08), 049 (11), 184–197
Filip Dujardin

ECAM
2014–22
Saint-Gilles, Brussels
7087 m²
client
Municipality of Saint-Gilles
procedure
Public tender (two-phase competition)
structure, techniques
JZH & Partners
energy
Enesta
landscape
Denis Dujardin
contractor
Thiran/In Advance
photography
p. 031 (01), 033 (04–07), 035 (13–14), 037 (15–17), 198–211
Séverin Malaud
p. 031 (03)
Delphine Mathy

BREDA
2013–20
Antwerp
4260 m²
client
City of Antwerp
procedure
Public tender (direct selection via a pool for small projects)
structure
JZH & Partners
techniques
Macobo
energy, security
Eveka
contractor
Dillen
photography
p. 029 (04–05), 212–213
Delphine Mathy
p. 214–217
Séverin Malaud

PRINS DRIES
2013–14
Antwerp
90.85 m²
client
City of Antwerp
procedure
Public tender (direct selection via a pool for small projects)
structure
JZH & Partners
security
Eveka
contractor
Sogiaf
photography
p. 218–219
Marie-Françoise Plissart

KRIEKELAAR
2013–15
Schaerbeek, Brussels
650 m²
client
VGC
procedure
Public tender (two-phase competition)
structure, Techniques
JZH & Partners
acoustics
Scala Consultants
security
Gbar
scenography
TTAS
contractor
Monument Vandekerckhove
photography
p. 220–225
Marie-Françoise Plissart

PÉRONNES
2009–ongoing
Péronnes-lez-Antoing
8500 m²
in collaboration with
Artgineering
client
Wallonia Brussels-Federation
procedure
Public tender (two-phase competition)
structure
Ney & Partners
techniques
Boydens
artist
Adrien Tritiaux
contractor
Dherte
photography
p. 019 (01–03), 020 (05), 021 (07)
Delphine Mathy
p. 226–233
Séverin Malaud

CARRÉ
2008–14
Mons
3000 m²
in collaboration with
Ney & Partners
client
Wallonia-Brussels Federation
procedure
Public tender (general tender)
structure
Ney & Partners
techniques
Boydens
acoustics
Khale Acoustics
photography
234–239
Marie-Françoise Plissart

PHILIPPEVILLE
2008
Philippeville
1024 m²
in collaboration with
Artgineering
client
Wallonia-Brussels Federation
procedure
Public tender (two-phase competition)
structure
Ney & Partners
techniques
Boydens

BPS22
2006
Charleroi
1500 m²
in collaboration with
Matador
client
Province of Hainaut
procedure
Public tender (two-phase competition)
structure
JZH & Partners
techniques
IRS
acoustics
Votre
landscape
Landinzicht
graphic designer
Coast

VERTIGO
2006–07
Wavre
400 m²
client
Walibi Belgium
procedure
Private competition
structure
Greisch
photography
241–243
Marie-Françoise Plissart

METAL
2006–09
Saint-Gilles, Brussels
1606 m²
in collaboration with
Ferrière Architectes
client
Municipality of Saint-Gilles
procedure
Public tender (general tender)
structure, techniques, energy
JZH & Partners
security
Abesco
contractor
M&M Sitty
photography
p. 004 (01)
Delphine Mathy
p. 005 (01), 007 (06), 244–245
Marie-Françoise Plissart
p. 246–253
Filip Dujardin

AgwA was founded between 2003 and 2006 by Harold Fallon, Benoît Vandenbulcke and Raphaël Cornelis (who left the office in 2008). After working for five years as a staff member, Benoît Burquel joined the board in 2017. AgwA has been nominated several times for national and international awards, including the Brussels Architecture Prize, the Gubbio Prize and the Belgian Architecture Award. Burquel, Fallon and Vandenbulcke are architectural engineers. They relate their architecture practice to research and teaching. In 2019 they began editing the *In Practice* book series and in 2018 they co-founded *Architecture in Practice*, an interuniversity research group for practising architects.

Benoît Burquel (b. 1981) graduated from ULiège in 2005 before specializing in human settlements at KU Leuven in 2007. He worked in Berlin, Ho Chi Minh City, Naples and Palestine before joining AgwA. He was working as a researcher at ULiège from 2013 before joining the Faculty of Architecture La Cambre-Horta of ULB in Brussels in 2018. In 2016 he co-founded Real Estate Architecture, a series of summer schools and publications that explore the potential of private real-estate production from the 1960s and 1970s in Belgium.

Harold Fallon (b. 1977) graduated from UCLouvain in 2001. He completed a PhD by design practice at RMIT University in Melbourne in 2012. After teaching for ten years at Sint-Lucas Hogeschool voor Wetenschap en Kunst in Ghent and Brussels (now KU Leuven Faculty of Architecture), he became a professor in 2017 and was a guest professor at UCLouvain in 2020. He regularly supervises PhDs and has been a partner in the research project 'Surviving Memory in Post-War El Salvador' since 2018.

Benoît Vandenbulcke (b. 1978) graduated from UCLouvain in 2001, where he also completed a PhD in engineering sciences in 2015. During five years, he worked for several offices in Belgium and in Austria. He taught for thirteen years at UCLouvain and since 2017 he has been a professor at the Faculty of Architecture in Liège. As an academic supervisor, he has overseen several master's theses and PhDs. He was a guest professor at TU Wien in 2022. He has also acted as a guest juror for many architecture faculties in Belgium and abroad.

TEAM

Julien Delmotte
  civil engineer architect KU Leuven 2007
  master's in management KU Leuven 2008
Sofie Devriendt
  civil engineer architect UGent 2013
  teaching assistant ULB
Mathias Elaerts
  architect ULiège 2021
  teaching assistant ULiège
Dorothée Fontignie
  architect UCLouvain 2019
  teaching assistant UCLouvain
Ali Ismail
  architect ULB 2018
Hélène Joos
  civil engineer architect UCLouvain 2013
Juliette Lucarain
  architect EPFL 2018
Louise Meersseman
  administrative assistant
Era Merkuri
  architect KIT 2020
Thomas Montulet
  civil engineer architect UGent 2013
  teaching and research assistant UCLouvain
Marie Pirard
  civil engineer architect UCLouvain 2012
  teaching and research assistant UCLouvain
Hannelore Thomas
  civil engineer architect KU Leuven 2015
Nicky Vancaudenberg
  civil engineer architect KU Leuven 2010

FORMER COLLABORATORS (2003–2022)

Joffrey About
Arvi Anderson
Guillaume Becker
Amelie Bimberg
Stefania Boca
Emily Bouché
Timothée Cadars
Jacopo Calafati
Jeremy Commenne
Raphaël Cornelis
  former partner 2003–2008
Frederik Dahlqvist
Pauline Degrand-Guillaud
Michiel De Potter
Damir Draganić
Léone Drapeaud
Manuel Léon Fanjul
Corentin Fivet
Charlotte Gaillard
Gaspard Geerts
Pierre Gréaume
Sophie Hazebrouck
Jan Hoffman
Moe Itaya
Laura Janssens
Florence Kaufmann
Griet Kuppens
Anne-Sophie Mahaux
Christophe Mattar
Jean-Guy Pecher
Bastien Pilet
Ionut Popa
François Ricciardi
Jochen Schamelhout
Thibault Schmitz
Julie Van Huynegem
Yannick Vergnaud
Elena Verelst
Heleen Verheyden
Kaat Volckaert
Friederike Vondran
Xander Wilhelm
Agnieszka Winiarska